IP ROUTING PRIMER

Robert Wright

Macmillan Technical Publishing
201 West 103rd Street
Indianapolis, Indiana 46290 USA

IP Routing Primer
Robert Wright

Copyright© 1998 Macmillan Technical Publishing

Cisco Press logo is a trademark of Cisco Systems, Inc.

Published by:
Macmillan Technical Publishing
201 West 103rd Street
Indianapolis, IN 46290 USA

Printed in the United States of America   3 4 5 6 7 8 9 0

Library of Congress Cataloging-in-Publication Number: 98-86497
ISBN: 1-57870-108-2

Warning and Disclaimer
This book is designed to provide information about IP routing configuration. Every effort has been made to make this book as complete and as accurate as possible, but no warranty or fitness is implied.

The information is provided on an "as is" basis. The author, Macmillan Technical Publishing, and Cisco Systems, Inc., shall have neither liability nor responsibility to any person or entity with respect to any loss or damages arising from the information contained in this book or from the use of the discs or programs that may accompany it.

The opinions expressed in this book belong to the author and are not necessarily those of Cisco Systems, Inc.

Feedback Information
At Cisco Press, our goal is to create in-depth technical books of the highest quality and value. Each book is crafted with care and precision, undergoing rigorous development that involves the unique expertise of members from the professional technical community.

Readers' feedback is a natural continuation of this process. If you have any comments regarding how we could improve the quality of this book, or otherwise alter it to better suit your needs, you can contact us at `ciscopress@mcp.com`. Please make sure to include the book title and ISBN in your message.

We greatly appreciate your assistance.

Associate Publisher	Jim LeValley
Executive Editor	Julie Fairweather
Cisco Systems Program Manager	H. Kim Lew
Managing Editor	Caroline Roop
Acquisitions Editor	Lynette Quinn
Development Editor	Kezia Endsley
Senior Editor	Dayna Isley
Copy Editor	Leah Williams
Technical Editors	Srinivas Vegesna
	Shankar Vemulapalli
Team Coordinator	Amy Lewis
Book Designer	Louisa Klucznik
Cover Designer	Karen Ruggles
Production Team	Argosy
Proofreader	Lynne Miles-Morillo
Indexer	Kevin Fulcher

Trademark Acknowledgments

All terms mentioned in this book that are known to be trademarks or service marks have been appropriately capitalized. Macmillan Technical Publishing or Cisco Systems, Inc. cannot attest to the accuracy of this information. Use of a term in this book should not be regarded as affecting the validity of any trademark or service mark.

About the Author

Robert Wright is a member of Cisco's Tools and Training team. Prior to that, he managed a team of Senior Customer Engineers responsible for providing dedicated, highly individualized technical support for some of the world's largest and fastest growing Internet service providers. He has also worked in Cisco's Critical Accounts group, in Cisco's Technical Assistance Center (TAC), and as a Systems Engineer for Cisco in the United Kingdom. Prior to joining Cisco, Robert worked for Texaco Ltd. in the United Kingdom. He worked in Texaco's LAN support group and supported the Cisco routers in the UK. He was also part of the team responsible for designing and installing Texaco's new data center in East London. He currently resides in San Jose, California, and enjoys riding his Icelandic horse, traveling with his wife, golfing, water skiing, snowboarding, and listening to his collection of Jimmy Buffett CDs.

Dedications

This book is dedicated to my wife, Lelia. She is always there for me and is my best friend.

Acknowledgments

I would like to thank the members of the Cisco ISP Expert Team who helped me validate many of the concepts presented in this material while I was developing it: Nga Vu for her perseverance in getting me to create the training document that was the genesis of this book and, finally, Shankar Vemulapalli and Srinivas Vegesna for their excellent technical editing. Finally, I would like to thank my wife, Lelia, for her support and motivation during the past year.

Contents

Contents

Introduction

Welcome to Cisco's *IP Routing Primer*! This book covers the generic behavior of IP routing and packet forwarding using Cisco routers. It goes into detailed analysis of several real-life scenarios to provide insight into the fundamentals of IP that everybody supporting IP in a network should know.

By providing examples taken directly from Cisco routers, this book enables the reader to associate theoretical behaviors discussed in many internetworking books with their real-life counterparts. The reader should find it much easier to understand statements such as "Split horizon refers to the concept of not advertising routes over the interface they were learned from . . ." when it is accompanied by actual screen output from a Cisco router as it sends a routing table update to an adjacent router.

By providing examples of IP routing behaviors taken directly from Cisco routers, this book avoids theoretical explanations that can vary from one networking engineer to another. Ask any 10 network engineers what a poison reverse update is, and you will likely receive 10 different answers. Refer to the section on Poison Reverse and Triggered Updates in Chapter 2 for a real-life example you can apply to any situation.

Objective of This Book

This book was written to fill the gap between internetworking books that are long on theory but short on practice and the high-level seminars on internetworking that cover real-life examples but lack depth. After reading this book, the reader should have a better understanding of the complexities involved in designing and supporting IP networks.

By presenting a few of the most common issues that can be encountered in managing an IP network, I hope to pique your curiosity to learn more by going into a networking lab and experimenting on your own.

Another goal of this book is to convey the idea that to be a successful internetworking engineer, it is more important to understand what needs to happen in a given situation to make something work than to memorize exactly what happens. For example, you can memorize the fact that before an IP host can send its first IP packet to another host, it must send an ARP request and receive an ARP reply. But what have you really learned? If you don't understand that the IP host was resolving a layer three address to a layer two address to avoid broadcasting all layer two frames to all hosts on the network, you haven't grasped a fundamental part of what makes an IP network work.

In addition, this book teaches some fundamental skills that anyone involved in internetworking should possess, such as binary and hexadecimal numbering and IP subnetting. It is almost impossible to be a successful network engineer if you do not have these skills mastered.

Keep in mind that this book is not intended to be an in-depth analysis of the individual routing protocols presented. This information is readily available in many other books, RFCs, and white papers. The goal is to present the behaviors exhibited by a couple of routing protocols (RIP and IGRP) to set the stage for reading and understanding the material available from other sources.

In addition, this book is not intended to be a design and implementation guide for building IP networks. Instead, it is meant to be a guide to issues that must be addressed when building IP networks. It gives readers a better idea of which questions to ask and which problems need to be solved when building their own networks.

Audience

This book is intended for anybody involved in supporting or designing IP networks—engineers, support personnel, and the like. It covers many basic internetworking concepts that people just starting out need to understand. It goes into great detail on some very sophisticated topics that even those with several years of experience supporting IP networks will find interesting.

Conventions Used in This Book

The routers in the topology and configuration section may appear in different topologies throughout this book. With the exception of removing some links in certain examples, the actual configurations do not change from those shown unless specifically noted.

Router commands referenced in paragraphs are in lowercase and italics, for example, *show ip route*.

Screen output from routers is presented in a monospaced font. For example:

```
RouterA#show ip route
Codes: C - connected, S - static, I - IGRP, R - RIP, M - mobile, B - BGP
       D - EIGRP, EX - EIGRP external, O - OSPF, IA - OSPF inter area
       E1 - OSPF external type 1, E2 - OSPF external type 2, E - EGP
       i - IS-IS, L1 - IS-IS level-1, L2 - IS-IS level-2, * - candidate default
       U - per-user static route

Gateway of last resort is 0.0.0.0 to network 0.0.0.0

     168.71.0.0/16 is subnetted, 5 subnets
C       168.71.9.0 is directly connected, Serial1
R       168.71.8.0 [120/1] via 168.71.9.2, 00:00:39, Serial1
R       168.71.7.0 [120/1] via 168.71.6.2, 00:00:11, Serial0
                   [120/1] via 168.71.9.2, 00:00:39, Serial1
C       168.71.6.0 is directly connected, Serial0
C       168.71.5.0 is directly connected, Ethernet0
S*   0.0.0.0/0 is directly connected, Ethernet0
RouterA#
```

Occasionally, a specific portion of the screen output is referenced by the surrounding text. In these cases, the output in question will be in bold.

For example, note that the update timer for 168.71.8.0 in the following output of the *show ip route* command from RouterA is now **39** seconds.

```
RouterA#show ip route
Codes: C - connected, S - static, I - IGRP, R - RIP, M - mobile, B - BGP
       D - EIGRP, EX - EIGRP external, O - OSPF, IA - OSPF inter area
       E1 - OSPF external type 1, E2 - OSPF external type 2, E - EGP
       i - IS-IS, L1 - IS-IS level-1, L2 - IS-IS level-2, * - candidate default
       U - per-user static route

Gateway of last resort is 0.0.0.0 to network 0.0.0.0

     168.71.0.0/16 is subnetted, 5 subnets
C       168.71.9.0 is directly connected, Serial1
R       168.71.8.0 [120/1] via 168.71.9.2, 00:00:39, Serial1
R       168.71.7.0 [120/1] via 168.71.6.2, 00:00:11, Serial0
                   [120/1] via 168.71.9.2, 00:00:39, Serial1
C       168.71.6.0 is directly connected, Serial0
C       168.71.5.0 is directly connected, Ethernet0
S*   0.0.0.0/0 is directly connected, Ethernet0
RouterA#
```

In addition, this book utilizes two other conventions:

NOTES

Margin notes—These are used to add additional points of interest to the reader without disrupting the flow of the main ideas presented.

HINT

Margin hints—These can be troubleshooting tips or additional procedures that are relevant to the current subject matter.

Organization

This book is divided into eight chapters and one appendix, as follows:

- Chapter 1, "Topology and Router Configurations"

  This chapter presents the routers and their configurations, which will form the basis of the scenarios presented in this book. It also introduces some of the basic functions of a router and some of the problems a router must solve to do its job successfully.

- Chapter 2, "Routing Metrics and Distances"

  This chapter explains what routing metrics are and how they can be calculated. It also describes Cisco's utilization of the distance function to determine which routing protocols take precedence when they run concurrently.

- Chapter 3, "Discontiguous Networks, Summarization, and Subnet 0"

  This chapter explains what the terms discontiguous networks, summarization, and subnet 0 mean and how they interact in a live network. It also includes scenarios in which functions have been used incorrectly to show the problems they can cause.

- Chapter 4, "Using IP Unnumbered and VLSM"

  This chapter describes IP unnumbered and Variable Length Subnet Masking (VLSM) and explains how they can be used as tools when building IP networks. It also includes scenarios in which these functions have been used incorrectly to show the problems they can cause.

- Chapter 5, "Default Routing"

  This chapter explains what default routing is and why it is necessary. Several scenarios are provided to show how default routing works and what can happen when it is not configured properly.

- Chapter 6, "IP Troubleshooting Scenarios"

  This chapter walks through common IP connectivity problems and introduces some tools and techniques to resolve them.

- Chapter 7, "Bridging IP Between Dissimilar Media"

  Many network engineers have made the mistake of attempting to bridge IP between Token Ring and Ethernet using Cisco routers. Cisco routers do not support this function. This chapter explains why this is the case.

- Chapter 8, "Hexadecimal and Binary Numbering and IP Addressing"

  This chapter describes the two numbering systems and explains why it is important to have mastered using them. It also covers IP addressing and subnetting.

- Appendix A, "RFCs"

  This chapter includes all of the RFCs referenced in this book, as well as a few that are useful for people just getting started in internetworking. In addition, there are several references to RFCs on more advanced topics.

It is recommended that you start with Chapter 1 because the concepts build on one another as the book progresses. Welcome again to Cisco's *IP Routing Primer*!

CHAPTER 1

Topology and Router Configurations

This chapter introduces routers and explains how they can be incorporated in networks to move data from one location to another. In addition, this chapter covers some basic IP concepts and background material that you need to understand in order to assimilate the information in later chapters. Included in this chapter are the following topics:

- Understanding the role of routers in networks

- Understanding topology and router configurations

- Understanding what a router does

- Understanding forwarding

UNDERSTANDING THE ROLE OF ROUTERS IN NETWORKS

Routers provide physical connectivity between networks by virtue of their physical attachments to either local-area networks (LANs), such as Token Ring or Ethernet, or wide-area networks (WANs), such as Frame Relay or ISDN.

A router can be used to connect only LANs together, only WANs together, or any other combination. The term *physical connection* should not be taken too literally. Many networks make use of Microwave links for WAN connectivity. This means that no actual physical connection exists between two connected routers communicating over microwave circuits.

The Router Interface

A router's attachment to a LAN or a WAN is usually referred to as an *interface* but may also be referred to as a *port*. For example, a connection to a Token Ring LAN is with a Token Ring interface. For consistency, the term *interface* is used throughout this book.

When discussing a router's connections to a network, it is common to say the following: "We connect the Finance department's Token Ring network to the corporate backbone via Bbone-1's first Token Ring interface." Bbone-1, in this case, is the logical name of a router in a corporate network. Routers are typically assigned names that provide some information about their locations and functions.

When a router is routing IP, each LAN or WAN it is connected to must have a unique IP network or subnetwork assigned to it. (In the case of some serial links, it must borrow an address from another interface. This borrowing, called *IP unnumbered*, is covered in Chapter 4, "Using IP Unnumbered and VLSM." Each interface on the router must have a valid IP host address for the subnet it is attached to. In most cases, a router can have only one connection to any single subnet. (One exception to this rule is that Cisco routers allow up to four serial links to share the same subnet, provided that they all terminate at the same destination router.)

Network Layer Addresses

In addition to providing physical connectivity between networks, routers also possess the capability to move information across multiple networks by forwarding *datagrams* based on their network layer addresses. In this case, the network layer is the third layer in the OSI seven-layer model. For IP, the layer three addresses are 32-bit binary numbers.

Datagrams

The term *datagram* is commonly used to describe any information generated by a higher-layer application or protocol that is being handled at the network layer in the OSI model. One example of a datagram is a Telnet login request from a host to a remote UNIX server.

The users indicate via their Telnet application—Telnet being an application layer function—that they want to log in to a server. The Telnet application passes this request to the next lower layer in the protocol stack—TCP, in this case—and waits for a response from the remote system.

The TCP layer adds its own information to what it received from the Telnet application and hands this combined message to the IP layer—the network layer—of the protocol stack. TCP will hold on to the request it received from Telnet in case the first attempt to contact the remote host fails. The message the IP layer receives from Telnet and TCP is called the datagram. The term *packet* is often used interchangeably with datagram.

NOTES

It is important to understand that IP datagrams are *connectionless*. This means that they are delivered once by the originator's IP layer and then discarded. If the destination host does not receive the datagram, some higher-layer protocol or application on the host that created the datagram must try again or give up.

If the destination host had not received the original IP datagram in the previous example, TCP would have made at least one more attempt to initiate the login. TCP would have handed another copy of its information to the IP layer, and IP would have attempted to deliver the datagram again.

NOTES

Using the example of users attempting to log in to a remote server with Telnet to explain datagrams necessarily omits many of the actual details involved in establishing a Telnet session. See *Network Protocol Handbook* by Matthew Naugle, published by McGraw-Hill (ISBN 0-07-046461-8) for more information on this subject.

When routers forward datagrams based on their level three addresses, all layer two information that arrived with the packet is discarded. The router recreates the required layer two information before forwarding the datagram to the next router, which allows routers to connect networks with different layer two frame and addressing formats. Sometimes certain routers are deployed only for the purpose of connecting dissimilar LAN or WAN types because it is usually impossible to bridge routable protocols (protocols with layer three addresses) in these situations.

MAC Addresses

Some routers are also able to move information across networks by forwarding frames based on their layer two addresses, which are more commonly known as *MAC* (*Medium Access Control*) addresses.

This activity is really *bridging*, not routing. Bridges forward frames based on their layer two addresses and leave the layer two packet and addressing formats unchanged. It is usually impossible for a host on an Ethernet network to exchange information with a host on a Token Ring network when one or more routers (acting as bridges) exists between them. The exception is when a bridge or a router acting as a bridge is set up to translate layer two addresses and frame formats between different types of LANs or WANs.

Several years ago, an attempt was made to call devices that performed both routing and bridging functions *brouters*. This never really took off. However, it is important to distinguish between a protocol being bridged or routed when configuring routers and a protocol being bridged or routed when troubleshooting network problems. Some protocols, such as DEC LAT, IBM SNA, and NetBIOS over 802.2, do not have layer three addresses and thus must be bridged using their layer two addresses. Routable protocols, such as IP and Novell's IPX, can be either bridged or routed.

NOTES

Many routers are not capable of bridging routable protocols between Ethernet and Token Ring. Ethernet and Token Ring use different bit ordering at the physical layer, which causes the MAC addresses to be ordered in opposite directions. When translating between Token Ring and Ethernet LANs, routers acting as translational bridges would have to modify layer three and higher information in certain datagrams passed between IP, AppleTalk, or IPX hosts to make this connectivity possible. No agreed-upon standard exists for performing this function. In many cases, vendors are unwilling to create proprietary code and instead tell their customers that they need to route protocols in this situation. See Chapter 7, "Bridging IP Between Dissimilar Media," for more information on this subject.

IP Address Formats

IP addresses are typically written in a format known as *dotted decimal* to avoid working with binary numbers (for example, writing 201.124.76.210 instead of 11001001.01111100. 01001100.11010010). Each of the four sections of the address represents one byte or eight bits. See Chapter 8, "Hexadecimal and Binary Numbering and IP Addressing," for more information on converting IP addresses from dotted decimal to binary format.

IP addresses are broken into two sections: a network section and a host section. Routers make decisions on forwarding datagrams based on the network portion of the IP address. The amount of an IP address allocated to the network portion is determined by the class of IP address in use and the subnet mask applied to it.

Assume, for example, that the address shown previously—201.124.76.210—has a subnet mask of 255.255.255.0. The subnet mask associated with this address (255.255.255.0) tells the router where the network portion stops and the host portion begins.

The router would only have to know where addresses with the prefix (network portion) 201.124.76.0 exist and forward the datagram accordingly. It is not necessary for the router to keep track of the entire address.

Network prefixes are stored in a router's memory in what is usually referred to as a *routing table*. The information a routing table contains can be learned by listening to information provided by other routers via a dynamic routing protocol (such as RIP or OSPF) or by information coded directly into it. Don't worry if you don't understand this completely yet. It should become clearer as the chapter progresses.

Network Reference Models

Figure 1–1 shows a representation of the OSI (Open System Interconnection) seven-layer model.

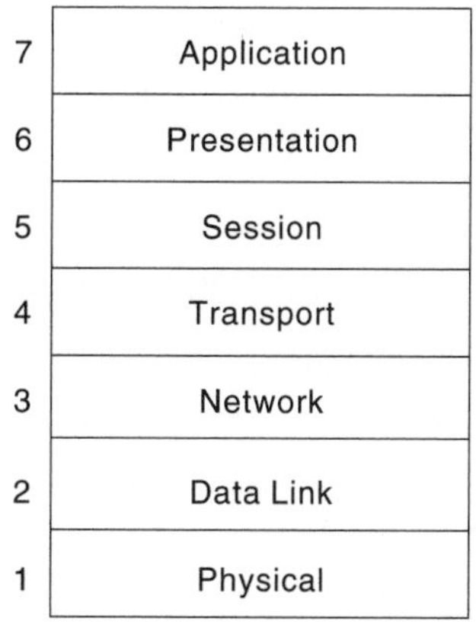

7	Application
6	Presentation
5	Session
4	Transport
3	Network
2	Data Link
1	Physical

Figure 1–1

A representation of the OSI seven-layer model. All layers are independent of on another.

The layers are as follows:

- Layer 7: Application layer

- Layer 6: Presentation layer

- Layer 5: Session layer

- Layer 4: Transport layer

- Layer 3: Network layer

- Layer 2: Data link layer

- Layer 1: Physical layer

It is important to note that, with few exceptions, most networks today are not based on the OSI seven-layer model. Instead, they are based on the IEEE LAN reference model or the Ethernet II standard.

Token Ring 802.5 and Ethernet 802.3 are two common IEEE LAN RM network protocols. Neither of these models contains a definition of the network layer or any layer above the network layer. The most common network layer protocols in use today are either proprietary, such as IPX, Appletalk, or part of an open standard, such as IP.

The IEEE LAN reference model consists of two primary layers, with the top layer broken into two sublayers. The bottom layer, called the physical layer, performs roughly the same function as its OSI equivalent. The top layer consists of two sublayers: a MAC sublayer and a logical link control sublayer (802.2), which is on top. These two sublayers combine to make up what the OSI model calls the data link layer, although the functions performed are not exactly the same. Figure 1–2 is a representation of this model.

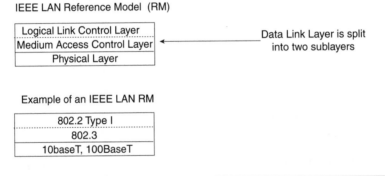

Figure 1–2

The IEEE LAN reference model.

The Ethernet II (DIX) model is the simplest of the two models. It contains a physical layer and a MAC layer. It was developed by Digital, Intel, and Xerox in the '70s. Figure 1–3 shows a representation of this model and compares it to the 802.5 Token Ring model and the 802.3 Ethernet model.

Note that no (802.2) data link layer is in the Ethernet II model.

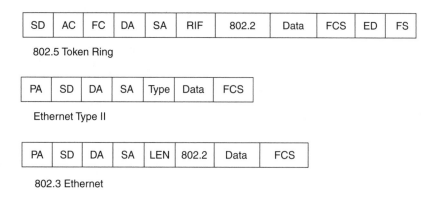

Figure 1–3

A comparison of the three most common LAN protocols.

UNDERSTANDING TOPOLOGY AND ROUTER CONFIGURATIONS

This section contains the original router configurations used for most of the examples in this book. Any time a change is made to one of these configurations in a subsequent chapter, a note is provided indicating what was changed and why.

Figure 1–4 shows the basic topology used unless otherwise noted. This three-router design uses the minimum number of routers required to present some fairly complex concepts. Adding additional routers is only necessary in a few instances, in which three routers are not sufficient to create a particular scenario.

In the network diagrams, SO and SI are used as shorthand for Serial Interface 0 and Serial Interface I, respectively.

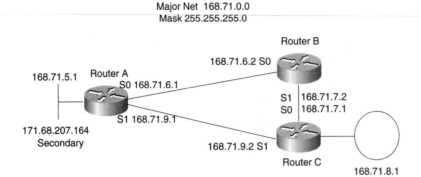

Major Net 168.71.0.0
Mask 255.255.255.0

Figure 1–4

Basic topology for most scenarios.

NOTES

RouterA as used in this chapter has a connection to the "real" Cisco network via its *secondary address*. Secondary addresses allow an interface to participate in more than one IP network at the same time. Although the secondary address space may not be mentioned again, look for references to it in the sections on summarization, default routes, and other issues that require access to networks the routers do not know explicitly.

RouterA's Configuration

The configuration for RouterA is as follows:

```
!
interface ethernet0
ip address 168.71.5.1 255.255.255.0
ip address 171.68.207.164 255.255.255.128 secondary
!
interface serial0
ip address 168.71.6.1 255.255.255.0
bandwidth 128
!
interface serial1
ip address 168.71.9.1 255.255.255.0
bandwidth 128
!
router rip
network 168.71.0.0
passive-interface Ethernet0
!
ip route 0.0.0.0 0.0.0.0 Ethernet0
!
```

This is the configuration for RouterA that is used in all future examples and scenarios unless otherwise noted. RouterA is running RIP. It is configured with a passive interface *Ethernet0* command that prevents RIP from advertising routing updates out *Ethernet0*, which is a connection to Cisco's corporate network.

NOTES

The addresses used in the examples and scenarios in this book are not part of Cisco's registered range of IP addresses. They were chosen entirely at random and may be assigned to another organization. For more information on using registered and unregistered IP addresses, see RFC 1918: "Address Allocation for Private Internets."

If RouterA inadvertently advertised the unregistered networks it has configured or learned from RouterB and RouterC to other Cisco routers, they might in turn advertise the networks to the Internet. If these addresses were actually in use by another organization, it is highly likely that some or all of the traffic for these networks would be directed from the Internet to Cisco. Users should always be aware of where a router will advertise its routes and, when necessary, prevent routing advertisements for certain networks to avoid connectivity problems caused by advertising false routes.

RouterB's Configuration

RouterB's configuration is very simple. RouterB only has two WAN interfaces, which is not a very common configuration. However, it does provide sufficient connectivity for most of the scenarios in this book. Adding additional interfaces would add unnecessary complexity.

RouterB has two bandwidth statements. This will affect any scenario using IGRP because IGRP used the bandwidth statement as part of the algorithm for determining routing metrics.

The configuration for RouterB is as follows:

```
!
interface serial0
ip address 168.71.6.2 255.255.255.0
bandwidth 128
!
interface serial1
ip address 168.71.7.2 255.255.255.0
bandwidth 64
!
router rip
network 168.71.0.0
!
```

RouterC's Configuration

RouterC has a Token Ring interface instead of an Ethernet interface. This interface is used to demonstrate that when routing protocols such as IP, IPX, and AppleTalk are used in conjunction with different types of LANs, routers automatically take care of creating the proper layer two packet and addressing formats for the destination interface.

RouterC also has two bandwidth statements. This will affect any scenario using IGRP because IGRP used the bandwidth statement as part of the algorithm for determining routing metrics.

The configuration for RouterC is as follows:

```
!
interface tokenring0
ip address 168.71.8.1 255.255.255.0
!
interface serial0
ip address 168.71.7.1 255.255.255.0
bandwidth 64
!
interface serial1
ip address 168.71.9.2 255.0.0.0
bandwidth 128
!
router rip
network 168.71.0.0
!
```

The previous sections introduced the concept of where routers can be deployed in a network and what types of functions they can perform. The format of IP addresses; as well as some possible issues when bridging routable protocols such as IP, IPX, and AppleTalk; were also introduced. Finally, the basic configurations used for the routers in many of the scenarios presented later in this book were provided. The next section goes into more detail on how routers forward packets through a network.

UNDERSTANDING WHAT A ROUTER DOES

The previous sections introduced some basic concepts about routers and discussed where they might be deployed. This section presents some advanced concepts in IP routing behavior, providing examples based on the network topology presented in the first sections.

You now know that a router has a routing table containing network prefixes for IP network addresses it knows about. This section explains how a router uses its routing table to determine which interface it should forward an IP datagram over in order to send it to its destination.

IP datagrams flow through a network one router at a time. Each router in a path must make its own decision about the best interface to forward a packet over to get it to its destination. This is what is meant by *hop-by-hop forwarding*.

Sample Network

The sample network has been simplified for this section by removing the serial link between RouterA and RouterC. This simple network is shown in Figure 1–5.

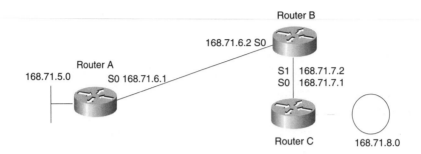

Figure 1–5
Simplified version of the sample network.

In most instances, the router forwarding a datagram does not know whether the next hop router is the final router in the chain or merely another hop in a longer chain.

In Figure 1–5, if RouterA received a packet for 168.71.8.2 (a host on the Token Ring attached to RouterC), it would simply forward the packet to RouterB. RouterA would neither know nor care that RouterB was not actually connected to 168.71.8.0 and thus would have to hand the packet off to yet another router.

As far as RouterA is concerned, the route to network prefix 168.71.8.0 is *known via* 168.71.6.2 over serial 0. "Known via" means that this is the IP address of the advertising router. In this case, RouterB advertised 168.71.8.0 to RouterA.

NOTES

Routers typically do not advertise networks back out the interface they are known via. This is called using a *Split Horizon*. Split Horizon is explained later in this chapter.

On a point-to-point link, such as a T1 connection, the advertising router is always the only other router on the link. On a multipoint link, such as Frame Relay, several routers may be advertising routes that arrive over a serial interface. In this case, it is imperative to store the next hop address to identify which router is advertising the routes. The multipoint example is covered later in this chapter.

___

NOTES

It is important to understand that the source and destination addresses of an IP packet never changes at it flows through the network unless the packet goes through a device that performs *network address translation (NAT)*. NAT devices can be used when you want to connect your private network to the Internet and you do not have officially registered IP addresses configured on your network devices. At a minimum, you need one valid IP address for use on your end of the connection to your Internet Service Provider (ISP). Your NAT device will use this address as the source address for any packets generated by your end systems. This book is focused on fundamental behaviors of IP in router-based networks. NAT is not a fundamental IP concept but rather an advanced application of IP address management, so it will not be covered in any further detail. You can assume that, in the context of the materials presented in this book, all IP addresses in all IP datagrams remain unchanged as the packets traverse the network scenarios presented. See RFC 1631 for more information on NAT.

___

How a Router Knows What to Do

Routers send each other information about networks they know about. They do this with different types of protocols that are generically referred to as *routing protocols*. Routers use this information to build a routing table that consists of the available networks, the costs associated with reaching the available networks, and the path to the next hop router.

In Figure 1–6, RouterA would like to advertise its connection to 168.71.5.0 to RouterB. RouterB would in turn like to advertise its connection to 168.71.8.0 to RouterA. The sample network in Figure 1.6 has been further simplified because only two routers are necessary to discuss this point.

Figure 1–6
A simplified view of the sample network.

The two primary classes of routing protocols in use today are link state and distance vector, described as follows:

- A router running a *link state protocol* sends updates that describe the state of the links attached to the router, the IP networks, or subnets assigned to the links and the costs associated with using those links. Other routers listen to these updates and then build a picture of the network's topology based on what networks the other routers have indicated they are connected to. The *metric* (unit of measurement) for link state protocols is typically cost based. A low-speed link costs more than a high-speed link in terms of performance. Paths that run over lower-cost higher-speed links are preferred.

- A router running a *distance vector protocol* sends updates that contain all of the networks that the router knows about, not just the networks it is connected to. The advertising router increases the metric (typically a hop count) of the routes it has heard about and advertises them to the next routers in the path.

Choosing Your Routing Protocol

In general, link state routing protocols such as ISIS and OSPF are more difficult to configure and troubleshoot than distance vector protocols, but they offer greater scalability when used in large, complex networks. In addition, link state protocols usually recover from network problems (converge) faster that distance vector protocols.

Distance vector protocols such as RIP and IGRP are easy to configure but may not work well in large, complex networks due to the length of time they can take to converge. Neither RIP V1 nor RIP V2 is capable of taking into account the speed of a link connecting two routers. This means that they will treat two parallel paths of unequal speeds between two routers as if they were the same speed and send the same number of packets over each link instead of sending more over the faster link and fewer or no packets over the slower link. (IGRP does understand the speed of a link and can handle parallel links of unequal speed to a certain degree.)

Some IP routing protocols, such as OSPF, ISIS, RIP V2, and EIGRP, support concepts such as *variable length subnet masking (VLSM)* and *non-contiguous major networks*.

In general, it is usually best to use the simplest routing protocol that meets your needs:

- In a network with no redundant links or parallel paths and no requirements for VLSM or discontiguous major networks, RIP V1 might be perfectly suitable.

- In a network that requires VLSM and or discontiguous major networks and that does not have redundant links or parallel paths, RIP V2 might be perfectly suitable.

- In a network that has redundant links or parallel paths and does not require VLSM or discontiguous major networks, IGRP might be perfectly suitable.

- In a network with parallel paths and/or redundant links and that requires VLSM or discontiguous major networks, use either OSPF, EIGRP, or ISIS for IP.

This book is not intended to be an in-depth study of IP routing protocols themselves. Routing protocols are mentioned because many fundamental behaviors of IP routing require some kind of routing protocol to be running.

The behaviors presented here apply universally to all IP routing protocols. You can configure a simple network using OSPF instead of RIP and use the scenarios that follow later in this book in the exact same way they are presented. The resulting behaviors are basically the same.

See *Interconnections* by Radia Perlman, published by Addison-Wesley (ISBN 0-201-56332-0) and *Internetworking With TCP/IP* by Douglas Comer, published by Prentice Hall (ISBN 0-13-474321-0) for more information on different types of routing protocols.

UNDERSTANDING HOW FORWARDING DECISIONS ARE MADE

IP routing is normally done on a next hop basis. For example, in Figure 1–7, RouterA may have told RouterB about subnet 168.71.5.0. RouterB doesn't really care whether RouterA is actually attached to 168.71.5.0. If RouterA says it can reach 168.71.5.0, that is sufficient for RouterB to make a forwarding decision to send packets destined for network address 168.71.5.0 to RouterA.

Performing Longest Match Lookups

Routers take an incoming IP packet and compare it to entries in their routing tables by performing a *longest match lookup*. Remember that IP addresses are really 32-bit binary numbers split between a network section and a host section. Only the network portion is stored in a routing table.

Performing a longest match lookup in a routing table is the same as saying the following: "Find the network address in the routing table with the most bits in common before a mismatch occurs with the destination network address of the packet being routed. Do this by reading each entry in the routing table from left to right, comparing each bit in sequence with the bits in the destination network address of the packet being routed. Stop the comparison process at the bit before the first bit that doesn't match in the routing table entry being compared."

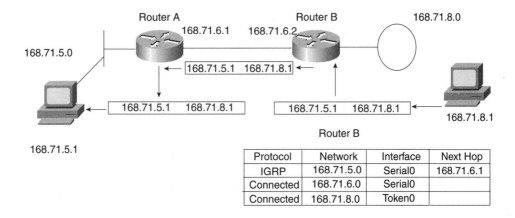

Protocol	Network	Interface	Next Hop
IGRP	168.71.5.0	Serial0	168.71.6.1
Connected	168.71.6.0	Serial0	
Connected	168.71.8.0	Token0	

Figure 1–7

An example of a simple routing table for RouterB.

Longest Match Lookup—A Simple Example

Start with the binary number 11111100. Compare it to the following binary numbers: (a) 11111000, (b) 11110000, and (c) 11100000. Which is the longest match?

The answer is (a). The original binary number starts with a string of six 1s, followed by two 0s. (a) starts with five 1s, followed by three 0s, so it has the longest matching number of bits before a mismatch.

Routers typically store entries in their tables in descending order. In this example, the numbers would be stored in the order: (a), (b), (c).

If a router were comparing these numbers, it would have started with
(a) and stored in memory how closely (a) matched the number being
compared (11111100) before a mismatched bit occurred.

The router would then proceed to do the same comparison for (b). The
router would have realized that (a) was a better match than (b) because (a) had five bits in common before a mismatch, whereas (b) had
only four.

The router would never have gotten around to checking (c) because it
would know that numbers are stored in descending order and that (c)
had to be a smaller number than (b) and therefore could not be a better match.

See the section on longest match lookups using VLSM in Chapter
3, "Discontiguous Networks, Summarization, and Subnet 0."
VLSM is also explained in Chapter 3.

Entries in a routing table are the network addresses that the
router knows about. It is common practice to refer to an entry
in a routing table as a *route*. Therefore, saying that RouterB
has a network entry in its routing table for network 168.71.5.0
is synonymous with saying "RouterB has a route to
168.71.5.0." This book uses both methods when discussing
the contents of a router's routing table.

Routers ignore the host section of the destination address.
They use only the network section when performing a longest
match lookup. Routers know how addresses should be broken
down because they store the subnet mask associated with each
route in its routing table.

NOTES

Routing tables normally include the subnet masks associated with the
network addresses, as well as the network addresses themselves.
Subnet masks are not given in the routing table in Figure 1–8 so that
it is easier to view. For reference, the mask for these routes is
255.255.255.0.

If a router finds a suitable match in its table for the network address of a packet it is trying to forward, it has what is sometimes referred to as an *explicit match*. In other words, the information in the routing table indicates explicitly where to send the packet.

If no explicit route is available, the router may choose to forward the packet to a gateway of last resort. This is covered in more detail in Chapter 4 in the section on gateways. In Figure 1–7, RouterB received a packet destined for 168.71.5.1.

The longest match in the routing table indicates that 168.71.5.0 is known via serial 0, with a next hop of 168.71.6.1. In this case, the next hop address is redundant because the serial link is point to point. There is only one router to forward this packet to. Remember that the actual destination IP address in the packet does not change. It remains 168.71.5.1.

Forwarding Decisions for Multipoint Interfaces

Figure 1–8 shows how the next hop interface of serial 0 is not sufficient for forwarding the packet to 168.71.5.1 accurately. The further distinction of a next hop IP address eliminates the ambiguity of only pointing to the serial interface. In this case, RouterB knows that the next hop is out serial 0 to the next hop address of 168.71.6.1. RouterB will have a Frame Relay map entry on serial 0 that indicates the appropriate DLCI (100) to send the packet to.

For Frame Relay, the DLCI address performs the same function as a MAC address on an Ethernet network. Frame Relay is a layer two protocol. Therefore, when a Frame Relay switch forwards an IP datagram encapsulated in a Frame Relay layer two frame, it does so by reading the layer two destination DLCI address contained in the frame.

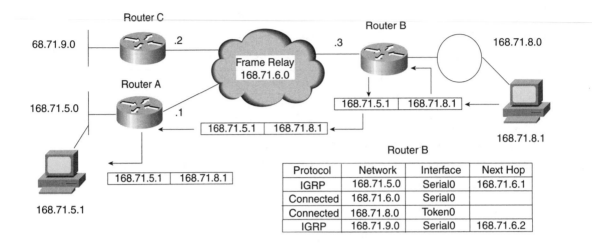

Figure 1–8

How forwarding decisions are made for multipoint interfaces.

The Frame Relay network switches the frame through the network and finally delivers it to RouterA. RouterA can then forward the datagram on to the ultimate host. See *Frame Relay Principles and Applications* by Philip Smith, published by Addison-Wesley (ISBN 0-201-62400-1), for more information on Frame Relay.

The Frame Relay map entry for IP address 168.71.6.1 to DLCI 100 is essentially an ARP entry for the layer two and layer three protocol addresses. It is similar to an Ethernet MAC address to IP address ARP entry:

```
RouterB#show frame-relay map
Serial0 (up): ip 168.71.6.1 dlci 100(0x64,0x1840), static,
              broadcast,
              CISCO
RouterB#
```

The Address Resolution Protocol (ARP) is used to resolve layer three (network) addresses to layer two (MAC) addresses so that frames can be forwarded to a particular host directly. If end systems were not able to store entries that mapped these two addresses, all frames would have to be broadcast at the MAC level. In addition, each end system would have to open every frame and de-encapsulate it to the network layer to see whether the frame's network layer address matched its own network layer address.

End Systems Sending Packets to Other Subnets

Before a router can even become involved in forwarding a packet from an end station, the end station must figure out how to get the packet to the router in the first place.

When an end system wants to send an IP packet to another end system, it compares the destination IP address with its own address. If the destination network address is within the same subnet (on the same local cable), the originating end station will ARP for the destination end system.

If the originating end system determines that the destination end system is on a different cable because it has a different subnet (network) address, it will send the packet to the MAC (cable address) of its gateway and the IP address of the destination end system.

In Figure 1–9, end system A wants to send a *PING* to end system B. End system A determines that end system B is on a different cable segment because the destination IP address is on a different subnet of 168.71.0.0. End system A is on subnet 168.71.5.0, and end system B is on subnet 168.71.8.0.

End system A has 168.71.5.2 configured as its gateway address. End system A will ARP for the MAC address of 168.71.5.2 so that it can use this address as the MAC address for delivering packets to 168.71.8.1. The layer two (MAC) addresses are specific to the link to which they are attached. The layer three (IP

addresses) are end to end. The layer two addresses for the serial
links have been omitted for clarity.

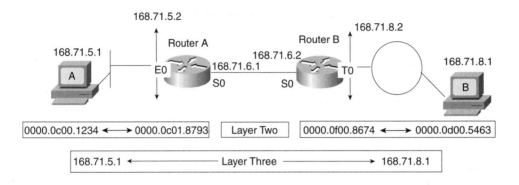

Figure 1–9

End system A sends a PING to end system B.

The IP address 168.71.5.2 and the MAC address
0000.0c01.8793 both belong to RouterA's Ethernet 0 interface. The IP address 168.71.8.2 and the MAC address
0000.0f00.8684 both belong to RouterB's Token Ring 0 interface. Gateways are covered in more detail in Chapter 5.

HINT

If you have a PC running TCP/IP, you may be able to see this for yourself. At a DOS prompt, type C:\> **arp -a**.

You should see the IP address and MAC address of your IP gateway.
You will probably not see entries for systems that are not on your subnet because your PC is sending these datagrams in frames that have
the MAC address of your IP gateway.

Entries for systems on your own subnet will have their own MAC addresses associated with their IP addresses. If you do not see any entries for systems on your subnet, try the following command at a DOS
prompt: C:\>**ping 255.255.255.255** . This is the IP broadcast address.
Then try C:\> **arp -a** again. If other IP hosts are on your subnet, they
may show up in your ARP table.

SUMMARY

Router-based internetworking is a very complex subject. Many of the concepts are interrelated and difficult to understand on their own. This chapter has introduced some of the terms used, as well as some fundamental concepts that provide the foundation upon which the remainder of this book is built. The next chapter introduces the concept of *convergence*, which allows routers to cope with changes in network topologies.

CHAPTER 2

Routing Metrics and Distances

This chapter focuses on convergence and parallel paths, primarily discussing their interaction with routing metrics and distances.

Convergence is the process routers go through when a route (network) or group of routes has become unavailable due to a link going down in the network or extreme packet loss on a link. This loss results in the routers flushing the lost routes and listening to see whether other routes are available. Routers usually store only the best route to a network in their routing tables. Other, higher-cost, routes may exist, but the router ignores them if it believes that the better route still exists.

In the example in Figure 2–1, RouterA converges on a new path to 168.71.8.1 because the link between RouterA and RouterC has failed.

PRIMARY ACTIVITIES OF CONVERGENCE

Convergence involves four primary activities: update, invalid, holddown, and flush, which are explained in Table 2–1. The following example, which uses the *show ip protocol* command at the command prompt of RouterA, shows the default timers used by RIP. These are the timers that a Cisco router uses to control the way RIP reacts to changes in its routing table. It is possible to override these defaults by using the *timers*

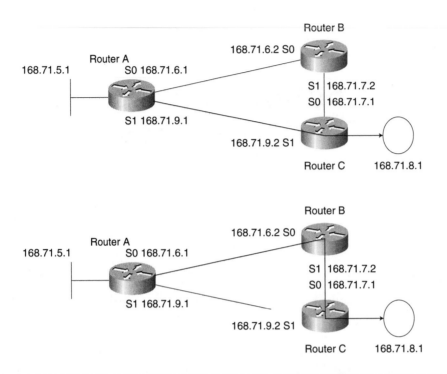

Figure 2–1
RouterA has to converge on a new path because the link to RouterC has gone down.

basic command. See the Cisco command reference for the version of IOS you are using for more information on this command.

NOTES

The *timers basic* command should be used with caution. Inappropriate use of this command can have a catastrophic effect on the IP routing functionality of your router.

```
RouterA#show ip protocol
Routing Protocol is "rip"
  Sending updates every 30 seconds, next due in 27 seconds
```

```
    Invalid after 180 seconds, hold down 180, flushed after 240
  .
  .
output deleted
  .
RouterA#
```

Table 2-1   **Primary Activities of Convergence**

Activity	Description
Update	The time between routing updates sent by a router.
Invalid	A term used to describe both a particular state that a route may be in and a timer that is used to monitor a route's status. The term *invalid* is used for routes that have not been heard from for the period of time that the invalid timer is set for. For example, if the invalid timer is for 60 seconds and an advertisement for a route from the router it is learned from has not been received for 61 seconds, the invalid timer expires and the route is considered invalid.
Hold down	A term used to describe both a particular state that a route may be in and a timer used to monitor the status of a route. The term *hold down* is used to refer to routes that have been marked as invalid (expired) but are not yet capable of being replaced with a new route of a higher metric. The hold down timer determines how long a route remains in hold down (unless the flush timer fires before the hold down timer finishes running).
Flush	A term for both a timer and the act of removing a route from the routing table. The flush timer restarts every time an update is received for a route from the router that it is learned from. It is important to note that the flush timer and the invalid timer restart at the same time and run concurrently. When the flush timer has expired for a route, the route is removed from the routing table. For RIP, the flush timer expires before the hold down timer, so hold down never runs for its complete cycle.

Viewing the Invalid Timers in a Routing Table

The following routing table from RouterA shows that the invalid timer for 168.71.8.0 from 168.71.9.2 (RouterC) was restarted 39 seconds ago.

```
RouterA#show ip route
Codes: C - connected, S - static, I - IGRP, R - RIP, M - mobile, B - BGP
       D - EIGRP, EX - EIGRP external, O - OSPF, IA - OSPF inter area
       E1 - OSPF external type 1, E2 - OSPF external type 2, E - EGP
```

```
      i - IS-IS, L1 - IS-IS level-1, L2 - IS-IS level-2, * - candidate default
      U - per-user static route
Gateway of last resort is 0.0.0.0 to network 0.0.0.0

     168.71.0.0/16 is subnetted, 5 subnets
C        168.71.9.0 is directly connected, Serial1
R        168.71.8.0 [120/1] via 168.71.9.2, 00:00:39, Serial1
R        168.71.7.0 [120/1] via 168.71.6.2, 00:00:11, Serial0
                    [120/1] via 168.71.9.2, 00:00:39, Serial1
C        168.71.6.0 is directly connected, Serial0
C        168.71.5.0 is directly connected, Ethernet0
S*   0.0.0.0/0 is directly connected, Ethernet0
RouterA#
```

The information immediately after the next hop IP address is the timer information. 00:00:00 is hh:mm:ss—hours, minutes, and seconds. The timer is reset to all 0s every time an update for the route is received.

Viewing an Expired Invalid Timer in a Routing Table

This scenario shows how to determine when a route—in this case, 168.71.8.0—is in hold down. For this example to work properly, the serial link between RouterA and RouterC has to remain up and RouterC has to stop advertising 168.81.8.0 to RouterA. If the serial link between the two routers were to fail, RouterA would immediately remove any routes from its routing table that it was using RouterC to reach without waiting for the hold down timer to expire.

In order to show what happens when a route is lost for a reason other than a directly attached link failing, it's necessary to stop RouterC from advertising 168.71.8.0 to RouterA. To do this, an access list is applied to the *router rip* section of RouterC's configuration. The new configuration for RouterC is as follows:

```
!
interface tokenring0
ip address 168.71.8.1 255.255.255.0
!
```

```
interface serial0
ip address 168.71.7.1 255.255.255.0
bandwidth 64
!
interface serial1
ip address 168.71.9.2 255.0.0.0
bandwidth 128
!
router rip
network 168.71.0.0
distribute-list 1 out serial1
!
access-list 1 deny 168.71.8.0 0.0.0.0
access-list 1 permit 0.0.0.0 255.255.255.255
!
```

NOTES

Refer to your Cisco IOS documentation for an explanation of access list configuration and use. The concept of using access lists to filter routing updates is explained in more detail in Chapter 5, "Default Routing."

In the following routing table from RouterA, you can see that RouterA's invalid timer has expired for 168.71.8.0 and that the route is marked "possibly down, routing via 168.71.9.2, Serial1." At this point, the route is considered to be in hold-down, and the 180-second holddown is now running.

There is another path via RouterB by which RouterA can reach 168.71.8.0. RouterA should converge on this path after it finally gives up on the original route via RouterC. In the meantime, RouterA will continue to use this route to reach 168.71.8.0.

```
RouterA#show ip route
Codes: C - connected, S - static, I - IGRP, R - RIP, M - mobile, B - BGP
       D - EIGRP, EX - EIGRP external, O - OSPF, IA - OSPF inter area
       E1 - OSPF external type 1, E2 - OSPF external type 2, E - EGP
       i - IS-IS, L1 - IS-IS level-1, L2 - IS-IS level-2, * - candidate default
       U - per-user static route
```

```
Gateway of last resort is 0.0.0.0 to network 0.0.0.0

     168.71.0.0/16 is subnetted, 5 subnets
C        168.71.9.0 is directly connected, Serial1
R        168.71.8.0/24 is possibly down,
            routing via 168.71.9.2, Serial1
R        168.71.7.0 [120/1] via 168.71.6.2, 00:00:24, Serial0
C        168.71.6.0 is directly connected, Serial0
C        168.71.5.0 is directly connected, Ethernet0
S*   0.0.0.0/0 is directly connected, Ethernet0
RouterA#
```

RouterA will continue to use this route to forward packets destined for subnet 168.71.8.0. This concept is explained in the next scenario.

HINT

If a network administrator discovers that a route is in holddown, he or she can attempt to clear the route manually to speed up convergence if a different path is available. If no other path is available, this command will probably not help resolve the connectivity loss problem created by the route going into holddown. The syntax for this command, using the route from this scenario, is as follows:

```
RouterA#clear ip route 168.71.8.0
```

This command was not used in this section because it would have invalidated the scenario being presented. This command can be used on routes that are in holddown with no negative effect. If it is used on an active route (one that is not in holddown), temporary connectivity loss can occur. It is best to experiment with this command in a lab environment to understand how it will affect IP connectivity before using it in a live environment.

The administrator can also use the *traceroute* command to find a router that has a connection to the network that is in holddown. Depending on the topology of the network and the status of the routing tables in the routers that the *traceroute* command encounters, it may actually end up at the router that was advertising the route that has gone into holddown. However, it is not really necessary to find the exact router that was sending the original route. Any router connected to the same network can be used to investigate what the problem is and possibly resolve it. It could be something like an Ethernet segment with excessive collisions that is constantly resetting or a beaconing Token Ring segment. The *traceroute* command is available on

Cisco routers and most other hosts that use TCP/IP. The syntax of this command on a Cisco router's command prompt is as follows:

```
RouterA#traceroute 168.71.8.0
```

In Figure 2–1, the *traceroute 168.71.8.0* command from RouterA would end up at RouterC using the path via RouterB after RouterA had converged on the new path. An investigation of RouterC would have turned up the fact that someone had configured an access list against RIP. The TraceRoute utility is described in more detail in Chapter 6, "IP Troubleshooting Scenarios." More information on TraceRoute can be found in RFC 1393 as well (see Appendix A, "RFCs").

Router Still Uses a Path

During the time RouterA has its route to 168.71.8.0 in hold-down, it continues to forward any packets it receives that are destined for subnet 168.71.8.0 to RouterC. This is standard behavior for a router running RIP, as well as for many other IP routing protocols.

One of the reasons for having routing protocols behave this way is based on the following assumption:

Temporary packet loss due to using routes to networks that might not be viable is better than immediately accepting a less desirable route to the destination network.

In this scenario, the less desirable path would be for RouterA to reach 168.71.8.0 via RouterB. If 168.71.8.0 went into hold-down in RouterA because of congestion on the link between RouterA and RouterC—which caused the packets with the routing updates to be dropped—packets from sessions between hosts on subnets 168.71.5.0 and 168.71.8.0 over the same link should be dropped as well.

By allowing these packets to be dropped instead of sending them via the less desirable path, RouterA and RouterC are giving the hosts a chance to react to the dropped packets by sending fewer packets at a time—and perhaps even sending smaller packets. This requires that either the applications in use or their underlying protocols keep track of packet loss and react in a network-friendly fashion.

HINT

In networks with very large routing tables, the updates might be split between multiple packets. If you have recently added several new routes and are having problems with these routes not being learned by other routers or other routes that were once stable suddenly disappearing—particularly over low-speed serial links—it is very probable that the same packets at the end of each update are getting lost. Routes are usually advertised in descending order: 134.67.0.0 would be sent before 120.34.0.0. If your lowest numbered routes are having problems, this is most likely what is happening.

If RouterA immediately accepted the less desirable route to 168.71.8.0 as soon as the invalid timer for 168.71.8.0 expired and forwarded all traffic to 168.71.8.0 over it, congestion on the more desirable path between RouterA and RouterC would cease to be a problem.

NOTES

Remember that holddown is both the name of a timer that routing protocols use and the name of a function. The holddown timer, which is 180 seconds for RIP, starts when the invalid timer expires. The holddown function is the same for all IP routing protocols. It is used to prevent a new, higher-cost (less desirable) route from being accepted for a route that has been marked invalid for the period of the holddown timer.

The routing updates that had been getting dropped due to congestion would start arriving again, and RouterA would immediately go back to using its link to RouterC to reach 168.71.8.0. At this point, the problem would start all over again.

This is referred to as *route flapping*, which is when a route continuously switches between two different next hop routers—RouterB and RouterC in this scenario.

If the traffic pattern that caused this problem is more than just an anomaly, it will be necessary to either increase the speed of the link between RouterA and RouterC or permanently configure the hosts to send fewer packets at a time (and possibly smaller packets as well) to prevent it from happening again.

In this scenario, Ping (Packet Internet Groper) will be used to generate IP packets to prove that a router will continue to forward packets to a network that it believes may be unreachable.

NOTES

Ping is a useful diagnostic tool that is available on all TCP/IP-capable systems. If you type **ping,** followed by an IP address, at a router console, the router attempts to send IP ping packets to the destination IP host. If the host is reachable, it should respond. The device sending the ping keeps track of the time it was sent and when a response was received so that it has a rough idea of how long it takes to send and receive IP packets with a remote host.

Cisco routers, as well as many other hosts using TCP/IP, run the Ping application as a very low priority task on the CPU. This can cause the round-trip times to appear longer than they really are. A better way to measure round-trip time is to analyze traffic from an actual application flow perspective. Most analyzers time stamp the packets they decode. For applications that send data in response to queries such as databases or Web pages, the time between the request and the response is the total network delay. However, this delay also includes any time the server took to process the request before replying.

Figure 2–2 shows that RouterA will continue to use its original route to 168.71.8.0 even though it is marked as "Possibly Down." Refer to the output of the *show ip route* command from RouterA that was presented at the end of the previous section.

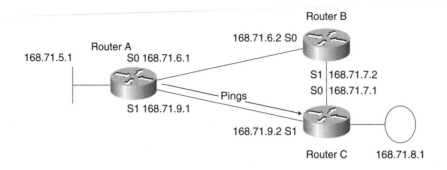

Figure 2–2

RouterA still uses the route to 168.71.8.0.

The following debug messages from RouterA show that RouterA still sends ping packets to 168.71.8.1 over the serial link to RouterC. The responses to the pings from RouterC to RouterA also show up in the debug messages. The last part of each message indicates whether the packet is being sent (*sending*) or received (*rcvd*). Refer to Figure 2–2 when reading the debug messages.

```
RouterA#deb ip packet
RouterA#ping 168.71.8.1
Type escape sequence to abort.
Sending 5, 100-byte ICMP Echos to 168.71.8.1, timeout is 2 seconds:
!!!!!
Success rate is 100  percent (5/5), round-trip min/avg/max = 20/23/24 ms
RouterA#
IP: s=168.71.9.1 (local), d=168.71.8.1 (Serial1), len 100, sending
IP: s=168.71.8.1 (Serial1), d=168.71.9.1 (Serial1), len 104, rcvd 3
IP: s=168.71.9.1 (local), d=168.71.8.1 (Serial1), len 100, sending
IP: s=168.71.8.1 (Serial1), d=168.71.9.1 (Serial1), len 104, rcvd 3
IP: s=168.71.9.1 (local), d=168.71.8.1 (Serial1), len 100, sending
IP: s=168.71.8.1 (Serial1), d=168.71.9.1 (Serial1), len 104, rcvd 3
IP: s=168.71.9.1 (local), d=168.71.8.1 (Serial1), len 100, sending
IP: s=168.71.8.1 (Serial1), d=168.71.9.1 (Serial1), len 104, rcvd 3
IP: s=168.71.9.1 (local), d=168.71.8.1 (Serial1), len 100, sending
IP: s=168.71.8.1 (Serial1), d=168.71.9.1 (Serial1), len 104, rcvd 3
RouterA
```

In the previous router output, you can see that RouterA sent five pings to a host on the 168.71.8.0 subnet; in this case, the host is RouterC's Token Ring interface. The pings were successful, as indicated by the exclamation points (!). This proves that even though RouterA thought its route to 168.71.8.0 was no longer valid, it still used it to forward packets.

NOTES

The preceding router output also shows the use of the *debug ip packet* command. When the router is Process Switching IP packets, this causes the router to display debug information for every IP packet that it either sends or receives. Process Switching is explained later in this chapter in the section on Process Switching versus Fast Switching. This command should be used with extreme care. It can cause a heavily loaded router to stop functioning. It is possible to use access lists in conjunction with some debugging commands (including *debug ip packet*) to reduce their performance impact on a router, which is explained in Chapter 5. If you are using a Telnet connection to a router, you need to enter the *terminal monitor* command in order to view the output of debug commands. You must do this for every new Telnet session. Check the version of Cisco IOS you are running to find out its default behavior for sending debug messages.

UNDERSTANDING CONVERGENCE

Recall that convergence involves four primary activities: update, invalid, holddown, and flush. These activities come into play any time a router experiences a change in its routing table, including when the router is powered on. This section includes a scenario that shows the process of convergence by causing RouterC to cease sending routing updates to RouterA. This section also introduces the concept of parallel paths in a routing table and discusses some of the issues they can create.

Parallel Paths

When a router has two or more routes to the same network with the same metric, these routes can be thought of as having an equal cost. The term *parallel paths* is a just a common way to refer to occurrences of equal-cost routes in a routing table.

The Effect of Parallel Paths on Convergence

If a router had two or more equal-cost paths (routes) to a network, it may use them concurrently. If a router loses one or more of the parallel paths, it will continue to use the paths that are still available. RouterA in Figure 2–3 has two equal-cost paths to 168.71.7.0. If it loses the route via serial 0, it can continue to use the route via serial 1. Convergence in this situation is simply a matter of removing any references in the routing table to the route that has ceased to exist.

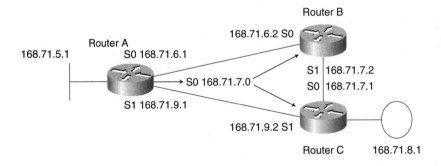

Figure 2–3

Parallel paths enable a router to continue to use whatever paths are available when some paths are down.

The arrows in Figure 2–3 show that RouterA has two routes (parallel paths) to subnet 168.71.7.0.

Looking at Parallel Paths in a Routing Table

The following routing table from RouterA has the two parallel paths, which are shown here in bold:

```
RouterA#show ip route
Codes: C - connected, S - static, I - IGRP, R - RIP, M - mobile, B - BGP
       D - EIGRP, EX - EIGRP external, O - OSPF, IA - OSPF inter area
       E1 - OSPF external type 1, E2 - OSPF external type 2, E - EGP
       i - IS-IS, L1 - IS-IS level-1, L2 - IS-IS level-2, * - candidate default
Gateway of last resort is 0.0.0.0 to network 0.0.0.0
168.71.0.0 255.255.255.0 is subnetted, 5 subnets
C       168.71.9.0 is directly connected, Serial1
R       168.71.8.0 [120/1] via 168.71.9.2, 00:00:15, Serial1
R       168.71.7.0 [120/1] via 168.71.6.2, 00:00:00, Serial0
                   [120/1] via 168.71.9.2, 00:00:15, Serial1
C       168.71.6.0 is directly connected, Serial0
C       168.71.5.0 is directly connected, Ethernet0
     171.68.0.0 is variably subnetted, 2 subnets, 2 masks
C       171.68.207.128 255.255.255.128 is directly connected, Ethernet0
S       171.68.0.0 255.255.0.0 [1/0] via 171.68.207.129
S*   0.0.0.0/0 is directly connected, Ethernet0
RouterA#
```

When parallel (equal-cost) paths are available to a network, the routing table displays the first entry with a character prefix indicating how it knows about the route and omits this prefix for all other paths to the same network. In the previous example, RouterA's routing table indicates that it has two paths to 168.71.7.0. Both are learned via RIP; however, only one of them has the R tag that indicates it is a RIP-derived route. The R is assumed for the other route. The first route has a next hop of 168.71.6.2. The second route has a next hop of 168.71.9.2. Refer to Figure 2–3 to compare the network diagram with the previous routing table.

The codes section of the routing table shows what routing protocols the various prefixes are used for.

Convergence in Action

This section presents a scenario that explains what happens
when a router running RIP has to converge on a new route
because an existing route has ceased to be advertised by the
router it was originally learned from.

Here is a review of the default timers RIP uses. These timers are
reflected in the behavior of RIP in this scenario.

```
RouterA#show ip protocol
Routing Protocol is "rip"
  Sending updates every 30 seconds, next due in 27 seconds
  Invalid after 180 seconds, hold down 180, flushed after 240
  .

  .
Output deleted
  .
RouterA#
```

The access list that was applied in the previous section to stop
RouterC from advertising 168.71.8.0 has been modified to
also block subnet 168.71.7.0. It has been applied to RouterC
again for this section.

This is RouterA's routing table before the invalid timer for the
route to 168.71.8.0 expires. Notice that the invalid timer is
already at 39 seconds. This means that the access list was
applied at least nine seconds ago.

```
RouterA#show ip route
Codes: C - connected, S - static, I - IGRP, R - RIP, M - mobile, B - BGP
       D - EIGRP, EX - EIGRP external, O - OSPF, IA - OSPF inter area
       E1 - OSPF external type 1, E2 - OSPF external type 2, E - EGP
       i - IS-IS, L1 - IS-IS level-1, L2 - IS-IS level-2, * - candidate default
       U - per-user static route

The gateway of last resort is 0.0.0.0 to network 0.0.0.0:
     168.71.0.0/16 is subnetted, 5 subnets
C       168.71.9.0 is directly connected, Serial1
R       168.71.8.0 [120/1] via 168.71.9.2, 00:00:39, Serial1
R       168.71.7.0 [120/1] via 168.71.6.2, 00:00:11, Serial0
                   [120/1] via 168.71.9.2, 00:00:39, Serial1
C       168.71.6.0 is directly connected, Serial0
C       168.71.5.0 is directly connected, Ethernet0
```

```
S*   0.0.0.0/0 is directly connected, Ethernet0
RouterA#
```

RouterA's invalid timers for the routes it has learned from RouterC will expire in 141 seconds.

Assume that 141 seconds have just passed. The following debug messages from RouterA show what happens when the invalid timers for the routes it has learned from RouterC fire.

```
RouterA#debug ip routing
RouterA#sh clock
20:33:30.246 UTC Fri Aug 2 1996
RouterA#debug ip routing
Aug  2 20:36:45: RT: flushed route to 168.71.8.0 via 168.71.9.2 (Serial1)
Aug  2 20:36:45: RT: no routes to 168.71.8.0, entering holddown
Aug  2 20:36:45: RT: flushed route to 168.71.7.0 via 168.71.9.2 (Serial1)
Aug  2 20:37:41: RT: garbage collecting entry for 168.71.8.0
Aug  2 20:37:50: RT: add 168.71.8.0/24 via 168.71.6.2, rip metric [120/2]
RouterA#
```

Notice in the debug that RouterA did not add a new route to 168.71.7.0 after removing the old routes from RouterC. This is because RouterA originally had two parallel paths to 168.71.7.0. The convergence process in this scenario involved removing any references to routes learned from RouterC and installing a route to 168.71.8.0 via RouterB.

NOTES

The preceding router output introduced the *debug ip routing* command. The *debug ip routing* command causes the router to create a message any time the status of the routing table changes. This change can be the addition of a new route or a change in the status of an existing route.

The Routing Table After Convergence

The following routing table from RouterA shows its new converged state. RouterA is now using RouterB to route packets to 168.71.8.0. Remember that RouterA did not lose its original route to 168.71.8.0 because there was a problem with RouterC's Token Ring interface. It lost the route because the access list applied to RouterC's configuration caused RouterC to stop advertising all of its routes to RouterA. RouterC never stopped advertising routes to RouterB.

```
RouterA#show ip route
Codes: C - connected, S - static, I - IGRP, R - RIP, M - mobile, B - BGP
       D - EIGRP, EX - EIGRP external, O - OSPF, IA - OSPF inter area
       E1 - OSPF external type 1, E2 - OSPF external type 2, E - EGP
       i - IS-IS, L1 - IS-IS level-1, L2 - IS-IS level-2, * - candidate default
       U - per-user static route
Gateway of last resort is 0.0.0.0 to network 0.0.0.0
     168.71.0.0/16 is subnetted, 5 subnets
C       168.71.9.0 is directly connected, Serial1
R       168.71.8.0 [120/2] via 168.71.6.2, 00:00:05, Serial0
R       168.71.7.0 [120/1] via 168.71.6.2, 00:00:06, Serial0
C       168.71.6.0 is directly connected, Serial0
C       168.71.5.0 is directly connected, Ethernet0
S*   0.0.0.0/0 is directly connected, Ethernet0
RouterA#
```

Notice the different metric in the partial routing tables shown here. When the route for 168.71.8.0 changed from RouterC to RouterB, the metric went from 1 to 2. The metric is the second number inside the []s. For example, [120/3] means a metric of 3. The next two bullet points illustrate the change from one metric to another.

- The original route via 168.71.9.2 has a metric of 1, as follows:

```
RouterA#show ip route 168.71.8.0 (output edited for clarity)
R       168.71.8.0 [120/1] via 168.71.9.2, 00:00:39, Serial1
```

- The metric changed to 2 after losing the original route via 168.71.9.2 and replacing it with the new route via 168.71.6.2:

```
RouterA#show ip route 168.71.8.0 (output edited for clarity)
R       168.71.8.0 [120/2] via 168.71.6.2, 00:00:05, Serial0
```

Keeping track of the metrics and next hop addresses in a routing table will help you when you are troubleshooting an IP routing problem. You will be able to determine the different routes your traffic is taking and compare them to your network diagrams.

Step-by-Step Review of Convergence

The following steps occurred at or close to the same time RouterC stopped advertising routes to RouterA. Refer to the time stamps on the previous debug messages.

1. Aug 2 20:33:45: Invalid timer restarted after the last routing update was received from RouterC. You know that this was the approximate time the last update was received because the invalid timer runs for 180 seconds (three minutes) before firing, and it fires at 20:36:45.

2. Aug 2 20:33:45: Flush timer restarted after the last routing update was received from RouterC. You know that this is the approximate time because the flush timer is reset every time the invalid timer is reset. The flush timer and the invalid timer run concurrently.

3. Aug 2 20:36:45: Invalid timer fires for networks that RouterA was using RouterC to reach.

4. Aug 2 20:36:45: Hold down timer starts for networks that RouterA was using RouterC to reach.

5. Aug 2 20:37:41: Flush timer fires and terminates hold-down timer for networks that RouterA was using RouterC to reach. This is allowed because the flush timer overrides the hold down timer.

Hold down didn't start until 20:36:45. The hold down timer is 180 seconds (three minutes); therefore, it should have run until 20:39:45.

Garbage collecting is Cisco-speak for totally removing (flushing) any remaining references to the routes in question.

6. Aug 2 20:37:50: RouterA receives RouterB's routing update and installs a route to 168.71.8.0. In this case, the update from RouterB arrived nine seconds after RouterA's flush timer fired.

NOTES

Because RIP only sends updates every 30 seconds, it could have taken anywhere from .01 second to 29.99 seconds (rounding to the nearest hundredth second) for RouterB's next update to arrive so that RouterA could accept the new route.

The total estimated time of convergence (from last update received to accepting the higher cost route) in this scenario was equal to the following:

 20:37:50 (finish)

−20:33:45 (start)

 00:04:05 Time to converge

You may have noticed that the times shown in the debug do not match the exact default timer intervals for RIP. This is because the router might take some time to get around to running the task. A RIP timer might expire and raise a flag to be serviced, but it might not be serviced for a few seconds after raising the flag. This is normal behavior and should be considered when determining maximum possible convergence times. Note that the update timer will vary by a random amount, helping prevent all routers from sending their updates at exactly the same time. RFC 1058, which is discussed in Appendix A, explains RIP timers in more detail.

It is important to note that RouterB was advertising 168.71.8.0 and 168.71.7.0 to RouterA every 30 seconds. RouterA was initially ignoring RouterB's advertisements for 168.71.8.0 because the metric from RouterB was 2, whereas the metric from RouterC was 1. RouterA already had RouterB's route to 168.71.7.0 installed in its routing table. Figure 2–4 maps the processes involved in convergence against a timeline.

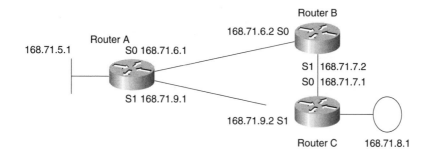

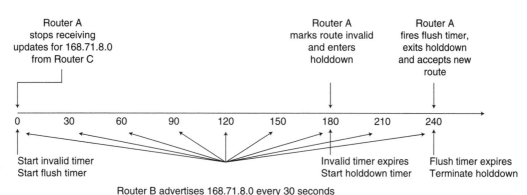

Router B advertises 168.71.8.0 every 30 seconds

a - Router C stops advertising 168.71.8.0 at 0 seconds.
b - Router A marks 168.71.8.0 as invalid and puts it into holddown at 180 seconds.
c - Router A exits holddown when flush timer expires and accepts new route via Router B at 240 seconds.

Figure 2–4
A timeline for convergence.

Debug Messages and Reality

Unfortunately, the debug messages in the previous example are somewhat misleading. Following are the original debug messages for reference:

```
RouterA#sh clock
20:33:30.246 UTC Fri Aug 2 1996
RouterA#debug ip routing
Aug  2 20:36:45: RT: flushed route to 168.71.8.0 via 168.71.9.2 (Serial1)
Aug  2 20:36:45: RT: no routes to 168.71.8.0, entering holddown
Aug  2 20:36:45: RT: flushed route to 168.71.7.0 via 168.71.9.2 (Serial1)
Aug  2 20:37:41: RT: garbage collecting entry for 168.71.8.0
Aug  2 20:37:50: RT: add 168.71.8.0/24 via 168.71.6.2, rip metric [120/2]
RouterA#
```

Here is what is really happening:

```
RouterA#sh clock
20:33:30.246 UTC Fri Aug 2 1996
RouterA#debug ip routing
Aug 2 20:36:45: RT: preparing to advertise 168.71.8.0 via 168.71.9.2 (Serial1) as unreachable
Aug 2 20:36:45: RT: invalid timer expired no routes to 168.71.8.0, entering holddown, marking
➥route as possibly down
Aug 2 20:36:45: RT: preparing to advertise 168.71.7.0 via 168.71.9.2 (Serial1) as unreachable
Aug  2 20:37:41: RT: flush timer expired terminating holddown for 168.71.8.0
Aug  2 20:37:50: RT: add 168.71.8.0/24 via 168.71.6.2, rip metric [120/2]
RouterA#
```

When Holddown Is Initiated

A router puts a route into holddown when one of the following happens:

- The router that was advertising the route stops advertising it for a period of time. This period of time is usually referred to as the *invalid period*.

- The router that advertised the original route sends a new advertisement for the same route with a metric greater than the metric stored in the routing table. This usually indicates that there is a *routing loop*, which causes the route to be immediately deleted and put into holddown instead of being forced to wait for the invalid timer to fire.

- The router that was advertising the route sends a new advertisement for the route with an unreachable metric, otherwise known as poisoning the route.

Understanding Parallel Paths and Their Effect on Packet Forwarding

Besides providing redundancy in case of a circuit failure, the availability of parallel paths enables a router to load balance packets over the available paths. This can lead to more efficient use of the available bandwidth. The two ways a router can load balance over parallel paths are as follows:

- Round robin on a packet-by-packet basis. *Packet by packet* means that the router sends one packet across each of the parallel links, one link at a time.

- Round robin on a session-by-session basis. *Session by session* means that instead of just keeping track of the destination subnet, the router stores the entire IP address of the destination host. Each packet to the same host uses the same link.

One type of load balancing is not necessarily better than another. Each type has its own set of benefits and drawbacks. Packet-by-packet load balancing is generally considered the better choice for parallel links that are slower than 64K. However, this method may deliver packets out of order in a network when the propagation delay (the time it takes a packet to reach the other end of a link) for the two paths is not the same.

In Figure 2–5, the PC has two equal-cost paths (parallel paths) available for subnet 168.71.7.0 to use for sending packets to 168.71.7.1 (the serial 1 interface on RouterB). Remember that routing decisions are most commonly made based only on the network portion of a destination address.

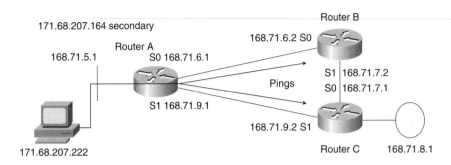

Figure 2–5

PC has two paths to reach subnet 168.71.7.0.

NOTES

It is possible to manually add a route in a routing table that uses an entire IP destination address. This is called a *static* (manually configured, not learned by a dynamic routing protocol) *host* (uses all bits in the destination IP host address) *route*. This concept is covered in more detail in Chapter 5 in the section on floating static routes.

RouterA could use packet-by-packet load balancing to forward ping packets from the PC to IP address 168.71.7.1, in which case one packet would go via RouterB directly and the other would go indirectly via RouterC.

The following debug messages from RouterA show RouterA using both paths to route pings to 168.71.7.1. Notice that the outbound interface alternates between (serial 0) and (serial 1).

```
RouterA#debug ip packet

RouterA#ping 168.71.7.1
Type escape sequence to abort.
Sending 5, 100-byte ICMP Echos to 168.71.7.1, timeout is 2 seconds:
!!!!!
Success rate is 100 percent (5/5), round-trip min/avg/max = 32/34/40 ms
IP: s=171.68.207.222 (Ethernet0), d=168.71.7.1 (Serial0), g=168.71.6.2, len
74, forward
IP: s=171.68.207.222 (Ethernet0), d=168.71.7.1 (Serial1), g=168.71.9.2, len 74, forward
IP: s=171.68.207.222 (Ethernet0), d=168.71.7.1 (Serial0), g=168.71.6.2, len 74, forward
IP: s=171.68.207.222 (Ethernet0), d=168.71.7.1 (Serial1), g=168.71.9.2, len 74, forward
IP: s=171.68.207.222 (Ethernet0), d=168.71.7.1 (Serial0), g=168.71.6.2, len 74, forward
```

The following is an important concept: Just because a path is equal cost from the perspective of one router doesn't mean that both paths have the same number of routers in them, even if the routing metric (unit of measurement) is hop-based.

RouterA has no way of knowing that 168.71.7.1 is assigned to a serial interface in RouterB. RouterA only understands that both RouterB and RouterC indicated that they are connected to subnet 168.71.7.0. RouterA listened to the routing advertisements from RouterB and RouterC indicating that each has a direct connection to 168.71.7.0. RouterA added one hop to the metric for each route because from its perspective, 168.71.7.0 is reachable over one hop (one router) via two different routers.

RouterA could also use session-by-session load balancing to forward the same ping packets. The following debug message from RouterA shows RouterA using a single path to forward the packets to 168.71.7.1.

However, the fact that only a single path is being used is obscured because the debug shows only the first packet used to set up the route cache when a router uses session-by-session load balancing. The remaining packets are hidden from the router's debug function because they are being forwarded by the router's CPU at interrupt level using the information from the route cache. If both paths had been used, there would have been a second debug message pointing to (serial 1).

```
RouterA#deb ip packet
RouterA#ping 168.71.7.1
Type escape sequence to abort.
Sending 5, 100-byte ICMP Echos to 168.71.7.1, timeout is 2 seconds:
!!!!!
Success rate is 100 percent (5/5), round-trip min/avg/max = 32/34/40 ms
IP: s=171.68.207.222 (Ethernet0), d=168.71.7.1 (Serial0), g=168.71.6.2, len 74, forward
```

PROCESS SWITCHING VERSUS FAST SWITCHING

The method chosen for packet forwarding is dependent on the type of switching the router is performing for IP datagrams. This book was written using Cisco 2500s running IOS version 11.1. Cisco 2500s running 11.1 only have the following two switching methods available:

- *Process switching* (performing packet-by-packet load balancing)
- *Fast switching* (performing destination-by-destination load balancing)

Process switching utilizes the CPU for looking up the next hop in the routing table for every packet that needs to be forwarded.

Fast switching, which uses a route cache of the destination IP address and the next hop IP address, is less CPU intensive than process switching. The first packet to any host is always process switched. If fast switching is enabled on the outbound interface, the router creates a cache entry for the destination host after forwarding the first packet. The CPU forwards the next packet destined for the same host based on the cache entry. Having the CPU do a route cache lookup is much faster than having it do a routing table lookup.

Cisco IOS actually has several different methods of switching IP packets from an inbound interface to an outbound interface. The methods available are dependent on the version of IOS in use and the hardware platform it is being run on. A thorough discussion of all Cisco switching methods is beyond the scope of this book. Refer to the Cisco IOS documentation for the hardware and software you are using for more information.

Configuring Process Switching

The following text shows how to configure a router to perform process switching on an interface, which causes the router to load balance on a packet-by-packet basis [the *no ip route-cache* command was also applied to Serial 1]:

```
RouterA#-config#interface serial 0
RouterA#-config-if#no ip route-cache
RouterA#-config-if#^Z
RouterA#sh ip int s 0
Serial0 is up, line protocol is up
  Internet address is 168.71.6.1/24
  Broadcast address is 255.255.255.255
  Address determined by non-volatile memory
  MTU is 1500 bytes
  Helper address is not set
  Directed broadcast forwarding is enabled
  Multicast reserved groups joined: 224.0.0.9
  Outgoing access list is not set
  Inbound  access list is not set
  Proxy ARP is enabled
  Security level is default
  Split horizon is enabled
  ICMP redirects are always sent
  ICMP unreachables are always sent
  ICMP mask replies are never sent
  IP fast switching is disabled
  IP fast switching on the same interface is disabled
  IP multicast fast switching is enabled
  Router Discovery is disabled
  IP output packet accounting is disabled
  IP access violation accounting is disabled
  TCP/IP header compression is disabled
  Probe proxy name replies are disabled
  Gateway Discovery is disabled
  Policy routing is disabled
RouterA#
```

In the following output, the debug IP packet from RouterA (which was captured as the PC in Figure 2–5 and sent four pings to 168.71.7.1), you can see the packets load balancing over serial 0 and serial 1. This occurs because there are two equal-cost routes to 168.71.7.0 and the pings are being process switched:

```
RouterA#debug ip packet
IP: s=171.68.207.222 (Ethernet0), d=168.71.7.1 (Serial1), g=168.71.9.2, len 74, forward
IP: s=171.68.207.222 (Ethernet0), d=168.71.7.1 (Serial1), g=168.71.9.2, len 74, forward
IP: s=171.68.207.222 (Ethernet0), d=168.71.7.1 (Serial0), g=168.71.6.2, len 74, forward
IP: s=171.68.207.222 (Ethernet0), d=168.71.7.1 (Serial1), g=168.71.9.2, len 74, forward
IP: s=171.68.207.222 (Ethernet0), d=168.71.7.1 (Serial0), g=168.71.6.2, len 74, forward
```

Configuring Fast Switching

The following text shows how to configure a router to perform fast switching on an interface. This will cause the router to load balance on a session-by-session basis [the *ip route-cache* command was also applied to Serial 1]:.

```
RouterA#-config#interface serial 0
RouterA#-config-if#ip route-cache
RouterA#-config-if#^Z
RouterA#sh ip int s 0
Serial1 is up, line protocol is up
  Internet address is 168.71.6.1/24
  Broadcast address is 255.255.255.255
  Address determined by non-volatile memory
  MTU is 1500 bytes
  Helper address is not set
  Directed broadcast forwarding is enabled
  Multicast reserved groups joined: 224.0.0.9
  Outgoing access list is not set
  Inbound  access list is not set
  Proxy ARP is enabled
  Security level is default
  Split horizon is enabled
  ICMP redirects are always sent
  ICMP unreachables are always sent
  ICMP mask replies are never sent
  IP fast switching is enabled
  IP fast switching on the same interface is enabled
  IP multicast fast switching is enabled
  Router Discovery is disabled
  IP output packet accounting is disabled
  IP access violation accounting is disabled
  TCP/IP header compression is disabled
  Probe proxy name replies are disabled
  Gateway Discovery is disabled
  Policy routing is disabled
RouterA#
```

The PC in Figure 2–5 is again sending four pings to 168.71.7.1. Notice that only one packet shows up in the debug. This is because debugging shows only the packets getting process switched. The final three pings in sequence were fast switched using the route cache entry created after the first ping was switched out serial 1. You can also see the IP cache becoming populated when the packets are forwarded because the *debug ip cache* command has been entered. Refer to Figure 2–6 to see the network topology used for this scenario.

```
RouterA#deb ip packet
RouterA#deb ip cache
IP: s=171.68.207.222 (Ethernet0), d=168.71.7.1 (Serial0), g=168.71.6.2, len 74, forward
IP: created cache entry for 168.71.7.1/32
```

The following text shows the output of entering the *show ip cache* command on RouterA. There are no entries for Ethernet0 because it was configured for process switching in this example.

```
RouterA#sh ip cache
IP routing cache 3 entries, 444 bytes
Minimum invalidation interval 2 seconds, maximum interval 5 seconds,
   quiet interval 3 seconds, threshold 0 requests
Invalidation rate 0 in last second, 0 in last 3 seconds
Last full cache invalidation occurred 0:00:25 ago
Prefix/Length      Age       Interface       Next Hop
168.71.7.1/32      0:00:08   Serial1         168.71.9.2
RouterA#
```

A thorough explanation of debugging the *ip route cache* is beyond the scope of this book. Refer to the Cisco IOS debug command reference for the IOS version you are using for more details on this command.

NOTES

The preceeding router output shows the use of the *debug ip cache* command. This command causes the router to display messages when changes occur in the IP forwarding cache.

UNDERSTANDING THE ROLE OF SPLIT HORIZON

Split horizon is the function of not advertising routes over an interface that the router is using to reach the route. The role of split horizon is to help avoid routing loops in a network. Split horizon prevents a router from advertising routes in its routing table that are known via a particular interface back out that same interface. This scenario explains how turning off split horizon can lead to routing loops.

Refer to Figure 2–6. RouterA would not advertise 168.71.8.0 to RouterC over serial 1 because RouterA learned about this subnet from RouterC over its serial 1 interface. However, RouterA does send and receive updates for 168.71.8.0 over serial 0 because RouterB is not the router that RouterA is using to access 168.71.8.0. RouterA's route to 168.71.8.0 is not known via this path.

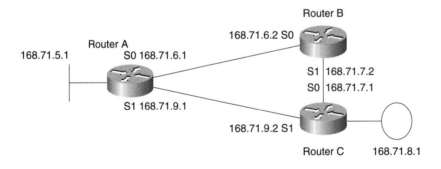

Figure 2–6

A review of the basic network topology.

Split horizon applies to connected routes as well. A *connected route* is a route to which the router has a direct physical attachment. In the previous example, RouterA has a connected route to 168.71.6.0 via interface serial 0. In other words, as far as RouterA is concerned, 168.71.6.0 is known via serial 0.

RouterA does not advertise 168.71.6.0 out serial 0 if split horizon is enabled on serial 0.

RouterA's preferred route (the route it has stored) to network 168.71.8.0 is out serial 1. When RouterA is due to send an update to RouterC, it builds an update that contains all of the routes in its routing table except for the routes known via serial 1. In this case, it does not contain 168.71.9.0, 168.71.8.0, or 168.71.7.0. It does contain 168.71.5.0 and 168.71.6.0.

The following is an edited version of RouterA's routing table for reference:

```
RouterA#show ip route (edited for clarity)
C       168.71.9.0 is directly connected, Serial1
R       168.71.8.0 [120/1] via 168.71.9.2, 00:00:24, Serial1
R       168.71.7.0 [120/1] via 168.71.9.2, 00:00:24, Serial1
                   [120/1] via 168.71.6.2, 00:00:19, Serial0
C       168.71.6.0 is directly connected, Serial0
C     168.71.5.0 is directly connected, Ethernet0
```

You need to refer back to this text as this scenario progresses.

Routing Advertisements with Split Horizon Enabled

In the following output of the *debug ip rip* command on RouterA, you can see RouterA both receiving and advertising 168.71.8.0 out serial 0. You can also see that RouterA does not advertise 168.71.8.0 out serial 1 to RouterC. Notice also that RouterA does not advertise the connected routes out the interfaces they are connected to.

```
RouterA#debug ip rip
Aug  2 23:02:03: RIP: received v1 update from 168.71.9.2 on Serial1
Aug  2 23:02:03:      168.71.8.0 in 1 hops
Aug  2 23:02:03:      168.71.7.0 in 1 hops
Aug  2 23:02:05: RIP: received v1 update from 168.71.6.2 on Serial0
Aug  2 23:02:05:      168.71.8.0 in 2 hops
Aug  2 23:02:05:      168.71.7.0 in 1 hops
Aug  2 23:02:16: RIP: sending v1 update to 255.255.255.255 via Serial0 (168.71.6.1)
Aug  2 23:02:16:      subnet  168.71.9.0, metric 1
Aug  2 23:02:16:      subnet  168.71.8.0, metric 2
Aug  2 23:02:16:      subnet  168.71.5.0, metric 1
```

```
Aug  2 23:02:16:        default, metric 1
Aug  2 23:02:16: RIP: sending v1 update to 255.255.255.255 via Serial1 (168.71.9.1)
Aug  2 23:02:16:        subnet  168.71.6.0, metric 1
Aug  2 23:02:16:        subnet  168.71.5.0, metric 1
Aug  2 23:02:16:        default, metric 1
RouterA#
```

Split horizon is enabled by default in most instances. It is possible to tell whether split horizon is on or off by entering the *show interface* command at a router prompt and examining the output.

```
RouterA#sh ip int s 1
Serial1 is up, line protocol is up
  Internet address is 168.71.9.1/24
  Broadcast address is 255.255.255.255
  Address determined by non-volatile memory
  MTU is 1500 bytes
  Helper address is not set
  Directed broadcast forwarding is enabled
  Multicast reserved groups joined: 224.0.0.9
  Outgoing access list is not set
  Inbound  access list is not set
  Proxy ARP is enabled
  Security level is default
  Split horizon is enabled
  ICMP redirects are always sent
  ICMP unreachables are always sent
  ICMP mask replies are never sent
  IP fast switching is enabled
  IP fast switching on the same interface is enabled
  IP multicast fast switching is enabled
  Router Discovery is disabled
  IP output packet accounting is disabled
  IP access violation accounting is disabled
  TCP/IP header compression is disabled
  Probe proxy name replies are disabled
  Gateway Discovery is disabled
  Policy routing is disabled
RouterA#
```

Routing Advertisements with Split Horizon Disabled

You want to disable split horizon when there is a need to send routing updates back out interfaces that they were learned over. The scenario on multipoint interfaces later in this chapter explains a circumstance you may want to disable split horizon for. It discusses how to disable split horizon, as well as the possible negative effects of doing so.

The following text shows how to disable split horizon and how to tell whether you have been successful [the *no ip split-horizon* command was also applied to Serial 1]:

```
RouterA#-config#interface serial 0
RouterA#-config-if#no ip split-horizon
RouterA#-config-if#^Z
RouterA#sh ip int s 0
Serial0 is up, line protocol is up
  Internet address is 168.71.6.1/24
  Broadcast address is 255.255.255.255
  Address determined by non-volatile memory
  MTU is 1500 bytes
  Helper address is not set
  Directed broadcast forwarding is enabled
  Multicast reserved groups joined: 224.0.0.9
  Outgoing access list is not set
  Inbound  access list is not set
  Proxy ARP is enabled
  Security level is default
  Split horizon is disabled
  ICMP redirects are always sent
  ICMP unreachables are always sent
  ICMP mask replies are never sent
  IP fast switching is enabled
  IP fast switching on the same interface is enabled
  IP multicast fast switching is enabled
  Router Discovery is disabled
  IP output packet accounting is disabled
  IP access violation accounting is disabled
  TCP/IP header compression is disabled
  Probe proxy name replies are disabled
  Gateway Discovery is disabled
  Policy routing is disabled
RouterA#
```

The configuration for RouterA would appear as follows with split horizon disabled on both serial interfaces:

```
!
interface ethernet0
ip address 168.71.5.1 255.255.255.0
!
interface serial0
ip address 168.71.6.1 255.255.255.0
bandwidth 128
```

```
no ip split-horizon
!
interface serial1
ip address 168.71.9.1 255.255.255.0
bandwidth 128
no ip split-horizon
!
router rip
network 168.71.0.0
passive-interface Ethernet0
!
ip route 0.0.0.0 0.0.0.0 Ethernet0
!
```

In the following output of the *debug ip rip* command on
RouterA, you can see RouterA advertising all of its routes out
both serial interfaces because split horizon has been disabled:

```
RouterA#debug ip rip
Aug  2 23:54:47: RIP: sending v1 update to 255.255.255.255 via Serial0 (168.71.6.1)
Aug  2 23:54:47:     subnet  168.71.9.0, metric 1
Aug  2 23:54:47:     subnet  168.71.8.0, metric 2
Aug  2 23:54:47:     subnet  168.71.7.0, metric 2
Aug  2 23:54:47:     subnet  168.71.6.0, metric 1
Aug  2 23:54:47:     subnet  168.71.5.0, metric 1
Aug  2 23:54:47:     default, metric 1
Aug  2 23:54:47: RIP: sending v1 update to 255.255.255.255 via Serial1 (168.71.9.1)
Aug  2 23:54:47:     subnet  168.71.9.0, metric 1
Aug  2 23:54:47:     subnet  168.71.8.0, metric 2
Aug  2 23:54:47:     subnet  168.71.7.0, metric 2
Aug  2 23:54:47:     subnet  168.71.6.0, metric 1
Aug  2 23:54:47:     subnet  168.71.5.0, metric 1
Aug  2 23:54:47:     default, metric 1
RouterA#
```

This output showed that RouterA advertised every route it
knew, including routes it is directly connected to back out the
connected interface.

To understand this point further, take a look at the edited
debug code that follows. It shows RouterA sending a route for
168.71.6.0 out serial 0 with split horizon disabled.

```
RouterA#debug ip rip
Aug  2 23:54:47: RIP: sending v1 update to 255.255.255.255 via Serial0 (168.71.6.1)
Aug  2 23:54:47:     subnet  168.71.9.0, metric 1
Aug  2 23:54:47:     subnet  168.71.8.0, metric 2
```

```
Aug  2 23:54:47:       subnet  168.71.7.0, metric 2
Aug  2 23:54:47:       subnet  168.71.6.0, metric 1
Aug  2 23:54:47:       subnet  168.71.5.0, metric 1
Aug  2 23:54:47:       default, metric 1
RouterA#
```

The following code shows that with split horizon enabled,
RouterA does not advertise 168.71.6.0 out serial 0:

```
RouterA#debug ip rip
Aug  2 23:02:16: RIP: sending v1 update to 255.255.255.255 via Serial0 (168.71.6.1)
Aug  2 23:02:16:       subnet  168.71.9.0, metric 1
Aug  2 23:02:16:       subnet  168.71.8.0, metric 2
Aug  2 23:02:16:       subnet  168.71.5.0, metric 1
Aug  2 23:02:16:       default, metric 1
RouterA#
```

Routing Loops Caused by Disabling Split Horizon

In this scenario, the IP address is removed from Ethernet0 on
RouterA (see Figure 2–7). The method for doing this follows.
Removing the IP address makes RouterA think it has lost its
route to 168.71.5.0. Because split horizon has been disabled
on RouterA's serial interfaces, this results in a temporary routing loop between RouterA and RouterC while the routing
tables in RouterA and RouterC reconverge.

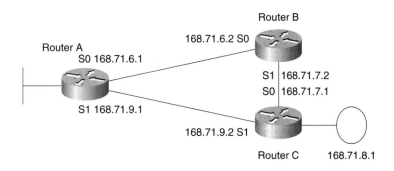

Figure 2–7

The IP address on Ethernet0 in RouterA is removed.

The following output of the *debug ip rip* and *debug ip route* commands on RouterA show RouterA's reaction to losing the IP address on Ethernet0.

The same debug messages are shown in each step. The messages appropriate to each section are in bold. Notice the progression as 168.71.5.0 is advertised back and forth between the routers until the metric is increased to 16.

> **NOTES**
>
> The *debug ip routing* command causes a router to create debug messages when significant changes, such as the loss of a route, occur in the routing table. The *debug ip rip* command causes the router to create a message whenever a RIP event takes place—in this case, when a routing update is either sent or received using the RIP protocol.

1. Notice what happens when the IP address is removed from RouterA:

```
RouterA#debug ip rip
RouterA#debug ip routing
RouterA#-config#interface ethernet 0
RouterA#-config-if#no ip address
RouterA#-config-if#^Z
RouterA#
Aug  3 01:14:01: RT: del 168.71.5.0/24 via 0.0.0.0, connected metric [0/0]
Aug  3 01:14:01: RT: delete subnet route to 168.71.5.0/24
Aug  3 01:14:02: RIP: received v1 update from 168.71.9.2 on Serial1
Aug  3 01:14:02:       168.71.5.0 in 2 hops
Aug  3 01:14:02: RT: add 168.71.5.0/24 via 168.71.9.2, rip metric [120/2]
Aug  3 01:14:02: RIP: sending v1 update to 255.255.255.255 via Serial0 (168.71.6.1)
Aug  3 01:14:02:       subnet  168.71.5.0, metric 3
Aug  3 01:14:02: RIP: sending v1 update to 255.255.255.255 via Serial1 (168.71.9.1)
Aug  3 01:14:02:       subnet  168.71.5.0, metric 3
Aug  3 01:14:02: RIP: received v1 update from 168.71.6.2 on Serial0
Aug  3 01:14:02:       168.71.5.0 in 16 hops (inaccessible)
Aug  3 01:14:02: RIP: received v1 update from 168.71.9.2 on Serial1
Aug  3 01:14:02:       168.71.5.0 in 16 hops (inaccessible)
Aug  3 01:14:02: RT: delete route to 168.71.5.0 via 168.71.9.2, rip metric [120/2]
Aug  3 01:14:02: RT: no routes to 168.71.5.0, entering holddown
RouterA#
```

2. Notice that RouterA receives an update for 168.71.5.0 with a metric of 2 from RouterC and installs it. At this point, RouterC thinks that RouterA has a path to 168.71.5.0, and RouterA thinks that RouterC has a path to 168.68.5.0. In other words, a loop exists. If RouterA received a packet destined for subnet 168.71.5.0 during this time, RouterA would forward it to RouterC, and RouterC would send it right back to RouterA.

```
RouterA#debug ip routing
RouterA#-config#interface ethernet 0
RouterA#-config-if#no ip address
RouterA#-config-if#^Z
RouterA#
Aug  3 01:14:01: RT: del 168.71.5.0/24 via 0.0.0.0, connected metric [0/0]
Aug  3 01:14:01: RT: delete subnet route to 168.71.5.0/24
Aug  3 01:14:02: RIP: received v1 update from 168.71.9.2 on Serial1
Aug  3 01:14:02:      168.71.5.0 in 2 hops
Aug  3 01:14:02: RT: add 168.71.5.0/24 via 168.71.9.2, rip metric [120/2]
Aug  3 01:14:02: RIP: sending v1 update to 255.255.255.255 via Serial0 (168.71.6.1)
Aug  3 01:14:02:      subnet  168.71.5.0, metric 3
Aug  3 01:14:02: RIP: sending v1 update to 255.255.255.255 via Serial1 (168.71.9.1)
Aug  3 01:14:02:      subnet  168.71.5.0, metric 3
Aug  3 01:14:02: RIP: received v1 update from 168.71.6.2 on Serial0
Aug  3 01:14:02:      168.71.5.0 in 16 hops (inaccessible)
Aug  3 01:14:02: RIP: received v1 update from 168.71.9.2 on Serial1
Aug  3 01:14:02:      168.71.5.0 in 16 hops (inaccessible)
Aug  3 01:14:02: RT: delete route to 168.71.5.0 via 168.71.9.2, rip metric [120/2]
Aug  3 01:14:02: RT: no routes to 168.71.5.0, entering holddown
RouterA#
```

3. In the following output, you can see that RouterA increases the metric to 3 and advertises the route back to RouterB and RouterC:

```
RouterA#debug ip routing
RouterA#-config#interface ethernet 0
RouterA#-config-if#no ip address
RouterA#-config-if#^Z
RouterA#-config-if#^Z
RouterA#
Aug  3 01:14:01: RT: del 168.71.5.0/24 via 0.0.0.0, connected metric [0/0]
Aug  3 01:14:01: RT: delete subnet route to 168.71.5.0/24
Aug  3 01:14:02: RIP: received v1 update from 168.71.9.2 on Serial1
```

```
Aug  3 01:14:02:        168.71.5.0 in 2 hops
Aug  3 01:14:02: RT: add 168.71.5.0/24 via 168.71.9.2, rip metric [120/2]
Aug  3 01:14:02: RIP: sending v1 update to 255.255.255.255 via Serial0 (168.71.6.1)
Aug  3 01:14:02:        subnet  168.71.5.0, metric 3
Aug  3 01:14:02: RIP: sending v1 update to 255.255.255.255 via Serial1 (168.71.9.1)
Aug  3 01:14:02:        subnet  168.71.5.0, metric 3
Aug  3 01:14:02: RIP: received v1 update from 168.71.6.2 on Serial0
Aug  3 01:14:02:         168.71.5.0 in 16 hops (inaccessible)
Aug  3 01:14:02: RIP: received v1 update from 168.71.9.2 on Serial1
Aug  3 01:14:02:         168.71.5.0 in 16 hops (inaccessible)
Aug  3 01:14:02: RT: delete route to 168.71.5.0 via 168.71.9.2, rip metric [120/2]
Aug  3 01:14:02: RT: no routes to 168.71.5.0, entering holddown
RouterA#
```

4. Notice in this final section that RouterB and RouterC send an advertisement for 168.71.5.0 back to RouterA with a metric of 16. This is in direct response to both RouterB and RouterC having noticed that RouterA increased the metric for 168.71.5.0 each time it advertised it. Receiving an advertisement from the same router with an increased metric usually means that the two routers are listening to each other's routes for the same network, thus creating a loop.

In order to stop this looping from going on until the increasing metric reaches the maximum amount—16 for RIP—the first router to notice the problem poisons the route to the other router by automatically marking the network as unreachable in its next update, which is called *poison reverse*. Poison reverse is explained in more detail later in this chapter.

```
RouterA#debug ip routing
RouterA#-config#interface ethernet 0
RouterA#-config-if#no ip address
RouterA#-config-if#^Z
RouterA#-config-if#^Z
RouterA#
Aug  3 01:14:01: RT: del 168.71.5.0/24 via 0.0.0.0, connected metric [0/0]
Aug  3 01:14:01: RT: delete subnet route to 168.71.5.0/24
Aug  3 01:14:02: RIP: received v1 update from 168.71.9.2 on Serial1
Aug  3 01:14:02:        168.71.5.0 in 2 hops
Aug  3 01:14:02: RT: add 168.71.5.0/24 via 168.71.9.2, rip metric [120/2]
```

```
Aug  3 01:14:02: RIP: sending v1 update to 255.255.255.255 via Serial0 (168.71.6.1)
Aug  3 01:14:02:       subnet  168.71.5.0, metric 3
Aug  3 01:14:02: RIP: sending v1 update to 255.255.255.255 via Serial1 (168.71.9.1)
Aug  3 01:14:02:       subnet  168.71.5.0, metric 3
Aug  3 01:14:02: RIP: received v1 update from 168.71.6.2 on Serial0
Aug  3 01:14:02:        168.71.5.0 in 16 hops (inaccessible)
Aug  3 01:14:02: RIP: received v1 update from 168.71.9.2 on Serial1
Aug  3 01:14:02:        168.71.5.0 in 16 hops (inaccessible)
Aug  3 01:14:02: RT: delete route to 168.71.5.0 via 168.71.9.2, rip metric [120/2]
Aug  3 01:14:02: RT: no routes to 168.71.5.0, entering holddown
RouterA#
```

RouterA's route to 168.71.5.0 has just entered holddown, as shown in the previous debug message. The events that occur in RouterA's routing table after the holddown timer expires will be the same as the events explained in the previous section on convergence.

NOTES

For brevity's sake, only RouterA's debug messages were provided in this section. RouterB and RouterC both went through a very similar scenario to that depicted for RouterA. They both lost their original routes to 168.71.5.0 and temporarily installed a loop, which eventually went into holddown, as did RouterA's route to 168.71.5.0.

Loss of a Connected Route Versus a Dynamic Route

Cisco routers react to losing a connected route differently than when they lose a dynamic route. Please refer to Figure 2–7 for the network topology used in this section.

In this scenario, split horizon has been disabled on all serial interfaces, and RouterA has had its IP address on Ethernet0 removed (see Figure 2–7). The debug messages shown here occur at the same time in both routers. Their clocks have been synchronized.

In the following debug messages from RouterA, you can see that RouterA immediately accepts RouterC's advertisement for 168.71.5.0 when it arrives. RouterC advertised 168.71.5.0 to RouterA because that split horizon has been disabled on RouterC's serial 1 interface.

```
RouterA#debug ip routing
Aug  5 23:11:04: RT: del 168.71.5.0/24 via 0.0.0.0, connected metric [0/0]
Aug  5 23:11:04: RT: delete subnet route to 168.71.5.0/24
Aug  5 23:11:15: RT: add 168.71.5.0/24 via 168.71.9.2, rip metric [120/2]
RouterA#
```

In the following debug from RouterC, you can see RouterC putting its route for 168.71.5.0 into holddown and waiting another 58 seconds before adding the new route:

```
RouterC# debug ip routing
Aug  5 23:47:40: RT: flushed route to 168.71.5.0 via 168.71.9.1 (Serial1)
Aug  5 23:47:40: RT: no routes to 168.71.5.0, entering holddown
Aug  5 23:48:38: RT: add 168.71.5.0 255.255.255.0 via 168.71.7.2, rip metric [120/2]
RouterC#
```

NOTES

The clocks in RouterA and RouterC are synchronized.

Split Horizon's Effect on Multipoint WAN Interfaces

Multipoint interfaces are physical interfaces that have the capability to reach multiple remote networks concurrently. Frame Relay and primary rate ISDN are two examples of interfaces with one physical connection. Through this connection, more than one remote network can be reached. The network diagram in Figure 2–8 has been changed to help explain how enabling split horizon causes problems on a Frame Relay network.

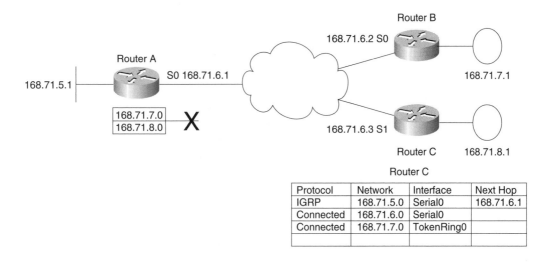

Router A			
Protocol	Network	Interface	Next Hop
Connected	168.71.5.0	Ethernet0	
Connected	168.71.6.0	Serial0	
IGRP	168.71.7.0	Serial0	168.71.6.2
IGRP	168.71.8.0	Serial0	168.71.6.3

Router B			
Protocol	Network	Interface	Next Hop
IGRP	168.71.5.0	Serial0	168.71.6.1
Connected	168.71.6.0	Serial0	
Connected	168.71.7.0	TokenRing0	

Router C			
Protocol	Network	Interface	Next Hop
IGRP	168.71.5.0	Serial0	168.71.6.1
Connected	168.71.6.0	Serial0	
Connected	168.71.7.0	TokenRing0	

Figure 2–8

RouterA can reach both RouterB and RouterC via serial 0.

Notice that the serial interfaces on all three routers are now part of subnet 168.71.6.0. This is because Frame Relay is a layer two protocol. All devices connected to a common layer two network usually share the same network address space.

NOTES

Address space is another way of referring to the network portion of an IP address. In this case, RouterA, RouterB, and RouterC are using up host addresses .1, .2, and .3 of the possible 254 host addresses available in address space 168.71.6.0.

A partial configuration for RouterA showing the use of a multipoint Frame Relay interface follows:

```
!
interface serial0
encapsulation frame-relay
ip address 168.71.6.1 255.255.255.0
frame-relay map ip 168.71.6.2 100 broadcast
frame-relay map ip 168.71.9.2 101 broadcast
!
```

HINT

Remember that split horizon is off by default on multipoint interfaces
for IP, which is why it doesn't appear in the previous configuration.

In the revised network diagram shown in Figure 2–8, RouterA
is the only router with a complete routing table. RouterA has
installed routes to subnets 168.71.7.0 and 168.71.8.0 that are
known via serial 0. Due to split horizon, RouterA does not
advertise either of these subnets back out serial 0. This prevents RouterB from learning about 168.71.8.0 and prevents
RouterC from learning about 168.71.7.0. A facsimile of the
actual routing tables for each router is included in Figure 2–8.

The *debug ip rip* messages from RouterA with split horizon
enabled show why having split horizon enabled causes
RouterB and RouterC to only have partial routing tables. Only
subnet 168.71.5.0 is being advertised.

```
RouterA#debug ip rip
Aug  2 23:03:21: RIP: sending v1 update to 255.255.255.255 via Serial0 (168.71.6.1)
Aug  2 23:03:21:      subnet  168.71.5.0, metric 1
RouterA#
```

The *debug ip rip* messages from RouterA with split horizon
disabled show why having split horizon disabled allows
RouterB and RouterC to obtain full routing tables.

```
RouterA#debug ip rip
Aug  2 23:10:51: RIP: sending v1 update to 255.255.255.255 via Serial0 (168.71.6.1)
Aug  2 23:10:51:      subnet  168.71.9.0, metric 1
Aug  2 23:10:51:      subnet  168.71.8.0, metric 2
Aug  2 23:10:51:      subnet  168.71.7.0, metric 2
Aug  2 23:10:51:      subnet  168.71.6.0, metric 1
Aug  2 23:10:51:      subnet  168.71.5.0, metric 1
RouterA#
```

This example shows why Cisco defaults to disabling split horizon on Frame Relay interfaces. However, the section on disabling split horizon and routing loops has shown that disabling split horizon can cause problems. A more effective solution is to use subinterfaces, as explained in the next section.

Using Subinterfaces to Avoid Problems Caused by Split Horizon

The term *subinterfaces* refers to the process of creating logical interfaces on a physical interface. It is better to use subinterfaces with Frame Relay because each logical interface is treated just like a real physical interface by routing protocols (see Figure 2–9).

RouterA's partial configuration with Frame Relay and subinterfaces on serial 0 look like the following output:

```
!
interface serial0
encapsulation frame-relay
!
interface serial0.1 point-to-point
ip address 168.71.6.1 255.255.255.0
frame-relay map ip 168.71.6.2 100 broadcast
!
interface serial0.2 point-to-point
ip address 168.71.9.1 255.255.255.0
frame-relay map ip 168.71.9.2 101 broadcast
!
```

Router A

Protocol	Network	Interface	Next Hop
Connected	168.71.5.0	Ethernet0	
Connected	168.71.6.0	Serial0.1	
IGRP	168.71.7.0	Serial0.1	168.71.6.2
IGRP	168.71.8.0	Serial0.2	168.71.9.2
Connected	168.71.9.0	Serial0.2	

Router B

Protocol	Network	Interface	Next Hop
IGRP	168.71.5.0	Serial0	168.71.6.1
Connected	168.71.6.0	Serial0	
Connected	168.71.7.0	TokenRing0	
IGRP	168.71.8.0	Serial0	168.71.6.1
IGRP	168.71.9.0	Serial0	168.71.6.1

Router C

Protocol	Network	Interface	Next Hop
IGRP	168.71.5.0	Serial0	168.71.9.1
IGRP	168.71.6.0	Serial0	168.71.9.1
IGRP	168.71.7.0	Serial0	168.71.9.1
Connected	168.71.8.0	TokenRing0	
Connected	168.71.9.0	Serial0	

Figure 2–9
An example of using subinterfaces to ensure full IP connectivity.

HINT

Remember that split horizon is on by default on point-to-point interfaces, which is why it doesn't appear in the configuration.

Using subinterfaces allows RouterB and RouterC to have full connectivity even though RouterA is running split horizon on subinterfaces 0.1 and 0.2.

The following *debug ip rip* messages from RouterA show that RouterA will now send advertisements to RouterB and RouterC that allow them to create a complete routing table.

```
RouterA#debug ip rip
Aug  3 03:07:01: RIP: sending v1 update to 255.255.255.255 via Serial0.1 (168.71.6.1)
Aug  3 03:07:01:      subnet  168.71.9.0, metric 1
Aug  3 03:07:01:      subnet  168.71.8.0, metric 2
Aug  3 03:07:01:      subnet  168.71.5.0, metric 1
Aug  3 03:07:01: RIP: sending v1 update to 255.255.255.255 via Serial0.2 (168.71.9.1)
Aug  3 03:07:01:      subnet  168.71.7.0, metric 2
Aug  3 03:07:01:      subnet  168.71.6.0, metric 1
Aug  3 03:07:01:      subnet  168.71.5.0, metric 1
RouterA#
```

POISON REVERSE AND TRIGGERED UPDATES

Poison reverse is when a router informs other routers that routes they were once capable of reaching via a particular interface are no longer reachable because the interface has gone down.

Routers normally react to a poison reverse message by immediately placing the poisoned routes into holddown instead of waiting for the invalid timer to expire. This saves convergence time, as much as 180 seconds (default invalid timer), depending on how soon after a regular update a poison reverse update arrives.

In Figure 2–10, RouterA's serial 1 interface is shut down. RouterA can no longer reach 168.71.9.0 and 168.71.8.0 out of serial 1.

By poisoning the routes out serial 0, RouterA is informing any other routers downstream from serial 0 that it can no longer reach these two subnets. This is, in essence, what a poison advertisement is.

When it receives these poison advertisements, RouterB deletes its references to the two subnets and puts them in holddown. This saves RouterB from having to wait until the invalid timers fire for these subnets to go into holddown.

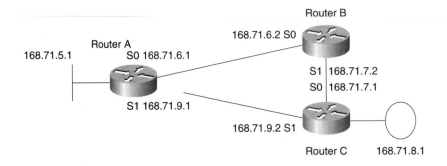

Figure 2–10

Serial 1 on RouterA has been shut down.

The debug messages in this scenario have been edited to only show activities related to subnets 168.71.8.0 and 168.71.9.0. Here, you can see the output of *debug ip rip* from RouterA when serial 1 is shut down. The *shutdown* command is shown on the line separating the two sections of the debug message.

```
RouterA#debug ip rip
RouterA#config term
RouterA-config#interface serial 1
RouterA#-config-if#
Oct  3 17:02:25: RIP: sending v1 update to 255.255.255.255 via Serial0 (168.71.6.1)
Oct  3 17:02:25:      subnet  168.71.9.0, metric 1
Oct  3 17:02:25:      subnet  168.71.8.0, metric 2
RouterA-config-if#shutdown
Oct  3 17:02:33: RIP: sending v1 update to 255.255.255.255 via Serial0 (168.71.6.1)
Oct  3 17:02:33:      subnet  168.71.9.0, metric 16
Oct  3 17:02:33:      subnet  168.71.8.0, metric 16
RouterA#
```

RouterA sent an update to RouterB just before the *shutdown* command was entered. Entering the *shutdown* command automatically triggered another update that poisoned the two routes. This process is sometimes referred to as a *triggered update*, meaning that an exception event occurred that required an out-of-cycle update to be sent. You can see that the poison update was out of cycle because only eight seconds separate the two messages. RIP's default update timer is 30 seconds. This example is yet another way router code can be written to speed convergence.

The following code shows the output of *debug ip rip* from RouterB's point of view. Notice that RouterB immediately reacts to RouterA's poisoning of the routes to both subnets by placing them in hold down.

```
RouterB#debug ip rip
Oct  3 17:02:31: RIP: received update from 168.71.6.1 on Serial0
Oct  3 17:02:31:      168.71.9.0 in 1 hops
Oct  3 17:02:31:      168.71.8.0 in 2 hops
Oct  3 17:02:40: RIP: received update from 168.71.6.1 on Serial0
Oct  3 17:02:40:      168.71.9.0 in 16 hops (inaccessible)
Oct  3 17:02:40:      168.71.8.0 in 16 hops (inaccessible)
```

This section covers a very important point. By using poison reverse and triggered updates instead of waiting for the entire 180-second invalid timer to expire, routers can learn much more quickly that a route may not be reachable via the path currently in their routing tables. Obtaining this information immediately rather than waiting for a series of scheduled updates to not arrive allows a router to place the lost routes into hold down much faster.

IGRP ROUTING METRICS (VARIABLES) AND CISCO ADMINISTRATIVE DISTANCES

This section covers two of the five possible variables of IGRP (Interior Gateway Routing Protocol) routing metrics— bandwidth and delay. It explains why only two are used and why it is usually best to accept the defaults for these two variables based on the type of link in use and its speed. It also discusses the concept of administrative distances.

IGRP Metrics (Variables)

IGRP can be configured to take the following variables into account when determining which routes to use:

- Bandwidth: This is a measure of the speed of the physical network connected to an interface. A 64K serial connection has a bandwidth of 64,000 bits per second. Cisco uses a factor of 1000 in the *bandwidth* command. Therefore, entering the command **bandwidth 64** on a serial interface results in a configured bandwidth of 64K.

- Delay: This is an arbitrary measurement of how long it takes an interface to serialize the maximum size of a packet that an interface can accept onto the physical media. Slower links have higher delays, and faster links have lower delays. The number used on the interface is not determined dynamically; it is configured to a static value by a network administrator or left at the Cisco default.

- Load: In Cisco terms, this is a measurement that is taken over a period of time and averaged. It doesn't reflect an exact instant in time but is meant to reflect the utilization of a link.

- Reliability: In Cisco terms, this is a measurement that is taken over a period of time and averaged. It doesn't reflect an exact instant in time but is meant to reflect the condition of a link. It can incorporate how often the link transitions from an up state to a down state, as well as the error rate of frames arriving on the link.

- MTU (maximum transmission unit): This represents the largest frame a link can accept.

Cisco recommends that only bandwidth and delay be used due to the following factors:

1. Load can be a very transient variable. Rerouting around an overloaded link reduces the load on the link and makes it more desirable. This causes the router to reconverge on the link it just rerouted around, and the cycle starts all over again.

2. Reliability is another transient condition; error conditions can come and go quickly. If a link is really so unreliable that it needs to be rerouted around, it should be shut down on the router until it can be repaired.

3. In addition to both of the points just made, convergence itself can take several minutes. In the meantime, the routers in the network may have paths that are really loops or black holes. Packets get forwarded to routers that do not have information sufficient to forward them further and consequently drop them.

4. Very few end systems constantly generate frames at the largest size a link is capable (MTU) of on a constant basis. Many applications, such as Telnet and HTTP Web traffic, generate many more smaller frames than maximum-sized frames. These applications tend to have asymmetric traffic patterns; larger frames travel in one direction while smaller frames travel in the other direction. Including the MTU in the equation complicates the decision of which route to use, and this problem isn't offset by the benefit it would provide.

Administrative Distances

The term *metric* has already been explained as describing the overall desirability of a route to a remote (not locally attached) network.

With Cisco routers, there is another concept called *administrative distance*, which is a subjective analysis of the believability of a routing protocol. In other words, if a router running two different routing protocols learns about the same network from both protocols, the protocol that has the lower distance associated with it will be the one whose entry is installed in the router's routing table. The types of distances used in the next scenario, which is on running multiple routing protocols concurrently, are as follows:

- Connected interface   Distance 0

  A subnet that is assigned to an interface in the router takes precedence over an advertised route for the same subnet. If RouterB advertised a route to 168.71.5.0, RouterA would ignore it because it has a connected route to this subnet already.

- Static route   Distance 1

  A route that has been manually configured into a router. If RouterA had a static route indicating that 168.71.8.0 was reachable via the next hop of 168.71.6.2 (RouterB), this route would override any dynamic route RouterA received from RouterC, even though the RouterA-to-RouterC path is actually shorter in terms of hops.

- IGRP   Distance 100

  Cisco's proprietary Interior Gateway Routing Protocol.

- RIP   Distance 120

  An IETF standard routing protocol.

There are several other types of routing protocols and associated distances. When using a combination of routing protocols, keep in mind that the default distance values may cause a router to use a path that you did not intend it to use.

Running Multiple Routing Protocols Concurrently

Two routers have been reconfigured for this scenario (see Figure 2–11). RouterA and RouterC are running both RIP and IGRP. RouterB is only running IGRP in order to demonstrate that when RouterC receives a one-hop route to 168.71.5.0 from RouterA via RIP, it will ignore it in lieu of the two hop IGRP route it receives from RouterB.

NOTES

Running multiple routing protocols is fairly common. Companies that have a lot of UNIX systems that use RIP but want to run IGRP on the routers use the RIP/IGRP combination. Distance will always play a part in configurations with more than one routing protocol running, regardless of the routing protocol combination used.

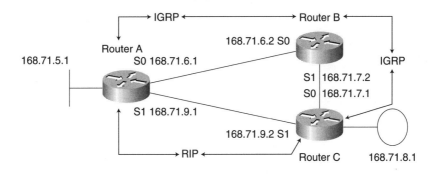

Figure 2–11
The network now has two routing protocols running.

In order to make this scenario work, RouterA and RouterC only send RIP advertisements over the link between them, which is accomplished by applying access lists to the RIP and IGRP sections of each router's configuration.

RouterA's new configuration is as follows:

```
!
interface ethernet0
ip address 168.71.5.1 255.255.255.0
!
interface serial0
ip address 168.71.6.1 255.255.255.0
bandwidth 128
!
interface serial1
ip address 168.71.9.1 255.255.255.0
!
router igrp 109
network 168.71.0.0
distribute-list 1 out serial1
router rip
network 168.71.0.0
distribute-list 1 out serial0
!
access-list 1 deny 0.0.0.0 255.255.255.255
!
```

RouterB's new configuration is as follows:

```
!
interface serial0
ip address 168.71.6.2 255.255.255.0
bandwidth 128
!
interface serial1
ip address 168.71.7.2 255.255.255.0
bandwidth 128
!
router igrp 109
network 168.71.0.0
!
```

RouterC's new configuration is as follows:

```
!
interface tokenring0
ip address 168.71.8.1 255.255.255.0
!
interface serial0
ip address 168.71.7.1 255.255.255.0
bandwidth 128
!
interface serial1
ip address 168.71.9.2 255.255.255.0
```

```
!
router igrp 109
network 168.71.0.0
distribute-list 1 out serial1
router rip
network 168.71.0.0
distribute-list 1 out serial0
!
access-list 1 deny 0.0.0.0 255.255.255.255
!
```

In the following output from the *debug ip rip* and *debug ip igrp transactions* commands, you can see the debug messages from both routing protocols as they arrive at RouterC.

```
RouterC#debug ip rip
Oct  7 22:33:10: RIP: received update from 168.71.9.1 on Serial1
Oct  7 22:33:10:      168.71.6.0 in 1 hops
Oct  7 22:33:10:      168.71.5.0 in 1 hops

RouterC#deb ip igrp transactions
Oct  7 22:35:59: IGRP: received update from 168.71.7.2 on Serial0
Oct  7 22:35:59:       subnet 168.71.6.0, metric 82125 (neighbor 80125)
Oct  7 22:35:59: subnet 168.71.5.0, metric 10004001 (neighbor 10002001)
```

NOTES

The *debug ip rip* and the *debug ip igrp transactions* commands perform the same function for their respective routing protocols. See the Cisco IOS documentation for more details on these two commands.

Notice in the following routing table from RouterC that the route to 168.71.5.0 is via serial 0 through RouterB even though the connection via serial 1 is only one hop. This is because, as previously explained, IGRP has a distance of 100, whereas RIP has a distance of 120. The smaller distance value overrides what appears to be a physically shorter route.

```
RouterC#show ip route
Codes: C - connected, S - static, I - IGRP, R - RIP, M - mobile, B - BGP
       D - EIGRP, EX - EIGRP external, O - OSPF, IA - OSPF inter area
       E1 - OSPF external type 1, E2 - OSPF external type 2, E - EGP
       i - IS-IS, L1 - IS-IS level-1, L2 - IS-IS level-2, * - candidate default
Gateway of last resort is 168.71.7.2 to network 10.0.0.0
```

```
I*    10.0.0.0 [100/180250] via 168.71.7.2, 00:00:47, Serial0
168.71.0.0 255.255.255.0 is subnetted, 5 subnets
C        168.71.9.0 is directly connected, Serial1
C        168.71.8.0 is directly connected, TokenRing0
C        168.71.7.0 is directly connected, Serial0
I        168.71.6.0 [100/82125] via 168.71.7.2, 00:00:47, Serial0
I        168.71.5.0 [100/10004001] via 168.71.7.2, 00:00:47, Serial0
R*     0.0.0.0 0.0.0.0 [120/1] via 168.71.9.1, 00:00:18, Serial1
RouterC#
```

If the links connecting RouterA to RouterB and RouterB to RouterC were both T1s (1.54MB), and the link between RouterA and RouterC were 256K (a fractional T1), the best path from a bandwidth perspective would be the one that IGRP selected in this instance. RIP lacks the capability to take into account the speed of the links it is being used over. If all of the routers in Figure 2–11 were running IGRP, the path from RouterA to 168.71.8.0 would be via RouterB.

Altering IGRP's Bandwidth and Delay Variables

This section further explains the functionality of the two IGRP metrics normally used: bandwidth and delay.

RIP will no longer be mentioned because Cisco routers do not have a function for manipulating RIP tables to make them override RIP's default hop-based metric. This means that if all of the routers in Figure 2–11 were running RIP, the links connecting RouterA to RouterB and RouterB to RouterC were both T1s (1.54MB), and the link between RouterA and RouterC was 256K (a fractional T1), RIP would still use the less desirable (slower) one-hop route.

RouterB would have to introduce significant *latency* (delay in switching a packet from one interface to another) to negate the speed benefit of sending a packet over the two hop routes.

As previously stated, IGRP is capable of using five metrics: bandwidth, delay, load, reliability, and MTU. Normally, only bandwidth and delay are considered. The overall IGRP metric for any path between a router and a remote network is based on the minimum bandwidth of any link in the path and the sum of all delays in the path.

This scenario proves this concept by configuring RouterC to load share traffic destined to 168.71.5.0 over its links to both RouterA and RouterB. In other words, RouterC still has two equal-cost routes to 168.71.5.0. All three routers are now running IGRP, as shown in Figure 2–12.

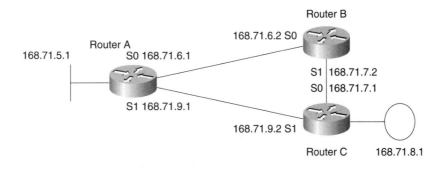

Figure 2–12

Review of the basic network topology—all routers are now running IGRP.

In the following routing table from RouterC, only one route is installed to 168.71.5.0. This is the normal condition before any manipulation of the IGRP variables has taken place.

```
RouterC#show ip route
Codes: C - connected, S - static, I - IGRP, R - RIP, M - mobile, B - BGP
       D - EIGRP, EX - EIGRP external, O - OSPF, IA - OSPF inter area
       E1 - OSPF external type 1, E2 - OSPF external type 2, E - EGP
       i - IS-IS, L1 - IS-IS level-1, L2 - IS-IS level-2, * - candidate default
Gateway of last resort is not set
I*   10.0.0.0 [100/180250] via 168.71.7.2, 00:00:42, Serial0
     168.71.0.0 255.255.255.0 is subnetted, 5 subnets
```

```
C        168.71.9.0 is directly connected, Serial1
C        168.71.8.0 is directly connected, TokenRing0
C        168.71.7.0 is directly connected, Serial0
I        168.71.6.0 [100/82125] via 168.71.9.1, 00:00:21, Serial1
                    [100/82125] via 168.71.7.2, 00:00:42, Serial0
I        168.71.5.0 [100/10002001] via 168.71.9.1, 00:00:21, Serial1
RouterC#
```

It is possible to convince RouterC to install the other path to 168.71.5.0 via RouterB by manipulating the *delay* command on RouterC's serial 1 interface. RouterC needs to believe that the total delay to 168.71.5.0 over its link to RouterA is equal to the total delay of the link to 168.71.5.0 over its link to RouterB. Remember from the earlier discussions that RouterC does not know that RouterB is not connected to 168.71.5.0 and has to forward packets destined to 168.71.5.0 to RouterA. All RouterC needs to believe is that RouterB is the next hop in the path to 168.71.5.0. Figure 2–13 shows where the increased delay is required.

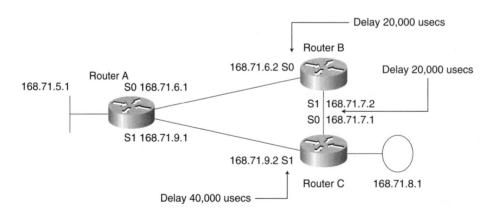

Figure 2–13
The delay is cumulative across all links in a path.

The following text shows how to configure the delay variable on an interface. This process is the same for all types of interfaces.

```
RouterC#conf term
RouterC(config)#int s 1
RouterC(config-if)#delay 4000
RouterC(config-if)#^Z
RouterC#
```

The following section of RouterC's configuration shows the result of increasing the delay on serial 1 to 40,000. The units are 10s, so 4000=40,000.

```
hostname RouterC
!
interface serial1
ip address 168.71.9.2 255.0.0.0
bandwidth 128
delay 4000
!
```

To view the results of the *delay* command on the interface itself, use the *show interface* command, as shown here:

```
RouterC#show interface serial 1
Serial1 is up, line protocol is up
   Hardware is HD64570
   Internet address is 168.71.9.2 255.255.255.0
   MTU 1500 bytes, BW 128 Kbit, DLY 40000 usec, rely 255/255, load 1/255
```

Now that the delay on RouterC's serial 1 interface has been changed to 40,000 usecs, the two paths to 168.71.5.0 should be installed in RouterC's routing table.

Using the *show ip route* command, followed by a subnet—in this case, 168.71.5.0—the router limits the output of the routing table to information relevant to the requested subnet. This can be very useful when a router has a large routing table. The output of this command shows that RouterC now has two equal-cost paths (parallel routes) to 168.71.5.0.

```
RouterC#show ip route 168.71.5.0
Routing entry for 168.71.5.0 255.255.255.0
   Known via "igrp 109", distance 100, metric 10004001
   Redistributing via igrp 109
   Advertised by igrp 109 (self originated)
   Last update from 168.71.7.2 on Serial0, 00:00:54 ago
   Routing Descriptor Blocks:
   * 168.71.9.1, from 168.71.9.1, 00:01:01 ago, via Serial1
```

```
    Route metric is 10004001, traffic share count is 1
    Total delay is 40010 microseconds, minimum bandwidth is 128 Kbit
    Reliability 255/255, minimum MTU 1500 bytes
    Loading 1/255, Hops 0
  168.71.7.2, from 168.71.7.2, 00:00:54 ago, via Serial0
    Route metric is 10004001, traffic share count is 1
    Total delay is 40010 microseconds, minimum bandwidth is 128 Kbit
    Reliability 255/255, minimum MTU 1500 bytes
    Loading 1/255, Hops 1
RouterC#
```

The following output of *debug ip igrp transactions* from RouterC shows both routes to 168.71.5.0 being advertised to RouterC with the same metric. The first message is from RouterA; the second is from RouterB. This is why the previous routing table has both routes in it.

```
RouterC#debug ip igrp transactions
Oct  8 16:57:59: IGRP: received update from 168.71.9.1 on Serial1
Oct  8 16:57:59:        subnet 168.71.6.0, metric 84125 (neighbor 80125)
Oct  8 16:57:59:        subnet 168.71.5.0, metric 10004001 (neighbor 10000001)
Oct  8 16:58:24: IGRP: received update from 168.71.7.2 on Serial0
Oct  8 16:58:24:        subnet 168.71.9.0, metric 84125 (neighbor 82125)
Oct  8 16:58:24:        subnet 168.71.6.0, metric 82125 (neighbor 80125)
Oct  8 16:58:24:        subnet 168.71.5.0, metric 10004001 (neighbor 10002001)
RouterC#
```

NOTES

A key point to understand is that a router uses the delay on an interface it receives a routing advertisement over to determine the metrics for the routes being advertised. In other words, delay is applied on inbound advertisements, not outbound. The delay variable was not changed on RouterA. Instead, it was changed on RouterC in order to force RouterC to accept RouterA's advertisement for 168.71.5.0.

RouterC now load balances over the two links in either a session-by-session basis or a packet-by-packet basis. This may result in better utilization of the links between RouterC and RouterA. However, if RouterB is already sending enough traffic to RouterA to keep the link nearly full, the extra traffic from RouterC may cause it to be oversubscribed. Care should always be used when manipulating routing tables to make them behave in a way that is different from their default behavior. The end results may not be what you expected.

Problems with Manipulating the Delay Variable

It is not possible to have both RouterB and RouterC load balance their traffic to 168.71.5.0. Figure 2–14 shows where the increased delay is required for RouterB to load balance.

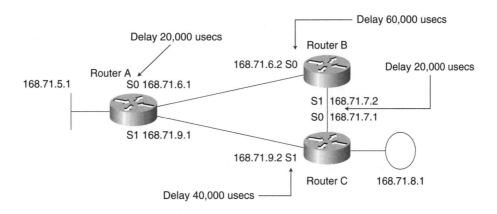

Figure 2–14

The delay is still cumulative across all links in a path, which prevents load balancing.

In order for RouterB to accept RouterC's and RouterA's advertisements for 168.71.5.0, the total delay on both paths from RouterB's perspective have to be equal. Because the delay on RouterC's serial 1 interface was changed to 40,000 usecs to force RouterC to load share, RouterB's serial 0 interface delay would have to be changed to 60,000 usecs—20,000 for the link to RouterC and an additional 40,000 for the link between RouterC and RouterA. This would affect the total delay that RouterC's path to 168.71.5.0 via RouterB encounters. RouterC would now have a path to 168.71.5.0 via RouterA with a delay of 40,000 usecs and a path to 168.71.5.0 via RouterB with a total delay of 80,000 usecs—20,000 for the link to RouterB and the additional 60,000 for RouterB's link to RouterA.

The next section illustrates what happens to the metrics advertised with routes when the delay variable is altered.

Understanding the Effects of Manipulating the Delay Variable

Increasing the delay on an interface causes the router to alter the metric it uses to advertise routes learned over the link to other routers. The delay on RouterB's serial 0 interface was changed to 40,000 usecs, which will cause RouterB to alter the metrics it uses for routes learned from RouterA when advertising them to RouterC. Figure 2–15 shows where the increased delay is applied.

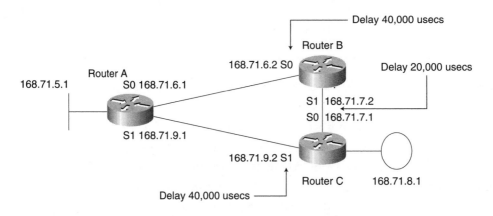

Figure 2–15

The delay parameter has been increased as shown.

The following output of the *show interface* command on RouterB shows that the delay on its serial 0 has been increased to 40,000:

```
RouterB#show interface serial 0
Serial0 is up, line protocol is up
  Hardware is HD64570
  Internet address is 168.71.6.2 255.255.255.0
  MTU 1500 bytes, BW 128 Kbit, DLY 40000 usec, rely 255/255, load 1/255
```

The following code is RouterC's entry for 168.71.5.0 now that RouterB has had the delay on serial 0 increased to 40,000 usecs. Note that the metric for this route is the same as before for serial 1: 10004001. The other route via serial 0 is not installed because the metric has increased from RouterB. The combined delay that RouterC sees for the path to 168.71.5.0 via RouterB is now 60,000 usecs—20,000 usecs for the link to RouterB and 40,000 usecs for the link between RouterB and RouterA.

The following output of *debug ip igrp transactions* from RouterC shows the advertisements for 168.71.5.0 arriving from RouterA and RouterB with different metrics. The first message is from RouterA and the second is from RouterB.

```
RouterC#debug ip igrp transactions
Oct  8 16:55:09: IGRP: received update from 168.71.9.1 on Serial1
Oct  8 16:55:09:        subnet 168.71.6.0, metric 84125 (neighbor 80125)
Oct  8 16:55:09:  subnet 168.71.5.0, metric 10004001 (neighbor 10000001)
Oct  8 16:55:29: IGRP: received update from 168.71.7.2 on Serial0
Oct  8 16:55:29:  subnet 168.71.6.0, metric 84125 (neighbor 82125)
Oct  8 16:55:29: subnet 168.71.5.0, metric 10006001 (neighbor 10004001)
```

The difference in the metrics is why the routing table from RouterC has only one route to 168.71.5.0 in it.

```
RouterC#show ip route 168.71.5.0
Routing entry for 168.71.5.0 255.255.255.0
  Known via "igrp 109", distance 100, metric 10004001
  Redistributing via igrp 109
  Advertised by igrp 109 (self originated)
  Last update from 168.71.9.1 on Serial1, 00:00:20 ago
  Routing Descriptor Blocks:
```

```
 * 168.71.9.1, from 168.71.9.1, 00:00:20 ago, via Serial1
     Route metric is 10004001, traffic share count is 1
     Total delay is 40010 microseconds, minimum bandwidth is 128 Kbit
     Reliability 255/255, minimum MTU 1500 bytes
     Loading 1/255, Hops 0
RouterC#
```

Compare the previous routing table, which was observed after RouterB's delay on serial 0 was increased to 40,000 usecs as shown in Figure 2-15, with the routing table and debug messages observed while RouterB's delay on serial 0 was still 20,000 usecs as shown in Figure 2-13:

```
RouterC#show ip route 168.71.5.0
Routing entry for 168.71.5.0 255.255.255.0
  Known via "igrp 109", distance 100, metric 10004001
  Redistributing via igrp 109
  Advertised by igrp 109 (self originated)
  Last update from 168.71.7.2 on Serial0, 00:00:54 ago
  Routing Descriptor Blocks:
  * 168.71.9.1, from 168.71.9.1, 00:01:01 ago, via Serial1
      Route metric is 10004001, traffic share count is 1
      Total delay is 40010 microseconds, minimum bandwidth is 128 Kbit
      Reliability 255/255, minimum MTU 1500 bytes
      Loading 1/255, Hops 0
    168.71.7.2, from 168.71.7.2, 00:00:54 ago, via Serial0
      Route metric is 10004001, traffic share count is 1
      Total delay is 40010 microseconds, minimum bandwidth is 128 Kbit
      Reliability 255/255, minimum MTU 1500 bytes
      Loading 1/255, Hops 1
RouterC#
```

The following output of *debug ip igrp transactions* from RouterC shows both routes to 168.71.5.0 being advertised to RouterC with the same metric. The first message is from RouterA; the second is from RouterB, which is why the previous routing table has both routes in it.

```
RouterC#debug ip igrp transactions
Oct  8 16:57:59: IGRP: received update from 168.71.9.1 on Serial1
Oct  8 16:57:59:        subnet 168.71.6.0, metric 84125 (neighbor 80125)
Oct  8 16:57:59:        subnet 168.71.5.0, metric 10004001 (neighbor 10000001)
Oct  8 16:58:24: IGRP: received update from 168.71.7.2 on Serial0
Oct  8 16:58:24:        subnet 168.71.9.0, metric 84125 (neighbor 82125)
Oct  8 16:58:24:        subnet 168.71.6.0, metric 82125 (neighbor 80125)
Oct  8 16:58:24:        subnet 168.71.5.0, metric 10004001 (neighbor 10002001)
RouterC#
```

This section has explained how manipulating the delay variable affects routing metrics and some of its limitations. The next section explains the role of the bandwidth variable in more detail.

Understanding the Effects of Manipulating the Bandwidth Variable

This scenario illustrates that the bandwidth variable is not cumulative. Only the lowest bandwidth in a path is taken into account when determining a metric for a route. This is illustrated by observing how changing the bandwidth on RouterB's serial 0 interface affects the metric RouterB advertises to serial 0's subnet—168.71.6.0—but does not affect the metric RouterC uses for its route to 168.71.6.0.

Figure 2–16 shows that the bandwidth on RouterB's serial 0 interface has been changed to that of a T1 connection— 1.54MB.

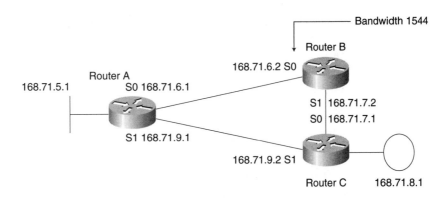

Figure 2–16

Changing the bandwidth on RouterB's serial 0 to a higher speed has no effect on RouterC.

The following output from RouterB shows how to change the bandwidth variable and how to tell whether the change has taken effect.

```
RouterB#config term
RouterB(config)#interface serial 0
RouterB(config-if)#bandwidth 1544
RouterB(config-if)#^Z

RouterB#show interface serial0
Serial0 is up, line protocol is up
  Hardware is HD64570
  Internet address is 168.71.6.2 255.255.255.0
  MTU 1500 bytes, BW 1544 Kbit, DLY 20000 usec, rely 255/255, load 1/255
```

The following output of the *debug ip igrp transactions* command on RouterC shows the metric advertised by RouterB to RouterC for 168.71.6.0 before the bandwidth on RouterB's serial 0 was changed.

```
RouterC#debug ip igrp transactions
Oct  8 16:58:24: IGRP: received update from 168.71.7.2 on Serial0
Oct  8 16:58:24:      subnet 168.71.6.0, metric 82125 (neighbor 80125)
RouterC#
```

In the previous debug output from RouterC, the bandwidth was 128, as indicated in the *show interface* command on RouterB provided here:

```
RouterB#show interface serial 0
Serial0 is up, line protocol is up
  Hardware is HD64570
  Internet address is 168.71.6.2 255.255.255.0
  MTU 1500 bytes, BW 128 Kbit, DLY 20000 usec, rely 255/255, load 1/255
```

The following output of the *debug ip igrp transactions* command on RouterC, which was taken after changing the bandwidth on RouterB's serial 0, shows that the change affects the advertised metric that RouterC receives from RouterB for 168.71.6.0 but does not affect the metric RouterC installs.

The installed metric is still 82125, even though the neighbor—RouterB—indicated that its metric was 8476. This is because the bandwidth on RouterC's serial 0 interface remained the same: 64K.

```
RouterC#deb ip igrp transactions
Oct  8 17:10:37: IGRP: received update from 168.71.7.2 on Serial0
Oct  8 17:10:37:        subnet 168.71.6.0, metric 82125 (neighbor 8476)
RouterC#
```

In the previous debug output from RouterC, the bandwidth on RouterB's serial 0 interface was 1544, as indicated in the output of the *show interface* command on RouterB provided here:

```
RouterB#show interface serial 0
Serial0 is up, line protocol is up
  Hardware is HD64570
  Internet address is 168.71.6.2 255.255.255.0
  MTU 1500 bytes, BW 1544 Kbit, DLY 20000 usec, rely 255/255, load 1/255
```

Experimenting with the delay and bandwidth parameters in a small network, such as the one used in this example, will probably not create major problems. However, experimenting with bandwidth and delay in a 1,000-router network in an attempt to achieve load balancing on some paths will almost certainly lead to more problems than it solves.

Calculating IGRP Metrics

In this book, only two of the five IGRP metrics are considered, which is the default behavior. The other three variables are set to 1.

The following text from Cisco's technical tips section on Cisco Connection Online (CCO) www.cisco.com explains in detail the formula for calculating IGRP metrics.

IGRP calculates the metric by adding together weighted values of different characteristics of the link to the network in question. These values (bandwidth, bandwidth divided by load, and delay) are weighted with the constants K1, K2, and K3. Here's the formula (BandW=bandwidth):

Metric = K1 * BandW + (K2 * BandW)/(256-load) + K3*Delay

The default constant values are K1=K3=1 and K2=K4=K5=0, so: Metric = BandW + Delay.

If K5 does not equal 0, an additional operation is done: Metric = Metric * [K5/(reliability + K4)]

To find BandW, find the smallest of all the bandwidths from outgoing interfaces and divide 10,000,000 by that number. (The bandwidth is scaled by 10,000,000 in kilobits per second.)

To find Delay, add all the delays from the outgoing interfaces and divide this number by 10. (The delay is in tens of microseconds.)

When the bandwidth was 128 and the delay was 20,000 usecs on RouterB's serial 0 interface, RouterB's advertised metric for the subnet assigned to serial 0 was 80125. This is shown by the [neighbor 80125] statement in bold taken from RouterC's debug messages. Following is RouterC receiving an update from RouterB:

```
RouterC#debug ip igrp transactions
Oct  8 16:58:24: IGRP: received update from 168.71.7.2 on Serial0
Oct  8 16:58:24:       subnet 168.71.6.0, metric 82125 (neighbor 80125)
RouterC#
```

The following output of the *show interface* command on RouterB shows that RouterB's serial 0 interface has the bandwidth set to 128K:

```
RouterB#show interface serial 0
Serial0 is up, line protocol is up
  Hardware is HD64570
  Internet address is 168.71.6.2 255.255.255.0
  MTU 1500 bytes, BW 128 Kbit, DLY 20000 usec, rely 255/255, load 1/255
```

The formula for determining the metric RouterB will use when advertising its connected route to 168.71.6.0 is as follows:

```
Bandwidth = 10,000,000/128,000  or 78125
Delay     = 20,000/10           or  2000
                                =  80125
```

When the bandwidth was 1544 and the delay was 20,000 usecs on RouterB's serial 0 interface, RouterB's advertised metric for the subnet assigned to serial 0 was 8476. This is shown by the [neighbor 8476] statement in bold taken from RouterC's debug messages. Following is RouterC receiving an update from RouterB:

```
RouterC#deb ip igrp transactions
Oct  8 17:10:37: IGRP: received update from 168.71.7.2 on Serial0
Oct  8 17:10:37:        subnet 168.71.6.0, metric 82125 (neighbor 8476)
RouterC#
```

The following output of the *show interface* command on RouterB shows that RouterB's serial 0 interface has the bandwidth set to 1544K:

```
RouterB#show interface serial 0
Serial0 is up, line protocol is up
  Hardware is HD64570
  Internet address is 168.71.6.2 255.255.255.0
  MTU 1500 bytes, BW 1544 Kbit, DLY 20000 usec, rely 255/255, load 1/255
```

The formula for determining the metric RouterB will use when advertising its connected route to 168.71.6.0 is as follows:

```
Bandwidth = 10,000,000/1,544,000  or 6476
Delay     = 20,000/10             or 2000
                                  = 8476
```

When the bandwidth was 128 and the delay was 20,000 usecs on RouterB's serial 0 interface, RouterC's installed metric for 168.71.6.0 was 82125. This is shown by the [metric 82125] statement in bold taken from RouterC's debug messages. Following is RouterC receiving an update from RouterB:

```
RouterC#debug ip igrp transactions
Oct  8 16:58:24: IGRP: received update from 168.71.7.2 on Serial0
Oct  8 16:58:24:        subnet 168.71.6.0, metric 82125 (neighbor 80125)
RouterC#
```

The following output of the *show interface* command on RouterC shows that RouterC's serial 0 interface has the bandwidth set to 128K:

```
RouterC#show interface serial 0
Serial0 is up, line protocol is up
  Hardware is HD64570
  Internet address is 168.71.7.1 255.255.255.0
  MTU 1500 bytes, BW 128 Kbit, DLY 20000 usec, rely 255/255, load 1/255
```

The formula for determining the metric RouterC will use for 168.71.6.0 is as follows:

```
Bandwidth = 10,000,000/128     or 78125
Delay     = 40,000/10          or  4000

                               =  82125
```

When the bandwidth was 1544 and the delay was 20,000 usecs on RouterB's serial 0 interface, RouterC's installed metric for 168.71.6.0 was still 82125. This is shown by the [metric 82125] statement in bold taken from RouterC's debug messages. This is RouterC receiving an update from RouterB:

```
RouterC#deb ip igrp transactions
Oct  8 17:10:37: IGRP: received update from 168.71.7.2 on Serial0
Oct  8 17:10:37:        subnet 168.71.6.0, metric 82125 (neighbor 8476)
RouterC#
```

The following output of the *show interface* command on RouterC shows that RouterC's serial 0 interface has the bandwidth set to 128K:

```
RouterC#show interface serial 0
Serial0 is up, line protocol is up
  Hardware is HD64570
  Internet address is 168.71.7.1 255.255.255.0
  MTU 1500 bytes, BW 128 Kbit, DLY 20000 usec, rely 255/255, load 1/255
```

The formula for determining the metric RouterC will use for 168.71.6.0 is the same because the lowest bandwidth in the path is still 128K.

```
Bandwidth = 10,000,000/128     or 78125
Delay     = 40,000/10          or  4000
                               =  82125
```

SUMMARY

This chapter is important to your overall understanding of routing metrics and distances. You need to understand the topics discussed in this chapter to be able to progress from here. You learned about convergence, which is the process that routers go through when a route has become unavailable. The primary activities of convergence are update, invalid, holddown, and flush. You also learned about parallel paths, the effect of parallel paths on convergence, the effect of parallel paths on packet forwarding, and how to review parallel paths in a routing table. The difference between process switching and fast switching was also discussed.

This chapter has touched upon the role of split horizon, including what it means for routing advertisements with split horizon enabled and disabled. Finally, IGRP routing metrics (variables) and Cisco administrative distances were explained. Chapter 3, "Discontiguous Networks, Summarization, and Subnet 0," continues the discussion by delving deeper into these topics.

CHAPTER 3

Discontiguous Networks, Summarization, and Subnet 0

This chapter groups together several concepts that affect network connectivity directly by altering the content of routing information shared between routers. These effects may be useful or detrimental, depending on how they are applied. These concepts are usually considered together in order to fully explain their interaction. This chapter covers discontiguous networks, subnet 0, and summarization, as the chapter title implies. Chapter 4, "Using IP Unnumbered and VLSM," continues this discussion.

NOTES

Only RIP V1 (version 1) and IGRP are mentioned in this chapter because RIP V1 and IGRP do not include the subnet masks associated with the routes they advertise. The routers receiving routing advertisements are forced to derive the correct subnet masks by using the mask on the interface that the route advertisements are received over (see Figure 3–1).

EIGRP, OSPF, and RIP V2 are not covered because they do advertise masks with their routing advertisements.

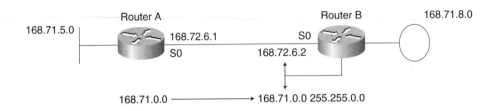

Figure 3–1
Advertisements don't include subnet masks; the receiving router must derive the mask.

NOTES

Notice in Figure 3–1 that the major network address of the link be-tween RouterA and RouterB has been changed. It is now 168.72.0.0. The configuration commands and related *show interface* commands are given in the section "Summarization Caused by Discontiguous Networks in Action."

INTRODUCTION TO TERMINOLOGY

Before proceeding any further in this chapter, it is important to lay the groundwork for the discussion by defining some terms, as follows:

- A *major net(work)* refers to the network-only portion of an Internet address. In Figure 3–1, the major net of subnet 168.71.5.0 is 168.71.0.0 because Class B addresses use only the first two of the four bytes in an IP address to determine the network address space. The other two bytes can be used for host addresses or a combination of subnets and host addresses. In other words, the term *major net* is used for the bytes of an address that are reserved for the network portion, based on the class of address in use. The major net for address 10.9.0.0 is 10.0.0.0. The major net for address

223.221.142.8 with a mask of 255.255.255.248 is 223.221.142.0.

- In a *discontiguous network*, IP subnet addresses from a major network are applied to physical networks that are separated by a network with a different major net. In Figure 3–1, the link between RouterA and RouterB has been configured with a different major network address (168.72.0.0).

- To *summarize* means to report only the major net portion of an address, even though there are subnets of the address in the routing table. In Figure 3–1, RouterB has a network with subnet 168.71.8.0 assigned. When RouterB is preparing a routing update to send out serial 0, it will notice that serial 0 is part of a different major net and send out only the summarized (in this case, major net) portion of the address.

- *Aggregation* is very similar to summarization. In fact, many people use the terms interchangeably. This book treats the terms as similar, but not identical, functions. In the context of this book, aggregation means reducing the number of subnets in a routing advertisement by advertising only the common portion of the subnet addresses that is required to provide full IP connectivity. If RouterA were connected to subnets 168.71.1.16, 168.71.1.32, and 168.71.1.48, and RouterB were connected to subnets 168.71.2.16, 168.71.2.32, and 168.71.2.48, each router could aggregate its connected subnets to the third byte. Full connectivity would be possible if RouterA advertised only 168.71.1.0 and RouterB advertised only 168.71.2.0. For a more detailed explanation, see the section on aggregation later in this chapter.

- A *major net boundary* is a router connected to two or more major nets. In Figure 3–1, RouterA is connected to two major nets: 168.71.0.0 and 168.72.0.0. The routing update for 168.71.5.0 that would be advertised over serial 0 to RouterB is encountering a major net boundary—168.71.0.0 >> 168.72.0.0. RouterA will summarize the 168.71.5.0 route to the major net of 168.71.0.0.

Now that you are familiar with the terms used in this chapter, you can move on to the heart of the matter—starting with discontiguous networks.

DISCONTIGUOUS NETWORKS USING RIP AND IGRP

In Figure 3–2, network 168.71.0.0 is no longer contiguous. It is separated by a serial link that has a different major network—168.72.0.0. This will cause both routers to summarize their subnets of 168.71.0.0 when sending advertisements. Summarization is explained in more detail later in this chapter.

Figure 3–2
Simplified network using different major network addresses.

For RIP, this means that neither router can reach the other's subnet of 168.71.0.0. The section on RIP that follows demonstrates this concept.

NOTES

For IGRP, the answer should have been the same as for RIP—neither router should have been able to reach the other's subnet of 168.71.0.0. However, while I was writing this book, an anomaly was discovered in IGRP that has since been fixed. This anomaly allowed IGRP to accept summarized routes for major networks when it should not have done so. The section on IGRP and discontiguous networks was left as originally written, with the anomaly still in effect.

The nature of the anomaly provides a great opportunity to discuss some interesting and fairly subtle IP connectivity problems and the methodologies used to track them down. More information on the anomaly is provided at the end of the IGRP section.

Before proceeding any further on the effects of discontiguous networks, the following fundamental principles need to be introduced:

- Understanding how a router derives the correct masks

- Understanding summarization

- Understanding subnet 0

- Summarized routes versus subnet 0

- Summarization caused by discontiguous networks in action

Understanding How a Router Derives the Correct Masks

Even when they are not dealing with discontiguous networks, routers running RIP V1 and IGRP must determine which masks to associate with the networks and subnetworks for which they receive route advertisements. When discontiguous networks are added to the picture, this process takes on even more significance. The normal methods these two protocols use to derive masks do not work properly with discontiguous networks. Later sections in this chapter explain these problems in more detail.

Routers receiving a RIP V1 or IGRP routing advertisement use two methods for deriving the correct mask to associate in the advertisement, as follows:

1. Advertisements for subnets that are part of the same major network as the IP address of the interface they are received over will have the subnet mask of the receiving interface applied to them.
2. All other networks in the advertisement should be for major networks, not subnets. This is because the router sending the advertisement should have summarized the subnets down to the major network before sending the advertisement. Therefore, the masks for all other networks should be the default mask for the class of address received.

In Figure 3–3, RouterA sends an advertisement for subnet 168.71.5.0 to RouterB as an example of what can go wrong when a router advertises subnets over a major net boundary. RouterB sees that 168.71.5.0 is in a different major net than its IP address on serial 0. RouterB knows that 168.71.5.0 is not a major net because it has bits set in the third byte (Class B address major net advertisements should have bits set only in the first two bytes).

RouterB has a few choices: ignore the route advertisement; install it with a mask of 255.255.255.255, indicating that it is a host route (has a full mask); or try to guess what mask should be used.

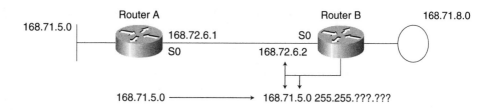

Figure 3–3
Advertising a subnet by mistake.

Attempting to guess the correct mask is difficult due to the many possible ways a subnet advertisement can be masked. *Mask ambiguity* is a situation in which a router can use many different masks on a subnet for which it receives an advertisement (see Figure 3–4).

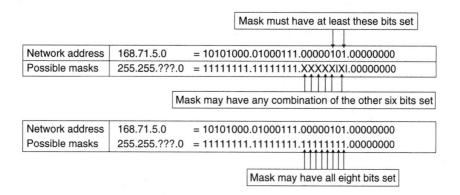

Figure 3–4
Many possible masks.

RouterB would analyze subnet 168.71.5.0, as shown in Figure 3–5. The bits for 1 and 4 must be set in the mask because these bits are set in the route advertisement and therefore must be set in the associated mask as well. Remember that 00000101 equals 5 in decimal notation. Subnet 168.71.5.0 can be masked in 65 $((2^6)+1)$ additional ways because 6 bits are left in the third byte that may be either 0 or 1. The +1 is added to the formula because all eight bits can be set to 1 as well. The number 65 assumes that the mask on the fourth octet is made up of all 0s.

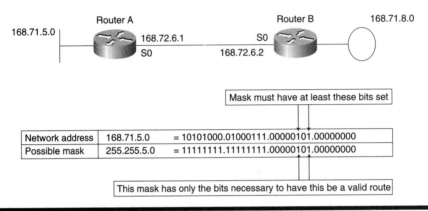

Figure 3–5

Masking from right to left instead of left to right.

Figure 3–5 shows an example of a mask that uses non-contiguous bits and does not work from left to right. This is a valid mask as far as IP addressing is concerned. However, as of 9.1, Cisco IOS supports only contiguous masks working from left to right.

Some vendors' implementations of IP masks do not have to be created working from left to right and do not have to utilize contiguous bits. However, it is highly discouraged to create masks that are not based on this model.

NOTES

RFCs 950 and 1219 are good references on subnet allocation. RFC 1219 states the following: "While RFC 950 allows the ones in the subnet mask to be non-contiguous, RFC 950 recommends that 1) they be contiguous and 2) that they occupy the most significant bits of the host portion of the Internet address." RFC 1219 also states that "RFC 950 did not specify whether different subnets of the same network may have different masks. This ambiguity was unfortunate, as it resulted in the development of routing protocols that do not support different masks"—specifically, RIP V1 and IGRP.

When deriving a major net mask, there is very little ambiguity in interpreting an advertised route if only the major network bits are used. In Figure 3–6, the only two choices are that 168.71.0.0 is a major network advertisement or that it is an advertisement of subnet 0. Subnet 0 is explained in the next section.

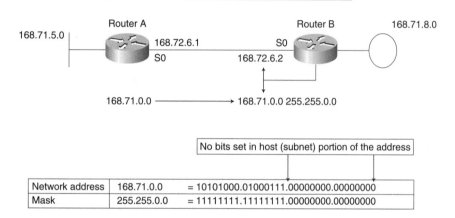

Figure 3–6
Deriving a mask for a major net.

Understanding Summarization (Summarized Routes)

Summarization is the process of advertising only the major network portion of subnets in a routing table. Figure 3–7 shows routers summarizing subnets.

Routers running RIP V1 or IGRP make decisions on whether to summarize a subnet based on the following rules:

1. If a network or subnet in the table is part of the same network address space (major net) and has the same mask as the outbound interface, it is advertised over the interface.
2. If a network or subnet is part of the same major net as the outbound interface but has a different mask, it is not advertised.

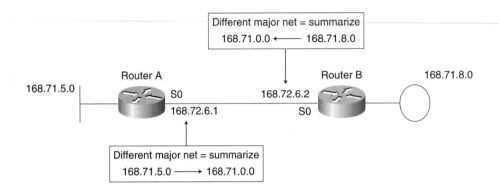

Figure 3–7
Routers summarizing subnets.

3. If a network or subnet is part of a different address space, the outbound interface mask is ignored and only the summarized major network portion of the route is advertised.

Understanding Subnet 0

Subnet 0 refers to the use of 0s in the subnet portion of an address covered by the subnet mask. In the following simple example of subnet 0, the subnet mask covers all bits in the third octet:

Network address 168.71.0.0   = 10101000.01000111.00000000.00000000

Possible mask   255.255.255.0 = 11111111.11111111.11111111.00000000

The IP address in this minitable is an example of subnet 0 because none of the bits in the third octet are turned on. If a router had this address configured on an interface and needed to advertise it with either RIP or IGRP, it would send out only the major network 168.71.0.0. A more complicated example of subnet 0 is shown in the following minitable. Here, the subnet mask covers all bits in the third octet and six of the bits in the fourth octet:

Network address 220.220.220.2   = 11011100.11011100.11011100.00000010

Possible mask   255.255.255.252 = 11111111.11111111.11111111.11111100

The preceding minitable shows a more complicated example of subnet 0 because bits within the first three octets are already used as part of the Class C Internet address. This means that subnets must be created using only the fourth byte. In this case, subnet 0 means that none of the 6 bits in the fourth byte covered by the mask of 252 are set to 1.

If a router advertised this subnet using RIP V1 or IGRP, the advertisement would be 220.220.220.0—the same as for the major net.

Summarized Routes Versus Subnet 0

Summarized routes look exactly like subnet 0 to routers running RIP V1 and IGRP. In Figure 3–8 and Table 3–1, you can see that as far as RouterA is concerned, the two advertisements are identical. This is because, as previously mentioned, neither RIP V1 nor IGRP includes a mask with the routes it advertises.

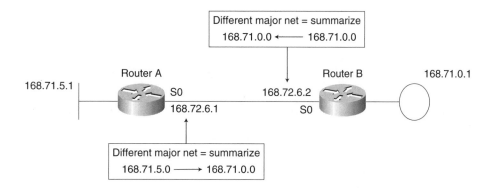

Figure 3–8

Sending a summarized route.

From a routing perspective, there is no difference between subnet 0 and the summarized route for 168.71.0.0, as shown in Table 3–1.

Table 3–1   *Binary Example of Subnet 0 Versus a Summarized Route*

Subnet 0		
Network address	168.71.0.0	= 10101000.01000111.00000000.00000000
Subnet 0 mask	255.255.255.0	= 11111111.11111111.11111111.00000000
Summarized Route		
Network address	168.71.0.0	= 10101000.01000111.00000000.00000000
Summarised mask	255.255.0.0	= 11111111.11111111.00000000.00000000

Summarization Caused by Discontiguous Networks in Action

This section provides real-life examples of summarization in action using RIP and IGRP.

Both routers have their configuration modified for the additional major network (see Figure 3–9). The *show interface* commands below the configuration commands show the new major net in place.

Figure 3–9

A reminder that a new major net has been configured on the serial link.

```
RouterA#conf t
RouterA#-config#interface s0
RouterA#-config-if# ip address 168.72.6.1 255.255.255.0
RouterA#-config-if#^Z
RouterA#

RouterA#show interface serial 0
Serial0 is up, line protocol is up
```

```
 Hardware is HD64570
 Internet address is 168.72.6.1 255.255.255.0
 MTU 1500 bytes, BW 128 Kbit, DLY 20000 usec, rely 255/255, load 1/255
RouterB#conf t
RouterB#-config#interface s0
RouterB#-config-if# ip address 168.72.6.2 255.255.255.0
RouterB#-config-if#^Z
RouterB#

RouterB#show interface serial 0
Serial0 is up, line protocol is up
 Hardware is HD64570
 Internet address is 168.72.6.2 255.255.255.0
 MTU 1500 bytes, BW 128 Kbit, DLY 20000 usec, rely 255/255, load 1/255
```

The portion of the configuration for adding 168.72.0.0 to the routing tables is the same for both routers. It is as follows:

```
!
router rip
network 168.71.0.0
network 168.72.0.0
!
```

RIP Cannot Reach Discontiguous Subnets

Routers running RIP ignore summarized routes for networks to which they have connections, which is one reason why RIP doesn't work with discontiguous networks (see Figure 3–10).

Recall that routers running RIP examine the network number and mask associated with an interface before advertising routes from the routing table over it. This was discussed previously in the section on understanding summarized routes.

In the following output of *debug ip rip* from RouterA, you can see RouterA sending and receiving advertisements for 168.71.0.0 with a metric of 1:

```
RouterA#deb ip rip
RIP: received update from 168.72.6.2 on Serial0
     168.71.0.0 in 1 hops
RIP: sending update to 255.255.255.255 via Serial0 (168.72.6.1)
     network 168.71.0.0, metric 1
```

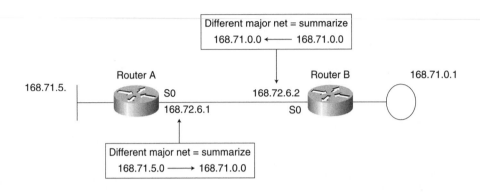

Figure 3–10
Summarized routes being advertised.

In the following routing table from RouterA, you can see that RouterA does not have a route installed to 168.71.0.0, even though RouterB is advertising it:

```
RouterA#show ip route
Codes: C - connected, S - static, I - IGRP, R - RIP, M - mobile, B - BGP
       D - EIGRP, EX - EIGRP external, O - OSPF, IA - OSPF inter area
       E1 - OSPF external type 1, E2 - OSPF external type 2, E - EGP
       i - IS-IS, L1 - IS-IS level-1, L2 - IS-IS level-2, * - candidate default

Gateway of last resort is 171.68.207.129 to network 10.0.0.0

168.72.0.0 255.255.255.0 is subnetted, 1 subnets
C       168.72.6.0 is directly connected, Serial0
     168.71.0.0 255.255.255.0 is subnetted, 1 subnets
C       168.71.5.0 is directly connected, Ethernet0
RouterA#
```

In the following output of *debug ip rip* from RouterB, you can see RouterB sending and receiving advertisements for 168.71.0.0 with a metric of 1:

```
RouterB#deb ip rip
RIP: received update from 168.72.6.1 on Serial0
     168.71.0.0 in 1 hops
RIP: sending update to 255.255.255.255 via Serial0 (168.72.6.2)
     network 168.71.0.0, metric 1
```

In the following routing table from RouterB, you can see that
RouterB does not have a route installed to 168.71.0.0, even
though RouterA is advertising it:

```
RouterB#show ip route
Codes: C - connected, S - static, I - IGRP, R - RIP, M - mobile, B - BGP
       D - EIGRP, EX - EIGRP external, O - OSPF, IA - OSPF inter area
       E1 - OSPF external type 1, E2 - OSPF external type 2, E - EGP
       i - IS-IS, L1 - IS-IS level-1, L2 - IS-IS level-2, * - candidate default

Gateway of last resort is 168.72.6.1 to network 0.0.0.0

     168.72.0.0 255.255.255.0 is subnetted, 1 subnets
C       168.72.6.0 is directly connected, Serial0
C    168.71.0.0 is directly connected, TokenRing0
RouterB#
```

In the following output of the *show interface* command from
RouterB, you can see that RouterB has 168.71.0.1 configured
on Token Ring 0:

```
RouterB#show interface tokenring 0
TokenRing0 is up, line protocol is up
  Hardware is TMS380, address is 0000.3062.676d (bia 0000.3062.676d)
  Internet address is 168.71.0.1 255.255.255.0
  MTU 4464 bytes, BW 16000 Kbit, DLY 630 usec, rely 255/255, load 1/255
```

In the following output from RouterA, you can see that
RouterA cannot ping 168.71.0.1, even though RouterB is
advertising 168.71.0.0:

```
RouterA#ping 168.71.0.1
Type escape sequence to abort.
Sending 5, 100-byte ICMP Echos to 168.71.0.1, timeout is 2 seconds:
.....
Success rate is 0 percent (0/5)
RouterA#
```

This section has explained why using discontiguous networks
with RIP does not work.

DISCONTIGUOUS NETWORKS, SUBNET 0, AND SUMMARIZATION USING IGRP

During the process of researching the material for this section,
an anomaly was discovered in the behavior of IGRP. IGRP

would install a summarized route for a major network when the router had a connection to a subnet of the same major net—which is not supposed to happen. Cisco engineers discovered this behavior while reviewing the material for this book prior to publication.

The Cisco engineers opened a bug against it—CSCdj03421— and fixed the bug so that IGRP now behaves as expected. In other words, it behaves now exactly as in the previous section on RIP. This bug has been integrated in IOS versions 11.0, 11.1 (and all 11.1-based releases), 11.2 (and all 11.2-based releases), and all releases that started shipping after IOS version 11.2 was first shipped.

NOTES

The remainder of this section should be treated as an exercise in analyzing anomalous behavior in a network and not as a representation of how IGRP really behaves.

The following two scenarios are presented in the remainder of this section:

- Discontiguous networks using two routers

- Discontiguous networks using three routers

Both routers have their configuration modified for running IGRP. The portion of the configuration for doing this in both routers is as follows:

```
!
router igrp 109
network 168.71.0.0
network 168.72.0.0
!
```

Recall that routers running IGRP examine the network number and mask associated with an interface before advertising routes from the routing table over it.

Discontiguous Networks Using Two Routers

Refer to Figure 3–10 for the network diagram used in this scenario. In the following output of the *debug ip igrp transactions* command from RouterB, you can see that RouterB advertises the major network of 168.71.0.0 to RouterA:

```
RouterB#deb ip igrp transactions
Oct 30 01:03:03: IGRP: sending update to 255.255.255.255 via Serial0 (168.72.6.2)
Oct 30 01:03:03:        network 168.71.0.0, metric=80125
```

NOTES

Variably subnetted means that the router has information that leads it to believe a major network address has been used with more than one mask. This is explained in more detail in Chapter 4 (in the section on VLSM). In the routing table from RouterA, major net 168.71.0.0 has two masks: 255.255.255.0 and 255.255.0.0.

In the following routing table from RouterA, you can see that RouterA believes that 168.71.0.0 is variably subnetted because of the local connection and the IGRP derived route from RouterB:

```
RouterA#show ip route
Codes: C - connected, S - static, I - IGRP, R - RIP, M - mobile, B - BGP
       D - EIGRP, EX - EIGRP external, O - OSPF, IA - OSPF inter area
       E1 - OSPF external type 1, E2 - OSPF external type 2, E - EGP
       i - IS-IS, L1 - IS-IS level-1, L2 - IS-IS level-2, * - candidate default

Gateway of last resort is 171.68.207.129 to network 10.0.0.0

S*   10.0.0.0 [1/0] via 171.68.207.129
     168.72.0.0 255.255.255.0 is subnetted, 1 subnets
C       168.72.6.0 is directly connected, Serial0
     168.71.0.0 is variably subnetted, 2 subnets, 2 masks
C       168.71.5.0 255.255.255.0 is directly connected, Ethernet0
I       168.71.0.0 255.255.0.0 [100/80188] via 168.72.6.2, 00:00:05, Serial0
RouterA#
```

In the following output from RouterA, you can see that RouterA can ping 168.71.0.1:

```
RouterA#ping 168.71.0.1
Type escape sequence to abort.
Sending 5, 100-byte ICMP Echos to 168.71.0.1, timeout is 2 seconds:
!!!!!
Success rate is 100 percent (5/5), round-trip min/avg/max = 4/4/4 ms
RouterA#
```

Recall that in the previous section on RIP, RouterA could not ping 168.71.0.1. For the next scenario, RouterC has been added to the network.

Discontiguous Networks Using Three Routers

This part of the scenario on using IGRP with discontiguous networks is split into additional sections:

- When connectivity to subnet 0 is possible from RouterA

- When connectivity to subnet 0 is not possible from RouterA

- Alternating paths for the first ping

Figure 3–11 shows that RouterC, which is also running IGRP, has been returned to the network.

NOTES

It is important to note that pings generated by a router are always *process-switched,* regardless of the switching method configured on the out-bound interfaces. If parallel paths exist, the router should load share pings across the available paths.

When Connectivity Is Possible

In this section, RouterA is able to ping RouterB's Token Ring port (168.71.0.1), even though it is using subnet 0. RouterA

can do this because it has a connection to the major net of
168.71.0.0, which it is advertising to RouterB and RouterC.
Don't worry if you don't understand this yet. It should become
clearer as this section progresses.

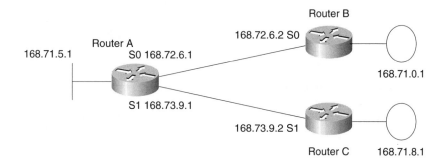

Figure 3–11

RouterC returns in the three-router scenario.

In the following routing table from RouterA, you can see that
RouterA now has two summarized routes to 168.71.0.0:

```
RouterA#show ip route
Codes: C - connected, S - static, I - IGRP, R - RIP, M - mobile, B - BGP
       D - EIGRP, EX - EIGRP external, O - OSPF, IA - OSPF inter area
       E1 - OSPF external type 1, E2 - OSPF external type 2, E - EGP
       i - IS-IS, L1 - IS-IS level-1, L2 - IS-IS level-2, * - candidate default

Gateway of last resort is 171.68.207.129 to network 10.0.0.0

S*   10.0.0.0 [1/0] via 171.68.207.129
     168.72.0.0 255.255.255.0 is subnetted, 1 subnets
C       168.72.6.0 is directly connected, Serial0
     168.73.0.0 255.255.255.0 is subnetted, 1 subnets
C       168.73.9.0 is directly connected, Serial1
     168.71.0.0 is variably subnetted, 2 subnets, 2 masks
C       168.71.5.0 255.255.255.0 is directly connected, Ethernet0
I       168.71.0.0 255.255.0.0 [100/80188] via 168.72.6.2, 00:00:02, Serial0
                               [100/80188] via 168.73.9.2, 00:00:10, Serial1
RouterA#
```

The arrows in Figure 3–12 show where these two routes point.

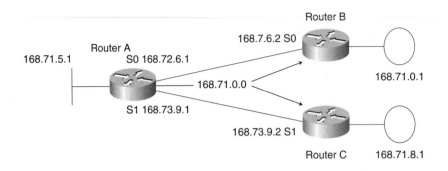

Figure 3–12

RouterA's two summarized routes to 168.71.0.0.

In the following output of the *show ip route 168.71.0.1* command from RouterA, you can see that RouterA uses the two summarized routes for 168.71.0.0 to reach 168.71.0.1:

```
RouterA#show ip route 168.71.0.1
Routing entry for 168.71.0.0 255.255.0.0
  Known via "igrp 109", distance 100, metric 80188
  Redistributing via igrp 109
  Advertised by igrp 109 (self originated)
  Last update from 168.73.9.2 on Serial1, 00:00:48 ago
  Routing Descriptor Blocks:
    168.72.6.2, from 168.72.6.2, 00:01:07 ago, via Serial0
      Route metric is 80188, traffic share count is 1
      Total delay is 20630 microseconds, minimum bandwidth is 128 Kbit
      Reliability 255/255, minimum MTU 1500 bytes
      Loading 1/255, Hops 0
  * 168.73.9.2, from 168.73.9.2, 00:00:48 ago, via Serial1
      Route metric is 80188, traffic share count is 1
      Total delay is 20630 microseconds, minimum bandwidth is 128 Kbit
      Reliability 255/255, minimum MTU 1500 bytes
      Loading 1/255, Hops 0
RouterA#
```

In the following output of the *ping* command from RouterA, you can see that RouterA can ping 168.71.0.1 successfully 100 percent of the time:

```
RouterA#ping 168.71.0.1
Type escape sequence to abort.
Sending 5, 100-byte ICMP Echos to 168.71.0.1, timeout is 2 seconds:
```

```
!!!!!
Success rate is 100 percent (5/5), round-trip min/avg/max = 28/30/32 ms
RouterA#
```

Looking back at the routing table from RouterA, it appears that some of the pings should have been sent to RouterB and others to RouterC. This is based on the following two facts, which were introduced previously:

- Pings generated by a router are always process-switched.

- Routers load share on a packet-by-packet basis when parallel routes exist and when the packets are being process-switched.

So, in theory, the pings to RouterC should have failed because RouterC doesn't own IP address 168.71.0.1—RouterB does.

The three possible reasons why these pings were successful are as follows:

- RouterA sent all of the pings to RouterB, even though it shouldn't have. This would have been a bug in the behavior of switching ping packets generated by the router itself.

- RouterC responded to the pings as if it owned 168.71.0.1. Because RouterC doesn't have an interface with 168.71.0.1 configured on it, this would have required a major bug in RouterC's operating system. (Note: it is possible to configure the same IP address in two or more routers by mistake. It is never a good idea.)

- RouterC was receiving the pings for 168.71.0.1 from RouterA and forwarding them back to RouterA. RouterA in turn forwarded them back to RouterC.

Fortunately, the answer is the last scenario: RouterC was forwarding them back to RouterA. The remainder of this section proves that this was the case.

The following output of the *debug ip packet* command is from RouterA as it sends five pings to 168.71.0.1. The output shows that some of the pings went out serial 1 to RouterC first and that RouterC sent them back to RouterA. RouterA then forwarded its own pings to RouterB. The *ping* command itself (*RouterA#ping 168.71.0.1*) and its related messages have been omitted for clarity.

NOTES

The pings are numbered (1), (2), (3), (4), and (5) so that you can see which events go together.

```
RouterA#debug ip packet
(1) IP: s=168.72.6.1 (local), d=168.71.0.1 (Serial0), len 100, sending
(1) IP: s=168.71.0.1 (Serial0), d=168.72.6.1 (Serial0), len 104, rcvd 3
(2) IP: s=168.72.6.1 (local), d=168.71.0.1 (Serial1), len 100, sending
(2) IP: s=168.72.6.1 (Serial1), d=168.71.0.1 (Serial0), g=168.72.6.2, len 104, forward
(2) IP: s=168.71.0.1 (Serial0), d=168.72.6.1 (Serial0), len 104, rcvd 3
(3) IP: s=168.72.6.1 (local), d=168.71.0.1 (Serial1), len 100, sending
(3) IP: s=168.72.6.1 (Serial1), d=168.71.0.1 (Serial0), g=168.72.6.2, len 104, forward
(3) IP: s=168.71.0.1 (Serial0), d=168.72.6.1 (Serial0), len 104, rcvd 3
(4) IP: s=168.72.6.1 (local), d=168.71.0.1 (Serial1), len 100, sending
(4) IP: s=168.72.6.1 (Serial1), d=168.71.0.1 (Serial0), g=168.72.6.2, len 104, forward
(4) IP: s=168.71.0.1 (Serial0), d=168.72.6.1 (Serial0), len 104, rcvd 3
(5) IP: s=168.72.6.1 (local), d=168.71.0.1 (Serial1), len 100, sending
(5) IP: s=168.72.6.1 (Serial1), d=168.71.0.1 (Serial0), g=168.72.6.2, len 104, forward
(5) IP: s=168.71.0.1 (Serial0), d=168.72.6.1 (Serial0), len 104, rcvd 3
RouterA#
```

The following text illustrates these steps:

1. The first ping (1) is sent out serial 0 to RouterB, and a response is received immediately.
2. Pings (2), (3), (4), and (5) take the other available path to 168.71.0.0 via serial 1 to RouterC.

3. RouterC forwards pings (2), (3), (4), and (5) back to RouterA.

4. RouterA forwards them on to RouterB.

5. Finally, RouterB responds to the pings.

This is exactly what should happen based on RouterA load sharing packets to 168.71.0.1 between serial 0 and serial 1. The next section explains in more detail the path that pings (2) and (3) take through the network.

NOTES

The remainder of this section explains the behavior just demonstrated. If you are comfortable with this material, feel free to skip this section and pick up at the next section, "When Connectivity Is Not Possible."

You now know that RouterC was forwarding RouterA's pings back to RouterA. You can explore the same issue from a more graphical point of view. In Figure 3–13, RouterA is load balancing between the two paths. Ping (2) goes out serial 0 to RouterC. RouterC does a longest match lookup and sees that 168.71.0.1 matches 168.71.0.0 that is known via serial 1 using RouterA.

RouterC forwards ping (2) back to RouterA. This is the second packet that RouterA has seen for the destination 168.71.0.1 (the first was when it sent ping (2) in the first place), so RouterA sends ping (2) out the next available path—serial 0 to RouterB.

In the following portion from the previous debug output, you can see RouterA load balancing between the two paths for pings, (1) and (2). The lines showing the two different paths are in bold.

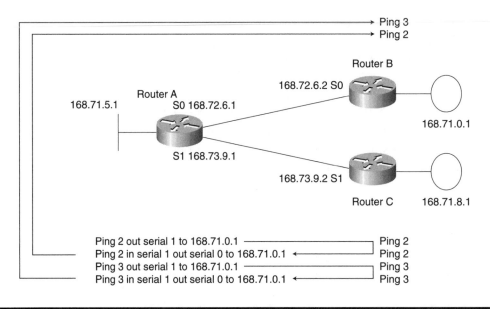

Figure 3–13

RouterA is load balancing between the two paths.

```
1) IP: s=168.72.6.1 (local), d=168.71.0.1 (Serial0), len 100, sending
1) IP: s=168.71.0.1 (Serial0), d=168.72.6.1 (Serial0), len 104, rcvd 3
2) IP: s=168.72.6.1 (local), d=168.71.0.1 (Serial1), len 100, sending
2) IP: s=168.72.6.1 (Serial1), d=168.71.0.1 (Serial0), g=168.72.6.2, len 104, forward
2) IP: s=168.71.0.1 (Serial0), d=168.72.6.1 (Serial0), len 104, rcvd 3
```

At the beginning of this section, you looked at RouterA's routes to 168.71.0.0. Now that you have seen how the network behaves, let's review the routing tables from RouterB and RouterC to understand why pings to 168.71.0.1 were routed as they were.

Following is RouterB's routing table, showing the summarized route to 168.71.0.0 that RouterA is advertising to it:

```
RouterB#show ip route
Codes: C - connected, S - static, I - IGRP, R - RIP, M - mobile, B - BGP
       D - EIGRP, EX - EIGRP external, O - OSPF, IA - OSPF inter area
       E1 - OSPF external type 1, E2 - OSPF external type 2, E - EGP
       i - IS-IS, L1 - IS-IS level-1, L2 - IS-IS level-2, * - candidate default
```

```
Gateway of last resort is 168.72.6.1 to network 10.0.0.0

I*   10.0.0.0 [100/160250] via 168.72.6.1, 00:00:49, Serial0
     168.72.0.0 255.255.255.0 is subnetted, 1 subnets
C       168.72.6.0 is directly connected, Serial0
I    168.73.0.0 [100/82125] via 168.72.6.1, 00:00:49, Serial0
168.71.0.0 is variably subnetted, 2 subnets, 2 masks
I       168.71.0.0 255.255.0.0 [100/10002001] via 168.72.6.1, 00:00:49, Serial0
C       168.71.0.0 255.255.255.0 is directly connected, TokenRing0
RouterB#
```

HINT

Using a full IP host address with the *show ip route* command is a good habit to get into. It ensures that the route displayed is the longest match in the routing table.

The following output of the *show ip route 168.71.0.1* command from RouterB shows that RouterB will use its route to 168.71.0.0 via RouterA to forward packets addressed to 168.71.0.1:

```
RouterB#show ip route 168.71.0.1
Routing entry for 168.71.0.0 255.255.0.0
  Known via "igrp 109", distance 100, metric 10002001
  Redistributing via igrp 109
  Last update from 168.72.6.1 on Serial0, 00:00:04 ago
  Routing Descriptor Blocks:
  * 168.72.6.1, from 168.72.6.1, 00:00:04 ago, via Serial0
      Route metric is 10002001, traffic share count is 1
      Total delay is 20010 microseconds, minimum bandwidth is 1 Kbit
      Reliability 255/255, minimum MTU 1500 bytes
      Loading 1/255, Hops 0

RouterB#
```

Following is RouterC's routing table, which shows the summarized route to 168.71.0.0 that RouterA is advertising to it:

```
RouterC#show ip route
Codes: C - connected, S - static, I - IGRP, R - RIP, M - mobile, B - BGP
       D - EIGRP, EX - EIGRP external, O - OSPF, IA - OSPF inter area
       E1 - OSPF external type 1, E2 - OSPF external type 2, E - EGP
       i - IS-IS, L1 - IS-IS level-1, L2 - IS-IS level-2, * - candidate default

Gateway of last resort is 168.73.9.1 to network 10.0.0.0

I*   10.0.0.0 [100/160250] via 168.73.9.1, 00:00:55, Serial1
I    168.72.0.0 [100/82125] via 168.73.9.1, 00:00:55, Serial1
```

```
    168.73.0.0 255.255.255.0 is subnetted, 1 subnets
C       168.73.9.0 is directly connected, Serial1
168.71.0.0 is variably subnetted, 2 subnets, 2 masks
C       168.71.8.0 255.255.255.0 is directly connected, TokenRing0
I       168.71.0.0 255.255.0.0 [100/10002001] via 168.73.9.1, 00:00:56, Serial1
RouterC#
```

Again, you can test whether the router will match the full IP host address (168.71.0.1) to the route:

```
RouterC#show ip route 168.71.0.1
Routing entry for 168.71.0.0 255.255.0.0
  Known via "igrp 109", distance 100, metric 10002001
  Redistributing via igrp 109
  Last update from 168.73.9.1 on Serial1, 00:01:09 ago
  Routing Descriptor Blocks:
  * 168.73.9.1, from 168.73.9.1, 00:01:09 ago, via Serial1
      Route metric is 10002001, traffic share count is 1
      Total delay is 20010 microseconds, minimum bandwidth is 1 Kbit
      Reliability 255/255, minimum MTU 1500 bytes
      Loading 1/255, Hops 0
RouterC#
```

When Connectivity Is Not Possible

In the previous section, RouterA was able to ping 168.71.0.1 100 percent of the time. It was able to do so because it was advertising the summarized route of 168.71.0.0 for its connection to 168.71.5.0 to RouterB and RouterC. RouterC used this summarized route to forward packets destined for 168.71.0.1 that were received from RouterA back to RouterA so that RouterA could forward them over the next available path to RouterB.

In Figure 3–14, RouterA no longer has a connection to a subnet of the 168.71.0.0 network, so it does not advertise the summarized route to RouterB and RouterC. RouterA still has two summarized routes to 168.71.0.0 via RouterB and RouterC. However, RouterA can no longer ping 168.71.0.1 100 percent of the time.

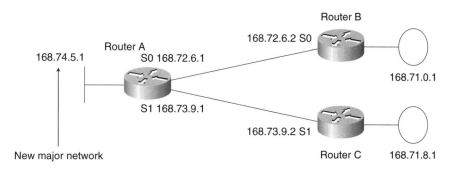

Figure 3–14
RouterA no longer has a connection to a subnet of the 168.71.0.0 network.

RouterB and RouterC are summarizing their local subnets of
168.71.0.0 because of the different major network applied to
their serial interfaces. However, RouterA will not forward
these entries to RouterB and RouterC due to a *split horizon*.
(Recall that the term split horizon means not advertising routes
back out the interface they were learned over.)

RouterA's new routing table shows the summarized routes to
168.71.0.0 and no local connection to 168.71.0.0:

```
RouterA#show ip route
Codes: C - connected, S - static, I - IGRP, R - RIP, M - mobile, B - BGP
       D - EIGRP, EX - EIGRP external, O - OSPF, IA - OSPF inter area
       E1 - OSPF external type 1, E2 - OSPF external type 2, E - EGP
       i - IS-IS, L1 - IS-IS level-1, L2 - IS-IS level-2, * - candidate default

Gateway of last resort is 171.68.207.129 to network 10.0.0.0

S*   10.0.0.0 [1/0] via 171.68.207.129
     168.72.0.0 255.255.255.0 is subnetted, 1 subnets
C       168.72.6.0 is directly connected, Serial0
     168.73.0.0 255.255.255.0 is subnetted, 1 subnets
C       168.73.9.0 is directly connected, Serial1
     168.74.0.0 255.255.255.0 is subnetted, 1 subnets
C       168.74.5.0 is directly connected, Ethernet0
I    168.71.0.0 [100/80188] via 168.72.6.2, 00:00:42, Serial0
              [100/80188] via 168.73.9.2, 00:00:04, Serial1
RouterA#
```

RouterB's new routing table shows the local connection to 168.71.0.0 and no summarized routes to 168.71.0.0:

```
RouterB#show ip route
Codes: C - connected, S - static, I - IGRP, R - RIP, M - mobile, B - BGP
       D - EIGRP, EX - EIGRP external, O - OSPF, IA - OSPF inter area
       E1 - OSPF external type 1, E2 - OSPF external type 2, E - EGP
       i - IS-IS, L1 - IS-IS level-1, L2 - IS-IS level-2, * - candidate default

Gateway of last resort is 168.72.6.1 to network 10.0.0.0

I*   10.0.0.0 [100/160250] via 168.72.6.1, 00:00:56, Serial0
     168.72.0.0 255.255.255.0 is subnetted, 1 subnets
C       168.72.6.0 is directly connected, Serial0
I    168.73.0.0 [100/82125] via 168.72.6.1, 00:00:56, Serial0
I    168.74.0.0 [100/10002001] via 168.72.6.1, 00:00:56, Serial0
168.71.0.0 255.255.255.0 is subnetted, 1 subnets
C       168.71.0.0 is directly connected, TokenRing0
RouterB#
```

In this output of *show ip route 168.71.0.0* from RouterB, you can see RouterB's connected route to 168.71.0.0. There is no summarized route to 168.71.0.0:

```
RouterB#show ip route 168.71.0.0
Routing entry for 168.71.0.0 255.255.255.0, 1 known subnets
  Attached (1 connections)
  Redistributing via igrp 109
  Advertised by igrp 109

C       168.71.0.0 is directly connected, TokenRing0
RouterB#
```

RouterC's new routing table shows the local connection to 168.71.8.0 and no summarized routes to 168.71.0.0:

```
RouterC#show ip route
Codes: C - connected, S - static, I - IGRP, R - RIP, M - mobile, B - BGP
       D - EIGRP, EX - EIGRP external, O - OSPF, IA - OSPF inter area
       E1 - OSPF external type 1, E2 - OSPF external type 2, E - EGP
       i - IS-IS, L1 - IS-IS level-1, L2 - IS-IS level-2, * - candidate default

Gateway of last resort is 168.73.9.1 to network 10.0.0.0

I*   10.0.0.0 [100/160250] via 168.73.9.1, 00:00:35, Serial1
I    168.72.0.0 [100/82125] via 168.73.9.1, 00:00:35, Serial1
     168.73.0.0 255.255.255.0 is subnetted, 1 subnets
C       168.73.9.0 is directly connected, Serial1
I    168.74.0.0 [100/10002001] via 168.73.9.1, 00:00:35, Serial1
168.71.0.0 255.255.255.0 is subnetted, 1 subnets
C       168.71.8.0 is directly connected, TokenRing0
RouterC#
```

In this output of *show ip route 168.71.0.0* from RouterC, you
can see RouterC is connected to 168.71.8.0. There is no summarized route to 168.71.0.0:

```
RouterC#show ip route 168.71.0.0
Routing entry for 168.71.0.0 255.255.255.0, 1 known subnets
  Attached (1 connections)
  Redistributing via rip, igrp 109
  Advertised by igrp 109

C       168.71.8.0 is directly connected, TokenRing0
RouterC#
```

In this configuration, you can see that RouterA is only 60 percent successful pinging 168.71.0.1:

```
RouterA#ping 168.71.0.1
Type escape sequence to abort.
Sending 5, 100-byte ICMP Echos to 168.71.0.1, timeout is 2 seconds:
!U!.!
Success rate is 60 percent (3/5), round-trip min/avg/max = 4/4/4 ms
RouterA#
```

In this output from the *debug ip packet* and *debug ip icmp*
commands from RouterA, taken while pinging 168.71.0.1,
you can see that pings (1), (3), and (5) are successful:

```
RouterA#debug ip packet
RouterA#debug ip icmp
(1) IP: s=168.72.6.1 (local), d=168.71.0.1 (Serial0), len 100, sending
(1) IP: s=168.71.0.1 (Serial0), d=168.72.6.1 (Serial0), len 104, rcvd 3
(1) ICMP: echo reply rcvd, src 168.71.0.1, dst 168.72.6.1
(2) IP: s=168.72.6.1 (local), d=168.71.0.1 (Serial1), len 100, sending
(2) IP: s=168.73.9.2 (Serial1), d=168.72.6.1, len 60, rcvd 4
(2) ICMP: dst (168.72.6.1) host unreachable rcv from 168.73.9.2
(3) IP: s=168.72.6.1 (local), d=168.71.0.1 (Serial0), len 100, sending
(3) IP: s=168.71.0.1 (Serial0), d=168.72.6.1 (Serial0), len 104, rcvd 3
(3) ICMP: echo reply rcvd, src 168.71.0.1, dst 168.72.6.1
(4) IP: s=168.72.6.1 (local), d=168.71.0.1 (Serial1), len 100, sending
(5) IP: s=168.72.6.1 (local), d=168.71.0.1 (Serial0), len 100, sending
(5) IP: s=168.71.0.1 (Serial0), d=168.72.6.1 (Serial0), len 104, rcvd 3
(5) ICMP: echo reply rcvd, src 168.71.0.1, dst 168.72.6.1
RouterA#
```

Figure 3-15 shows the paths that the pings in this example took
through the network.

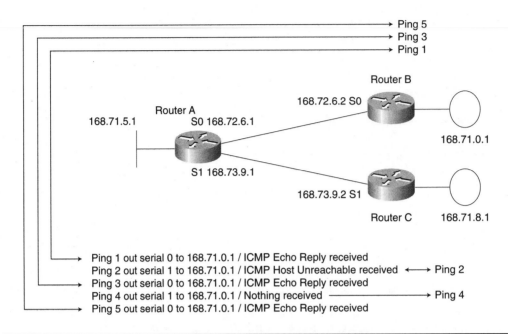

Figure 3–15
A graphical representation of the paths used by the pings in this example.

NOTES

debug ip icmp allows you to see exactly what ICMP messages are being received. Note that only one ICMP Host Unreachable is sent to RouterA. Having the routers limit ICMP Host Unreachable messages to hosts (in this case RouterA) that send more than one IP packet to an unreachable host over a short period of time keeps routers from being overwhelmed by the task of creating and sending the ICMP messages.

In the debug messages from RouterA, the ICMP host unreachable message from RouterC is in response to ping (2). RouterC does not send an IP ICMP unreachable message for ping (4) because routers protect themselves from having to respond to too many packets for unreachable hosts by ignoring some of them. Otherwise, malicious people could tie up a router's CPU by barraging the router with packets to unreachable hosts.

The following extract from the output of the *debug ip packet* and *debug ip icmp* commands from RouterC shows only the messages related to the packets RouterA sent to RouterC:

```
RouterC#debug ip packet
RouterC#debug ip icmp
(2) IP: s=168.72.6.1 (Serial1), d=168.71.0.1, len 104, unroutable
(2) ICMP: dst (168.71.0.1) host unreachable sent to 168.72.6.1
(2) IP: s=168.73.9.2 (local), d=168.72.6.1 (Serial1), len 32, sending
(4) IP: s=168.72.6.1 (Serial1), d=168.71.0.1, len 104, unroutable
RouterC#
```

Alternating Paths for the First Ping

If you stage a scenario like the previous one in a lab, you will notice that the number of successful pings will be inconsistent from one test to another. This is because when a router believes that it has two or more viable paths to a destination, it will alternate between them when sending the first ping. The remainder of this section explains this phenomenon in more detail. This behavior is not related to the routing protocol in use.

The following output from RouterA shows that RouterA will alternate which route to 168.71.0.0 it uses first so that the failures will vary from time to time.

Using serial 1 first results in the following output:

```
RouterA#ping 168.71.0.1
Type escape sequence to abort.
Sending 5, 100-byte ICMP Echos to 168.71.0.1, timeout is 2 seconds:
U!.!U
Success rate is 40 percent (2/5), round-trip min/avg/max = 4/4/4 ms
```

Using serial 0 first results in the following output:

```
RouterA#ping 168.71.0.1
Type escape sequence to abort.
Sending 5, 100-byte ICMP Echos to 168.71.0.1, timeout is 2 seconds:
!U!.!
Success rate is 60 percent (3/5), round-trip min/avg/max = 4/4/4 ms
RouterA#
```

This is normal load-balancing behavior. The percentage of successful pings varies, depending on which interface is selected first.

Using Other Routing Protocols

It is possible to create very similar problems to those just presented using IP routing protocols that allow for discontiguous networks, such as EIGRP, RIP V2, and OSPF. You can create a situation in which one remote location is advertising a summarized major net and another site is advertising subnet 0 for the same major net. The results will be very similar to the results documented here.

For example, suppose you are using EIGRP. If RouterA has a route via RouterB to 168.71.0.0 with a mask of 255.255.0.0, and another route for 168.71.0.0 with a mask of 255.255.255.0 via RouterC, you may find that packets you intend to reach RouterB (168.71.0.1) end up at RouterC. This may take place because it is a longer match (the mask is longer, so there are more bits to compare to the destination IP address).

This section introduced a new debug command, *debug ip icmp*, as well as some interesting packet-forwarding behavior. Pings were successful in some cases—but not always by using the most obvious path. Remember that the section on IGRP is only applicable in real life if you are running a version of Cisco IOS that doesn't have the fix—CSCdj03421.

The next section discusses how summarization can be used as a network design tool when creating complex IP networks.

USING AGGREGATION AS A TOOL

Summarization has already been introduced as a function that routers running RIP and IGRP perform when sending routing advertisements over interfaces whose IP addresses are in different major nets than the routes being advertised.

In the following scenario, aggregation will be manually configured to avoid sending unnecessary routing advertisements to certain routers. This can be done by using access lists to block the advertisement of certain subnets (see Figure 3–16).

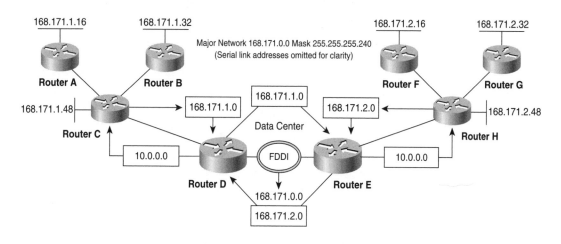

Figure 3–16

Summarization reduces the content of routing advertisements.

Figure 3–16 also introduces a classic hierarchical design for building networks and implementing IP addresses. RouterA, RouterB, RouterF, and RouterG are remote sites. RouterC and RouterH are distribution sites. RouterD and RouterE are core routers. Any traffic from RouterA or RouterB that is destined for RouterF or RouterG must go through the distribution and core routers, and vice versa.

The goal for this scenario is to have full connectivity while advertising only a few subnets. Each router should have only as much routing information as absolutely necessary.

The FDDI ring has 10.0.0.0 assigned to it. RouterD and RouterE each advertise this major net to their distribution routers, which accept it as a major net advertisement. The distribution routers advertise this major net to their respective remote routers, which also accept it as a major net advertisement.

All distribution and remote routers are configured to use their routes to 10.0.0.0 to forward packets for networks they have no knowledge of. The method for doing this is explained in more detail in Chapter 5, "Default Routing."

The distribution routers must know about the subnets their remote routers have configured. RouterC must know that RouterA has 168.71.1.16 and that RouterB has 168.71.1.32. This can be done by manually configuring these routes into RouterC or by allowing RouterA and RouterB to advertise their networks to RouterC. RouterC already knows it is connected to 168.71.1.48.

In any case, RouterC only needs to advertise subnet 168.71.1.0 to RouterD because all subnets that start with the prefix 168.71.1.0 are in some way reachable via RouterC. The same holds for RouterH—it only has to advertise the prefix 168.71.2.0 to RouterE because all subnets with this prefix are reachable via RouterH. Only RouterD and RouterE need to know how to reach prefixes 168.71.1.0 and 168.71.2.0.

You can see that, in this design, all packets for subnets that the distribution and remote routers have no knowledge of will eventually arrive at the core routers. The core routers will drop any packets destined to subnets that they have no knowledge of.

It is imperative that the core routers are not configured to send any packets for subnets they have no knowledge of to each other—this would result in a loop.

This scenario shows how careful use of subnetting at distribution and remote sites can greatly reduce the amount of routing information necessary to maintain full connectivity throughout a network.

SUMMARY

This chapter has covered the problems that can occur when using subnet 0, discontiguous networks, and summarized routes with RIP and IGRP. The use of discontiguous networks to cause summarization was discussed. Summarized routes were compared to subnet 0 in order to explain how they can be confused with one another. Recall that IGRP worked in some scenarios because of the anomalous behavior that allowed it to accept a major net advertisement even though it had a local connection to the same major net. In fact, RIP and IGRP should behave exactly the same when faced with major net advertisements for networks they have direct connections to—they should ignore the major net advertisement.

EIGRP, OSPF, and RIP V2 were not covered because they have built-in methods for coping with these issues. However, even EIGRP, OSPF, and RIP V2 can fail when using subnet 0 and summarization if configured incorrectly. The information provided in this chapter also explained why RIP and IGRP fail when using discontiguous networks.

Using aggregation as a tool in designing networks was also discussed. It can greatly simplify routing tables and the debugging of IP connectivity problems. Chapter 4 continues this discussion with explanations of IP unnumbered and VLSM.

Using IP Unnumbered and VLSM

This chapter is broken into two sections. The first section discusses IP unnumbered. It provides scenarios showing how it works when properly configured and how it breaks when improperly configured.

The second section discusses variable length subnet masking (VLSM). It provides scenarios showing how it works when properly configured and how it breaks when improperly configured.

Before proceeding any further in this chapter, it is important to lay the groundwork for the discussion by defining the following terms:

- *IP unnumbered* refers to using the network or subnet address of a local LAN interface as the router's network or subnetwork address for a point-to-point serial link. The term *point-to-point* means that only two devices are on the link, as is the case on a T1 connection between two routers or a point-to-point sub-interface to a Frame Relay network. Normally, a serial link has its own unique network or subnetwork address. IP unnumbered allows a network administrator to conserve network or subnetwork addresses. IP unnumbered is especially valuable for networks running IP routing protocols such as RIP V1 and IGRP, which do not support VLSM. Without VLSM support, a network must use the same subnet mask on its serial (WAN) interfaces as it does on its LAN interfaces.

For a company using an 24-bit (255.255.255.0) mask on a Class B address, this means applying a subnet capable of supporting 253 hosts on a WAN link that never has more than two hosts. See Chapter 8, "Hexadecimal and Binary Numbering and IP Addressing," for more information on IP subnetting.

- *VLSM* means applying different subnet masks to the same major net. With VLSM, a Class B address can be subnetted with a 253–host, 24-bit mask (255.255.255.0) for the LAN subnets and a two–host, 30-bit mask (255.255.255.252) for the WAN subnets.

- *Host routes* are routes whose associated subnet mask is set to all 1s (255.255.255.255). Remember that the subnet mask is used to separate the bits that are part of the network address from the bits that are part of the host address. In this case, the mask covers all of the bits, leaving no bits for the host portion. Because a subnet that is all network with no hosts would be of little use, it was decided that this subnet mask would be used as a host route pointing to a particular host. The section covering host routes in dial-on-demand routing (DDR) network configurations helps clarify this point.

- *DDR* is providing temporary connections between networks or between users who are not based at the same site. DDR is often used when a permanent connection is not cost-efficient because data is only exchanged sporadically. Automated teller machines (ATMs) use DDR to contact their central host when verifying a transaction. This is typically done using a dial-up connection, such as a telephone line or an Integrated Services Digital Network (ISDN) connection.

UNDERSTANDING IP UNNUMBERED

One of the reasons IP unnumbered is possible is that with only two hosts on any serial link—when the routers are at either end—there is no confusion about which device a packet is originating from or destined for. The following are a few rules that apply to using IP unnumbered:

- The serial interface must be a point-to-point link.

- You must use the same major network with the same mask on both sides of the WAN link.

  or

- You must use different major nets with no subnetting on both sides of the WAN link.

These rules are discussed in more detail in the following sections.

IP Unnumbered Causes Host Routes and Lost Connectivity

This section provides some background on IP unnumbered and some real-life scenarios of IP unnumbered in action. Figure 4–1 represents the network topology used for most of this section.

In Table 4.1, the routing update from RouterC has a bit (1) set in the fourth octet (.1 = 00000001). RouterA compares this update with the mask of the IP address and the mask used by the unnumbered *ethernet0* command. RouterA will discover that a bit is set outside the range of the mask, which must be interpreted as a host route.

Figure 4–1

Simplified network using IP unnumbered.

Table 4–1 *Binary example of an advertisement/mask mismatch.*

Advertised mask	168.71.8.1	= 10101000.01000111.00001000.00000001
Router's mask	255.255.255.0	= 11111111.11111111.11111111.00000000

See the section on mask ambiguity in Chapter 3, "Discontiguous Networks, Summarization, and Subnet 0," for more information on this issue.

Host Routes

As previously explained, a *host route* refers to a route whose associated mask has all 32 bits set to 1—255.255.255.255. For an address and mask such as this, there can be only one host.

One common cause of host routes is a route advertisement that has bits set in the range that the receiving router interprets as outside of the subnet mask. In this case, the router compared the advertisement received from an adjacent router with the mask of the interface it was received over and found a mismatch. This is how RIP V1 and IGRP determine the mask to apply to advertisements they receive.

Table 4.1 shows an example of an advertisement that has a bit set to 1 in a region of the address not covered by the subnet mask in use.

Another common cause of host routes is a routing update explicitly advertised with a mask of 255.255.255.255. Routing protocols such as OSPF and EIGRP include the masks associated with the routes in their routing updates.

Host routes are also often manually configured to resolve routing problems related to configuring dial-on-demand routing (DDR). The following section on DDR goes into more detail on this subject.

Hosts Routes Using DDR

Dial-up users may require host routes to ensure that they have full connectivity to the network. Although dial-up networking is beyond the scope of this book, this section attempts to clarify when host routes can be useful. In the scenario in Figure 4–2, hosts A and B use modems to dial into the corporate network.

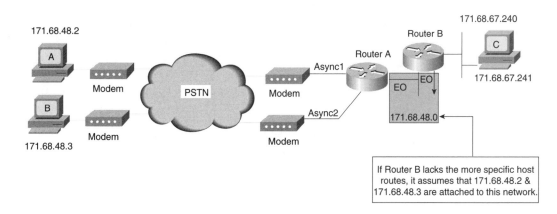

Figure 4–2
Async dial-up network using IP unnumbered without host routes.

In Figure 4–2, RouterA is using *IP unnumbered ethernet 0* on its Async interfaces. This results in multiple Async interfaces sharing the same subnet as a local Ethernet. However, the router needs to be able to keep track of the interfaces as separate subnets in order to route traffic correctly.

Remember that one of the rules of IP unnumbered is that it must be used only for point-to-point network connections. Extending the mask already applied to RouterA's Ethernet 0 interface when the addresses are configured on the asynchronous interfaces provides this point-to-point connection. Interface Async1 has an address of 168.71.48.2 255.255.255.255, and interface Async2 has an address of 168.71.48.3 255.255.255.255.

When all of the hosts are connected to RouterA (they have dialed in to the network), they will have their own unique routes (their host routes) in RouterA's routing table. If RouterA receives a packet for 168.71.48.4 from HostA, it does a longest match lookup of its routing table and determines that the best match is the subnet applied to its Ethernet 0 interface: 168.71.48.0. It forwards the packet out of that interface.

On the other hand, if RouterA receives a packet for 168.71.48.2 from HostB, the longest match lookup results in a match for the host route applied to Asynch1: 168.71.48.2. The packet is forwarded out that interface to HostA (assuming either that the link to HostA is already up or that RouterA is configured to place a call to HostA when it receives a packet for it).

Without host routes being advertised by RouterA to RouterB for end systems A and B, RouterB assumes that an IP packet to 171.68.48.2 or 171.68.48.3 is for an end system on the Ethernet network connecting RouterA and RouterB. The gray box surrounding the (E0) interfaces for routers A and B in Figure 4–2 shows where RouterB assumes that addresses 171.68.48.2

and 171.68.48.3 reside. RouterB ARPs (attempts to determine the layer two MAC address) for 171.68.48.2 or 171.68.48.3 directly instead of forwarding the packet to RouterA to reach end system A.

NOTES

If you do not understand the role of the Address Resolution Protocol (ARP), refer to Chapter 7, "Bridging IP Between Dissimilar Media," or RFC 826.

In Figure 4–3, RouterA is advertising the host routes for end systems A and B. RouterB will do a longest match lookup for packets to either 171.68.48.2 or 171.68.48.3 and discover that the connected route to 171.68.48.0 is not the longest match. RouterB will determine that these routes are reachable via its Ethernet 0 address, using RouterA as the next hop.

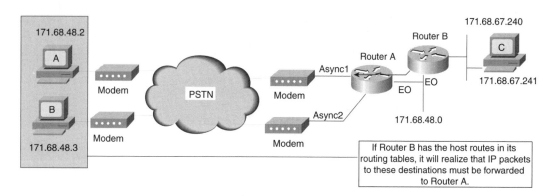

Figure 4–3
Async dial-up network using IP unnumbered with host routes.

The gray box surrounding HostA and HostB in Figure 4–3 shows where RouterB will assume that addresses 171.68.48.2

and 171.68.48.3 reside now that the correct host routes are being advertised by RouterA.

This section has given you an intentionally simplistic example of DDR. DDR is an incredibly complex subject that can take up an entire book all by itself. Consult the documentation for the version of Cisco IOS you are using for more information on DDR internetworking. The next section explains how to configure IP unnumbered in non-DDR situations.

CONFIGURING IP UNNUMBERED ON SERIAL INTERFACES

Configuring IP unnumbered for RIP and IGRP is done in the same way as explained previously. The excerpts from the configurations of RouterA and RouterC that follow show how to configure IP unnumbered on a serial interface.

```
!
hostname RouterA
!
interface serial1
ip unnumbered Ethernet0
!

!
hostname RouterC
!
interface serial1
ip unnumbered TokenRing0
!
```

The following *show interface* commands from RouterA and RouterC show that IP unnumbered is now in use on both serial interfaces.

```
RouterA#show interface serial 1
Serial1 is up, line protocol is up
  Hardware is HD64570
  Interface is unnumbered.  Using address of Ethernet0 (168.71.5.1)
  MTU 1500 bytes, BW 128 Kbit, DLY 20000 usec, rely 255/255, load 1/255

RouterC#show interface serial 1
Serial1 is up, line protocol is up
```

```
Hardware is HD64570
Interface is unnumbered.  Using address of TokenRing0 (168.71.8.1)
MTU 1500 bytes, BW 128 Kbit, DLY 20000 usec, rely 255/255, load 1/255
```

RIP and IGRP Behave the Same

The rules governing the successful configuration of IP unnumbered that were given at the start of this chapter apply to RIP V1 and IGRP equally. When properly configured, both protocols behave in the same manner. All of the material presented in the following scenario, which shows the proper configuration of IP unnumbered using RIP, applies to IGRP as well.

Improper configuration of IP unnumbered causes both RIP V1 and IGRP to lose IP connectivity for the misconfigured subnets. The failure modes for RIP and IGRP are slightly different because IGRP doesn't support host routes as well as RIP. However, this difference is not sufficient to warrant providing separate scenarios that show both routing protocols failing when IP unnumbered is misconfigured. By applying the concepts presented in this scenario, you should be able to understand what is going wrong when you are faced with a network in which IGRP has been configured with an improper use of IP unnumbered.

This section is broken into the following three scenarios:

- *RIP with IP unnumbered configured properly.*

  This section shows IP unnumbered working as intended and provides insights into proving that it is working as intended.

- *RIP with IP unnumbered configured improperly—a different subnet mask was used.*

  This section shows IP unnumbered not working as intended because an improper subnet mask has been applied. It also provides some insights into proving that it is not working as intended.

- *RIP with IP unnumbered configured improperly—a different subnet mask and a different major net were used.*

This section combines the use of different major networks with a misconfiguration caused by using a subnet mask on one of the networks. It shows how IP unnumbered works with different major nets as well as how the use of a subnet masked major net can cause problems in some configurations.

RIP with IP Unnumbered Configured Properly

In this scenario, RIP has been properly configured with IP unnumbered. The examples show how to verify the proper configuration of IP unnumbered.

Displaying the Routes

In the following output of the *show ip route* command from RouterA, you can see that RouterA has a route to 168.71.8.0:

```
RouterA#show ip route 168.71.8.1
Routing entry for 168.71.8.0 255.255.255.0
  Known via "rip", distance 120, metric 1
  Redistributing via rip
  Last update from 168.71.8.1 on Serial1, 00:00:13 ago
  Routing Descriptor Blocks:
  * 168.71.8.1, from 168.71.8.1, 00:00:13 ago, via Serial1
      Route metric is 1, traffic share count is 1
RouterA#
```

In the following output of the *show ip route* command from RouterC, you can see that RouterC has a route to 168.71.5.0:

```
RouterC#show ip route 168.71.5.1
Routing entry for 168.71.5.0 255.255.255.0
  Known via "rip", distance 120, metric 1
```

```
Redistributing via rip
Advertised by rip (self originated)
Last update from 168.71.5.1 on Serial1, 00:00:13 ago
Routing Descriptor Blocks:
* 168.71.5.1, from 168.71.5.1, 00:00:13 ago, via Serial1
    Route metric is 1, traffic share count is 1
RouterC#
```

Notice that in both of the previous routing tables, the last update from address is the same as the actual address used in the *show ip route* command. Note that the routing entry indicates that this is a subnetted Class B address and not a host route because the mask is *255.255.255.0*. This is the expected behavior when IP unnumbered is configured correctly. If IP unnumbered had been configured incorrectly, the routing entry would have a host route mask of *255.255.255.255*.

Sending Routing Updates

The following output of *debug ip rip* from RouterA shows RouterA advertising the summarized major network of 168.71.0.0:

```
RouterA#debug ip rip
RIP: sending update to 255.255.255.255 via Serial1 (168.71.5.1)
    subnet 168.71.5.0, metric 1
    default 0.0.0.0, metric 1
    network 168.71.0.0, metric 1
RIP: received update from 168.71.8.1 on Serial1
    168.71.8.0 in 1 hops
    168.71.0.0 in 1 hops
```

The following output of *debug ip rip* from RouterC shows RouterC advertising the summarized major network of 168.71.0.0:

```
RouterC#deb ip rip
RIP: sending update to 255.255.255.255 via Serial1 (168.71.8.1)
    subnet 168.71.8.0, metric 1
    network 168.71.0.0, metric 1
RIP: received update from 168.71.5.1 on Serial1
    168.71.5.0 in 1 hops
    0.0.0.0 in 1 hops
    168.71.0.0 in 1 hops
```

Although both routers are advertising the summarized major net of 168.71.0.0 to each other, neither router will install the route while using RIP because they have local connections to the 168.71.0.0 major net. This was explained in Chapter 3 in the section on summarization.

Pinging the Interfaces

In the following output, which is from RouterA pinging 168.71.8.1, you can see that the pings are successful:

```
RouterA#ping 168.71.8.1
Type escape sequence to abort.
Sending 5, 100-byte ICMP Echos to 168.71.8.1, timeout is 2 seconds:
!!!!!
Success rate is 100 percent (5/5), round-trip min/avg/max = 16/17/20 ms
RouterA#
```

In the following output, which is from RouterC pinging 168.71.5.1, you can see that the pings are successful:

```
RouterC#ping 168.71.5.1
Type escape sequence to abort.
Sending 5, 100-byte ICMP Echos to 168.71.5.1, timeout is 2 seconds:
!!!!!
Success rate is 100 percent (5/5), round-trip min/avg/max = 16/16/16 ms
RouterC#
```

The fact that the pings are successful is the final proof that IP unnumbered has been configured correctly. Strictly speaking, this step is unnecessary as long as the results from the *show ip route* command indicate that proper routes have been installed. However, it is always better to double-check proper configuration by pinging the addresses.

The next section is a scenario about what happens when IP unnumbered has been misconfigured.

RIP with IP Unnumbered Configured Improperly

This scenario shows what happens when the rule is violated that requires the same mask to be used on all occurrences of the same major network's subnets. In Figure 4–4, RouterC's Token Ring interface now has a mask of 255.255.255.240. This is an example of variable length subnet masking (VLSM). In this case, major network 168.71.0.0 now has two masks: 255.255.255.0 and 255.255.255.240. VLSM is discussed in more detail in the next section.

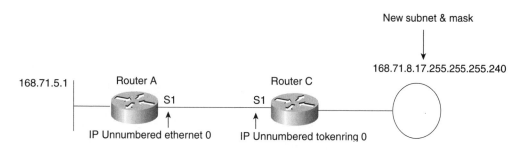

Figure 4–4
An incorrect mask has been applied to RouterC's Token Ring interface.

In the following output of the *show interface* commands from RouterC, you can see the new mask in use. Note that no reference to the mask used on Token Ring 0 is in the output from serial 1. You must always check the interface that the address is being derived from to determine which subnet mask is in use.

```
RouterC#show interface tokenring 0
TokenRing0 is up, line protocol is up
  Hardware is TMS380, address is 0000.30c8.ab75 (bia 0000.30c8.ab75)
  Internet address is 168.71.8.17 255.255.255.240

RouterC#show interface serial 1
Serial1 is up, line protocol is up
  Hardware is HD64570
  Interface is unnumbered.  Using address of TokenRing0 (168.71.8.17)
  MTU 1500 bytes, BW 128 Kbit, DLY 20000 usec, rely 255/255, load 1/255
```

> ### HINT
>
> When you are troubleshooting IP unnumbered problems always check the *show interface* command from the interface that is providing the address.

Examples of Routing Updates

The output of the *debug ip routing* and *ip rip* commands from RouterA shows what happens when RouterA adds the subnet route to 168.71.8.16. Note the statement indicating that network 168.71.0.0 is now variably masked. This is in response to RouterA comparing the routing update to its IP address and mask on *ethernet 0*. Note also that RouterA believes that the next hop address for 168.71.8.16 255.255.255.255 is 168.71.8.17.

```
RouterA#debug ip routing
RouterA#debug ip rip
RouterA# clear ip route 168.71.8.16
RT: del 168.71.8.16 255.255.255.255 via 168.71.8.17, rip metric [120/1]
RT: delete subnet route to 168.71.8.16 255.255.255.255
RIP: received update from 168.71.8.17 on Serial1
     168.71.8.16 in 1 hops
     168.71.0.0 in 1 hops
RT: network 168.71.0.0 is now variably masked
RT: add 168.71.8.16 255.255.255.255 via 168.71.8.17, rip metric [120/1]
RouterA#
```

RouterA has now installed a host route to 168.71.8.16 in its routing table because the advertisement received from RouterC had bits set in what RouterA believes is the host portion of the address.

RouterA's mask for the 168.71.0.0 network is 255.255.255.0. The advertisement was for 168.71.8.16. The 16 in the fourth octet should not be there for a routing advertisement of a subnet with a 255.255.255.0 mask. Routers use the mask of the interface that received the update to determine the appropriate mask to apply.

```
RouterA#show ip route
Codes: C - connected, S - static, I - IGRP, R - RIP, M - mobile, B - BGP
       D - EIGRP, EX - EIGRP external, O - OSPF, IA - OSPF inter area
       E1 - OSPF external type 1, E2 - OSPF external type 2, E - EGP
       i - IS-IS, L1 - IS-IS level-1, L2 - IS-IS level-2, * - candidate default

Gateway of last resort is 171.68.207.129 to network 10.0.0.0

S*   10.0.0.0 [1/0] via 171.68.207.129
168.71.0.0 is variably subnetted, 2 subnets, 2 masks
C       168.71.5.0 255.255.255.0 is directly connected, Ethernet0
R       168.71.8.16 255.255.255.255 [120/1] via 168.71.8.17, 00:00:13, Serial1
S*   0.0.0.0 0.0.0.0 [1/0] via 171.68.207.129
RouterA#
```

Host Route Problem

The following output of the *show ip route* command and the routing table from RouterA shows that RouterA does not have a route it can use for a packet to 168.71.8.17. Even though it has a route to 168.71.8.16, the subnet that the host address of 168.71.8.17 should be on, RouterA does not have such a route because the route to 168.71.8.16 is a host route.

```
RouterA#show ip route 168.71.8.17
% Subnet not in table
RouterA#

RouterA#show ip route 168.71.0.0
Routing entry for 168.71.0.0 255.255.0.0, 2 known subnets
  Attached (1 connections)
  Variably subnetted with 2 masks
  Redistributing via rip
  Advertised by rip

C       168.71.5.0 255.255.255.0 is directly connected, Ethernet0
R       168.71.8.16 255.255.255.255 [120/1] via 168.71.8.17, 00:00:01, Serial1
RouterA#
```

When RouterA does a longest match lookup for the destination IP address 168.71.8.17 in its routing table, the mask associated with the route determines the number of bits that must match. In the case of its route to 168.71.8.16, all 32 bits would have to match exactly because the mask is 255.255.255.255.

168.71.8.16 and 168.71.8.17 are different at the 32nd bit and are therefore not a match.

The routing table also shows that RouterA does not have a summarized route to 168.71.0.0, even though RouterC is advertising it.

Lost Routes Problem

In the following routing table from RouterC, you can see that RouterC has a route to 168.71.5.0, which it uses to route packets destined for 168.71.5.1:

```
RouterC#show ip route
Codes: C - connected, S - static, I - IGRP, R - RIP, M - mobile, B - BGP
       D - EIGRP, EX - EIGRP external, O - OSPF, IA - OSPF inter area
       E1 - OSPF external type 1, E2 - OSPF external type 2, E - EGP
       i - IS-IS, L1 - IS-IS level-1, L2 - IS-IS level-2, * - candidate default

Gateway of last resort is 168.71.5.1 to network 0.0.0.0

R    10.0.0.0 [120/1] via 168.71.5.1, 00:00:14, Serial1
168.71.0.0 255.255.255.240 is subnetted, 2 subnets
R       168.71.5.0 [120/1] via 168.71.5.1, 00:00:15, Serial1
C       168.71.8.16 is directly connected, TokenRing0
R*   0.0.0.0 0.0.0.0 [120/1] via 168.71.5.1, 00:00:15, Serial1
RouterC#
```

In the following output of the *debug ip packet* command from RouterC, you can see that RouterC sends the pings destined for 168.71.5.1 out serial 1. Note that the source address of the pings is 168.71.8.17. This is the host address that RouterA cannot reach because the route it should use to the subnet of 168.71.8.16 has the wrong mask.

```
RouterC#deb ip packet
RouterC#ping 168.71.5.1
Type escape sequence to abort.
Sending 5, 100-byte ICMP Echos to 168.71.5.1, timeout is 2 seconds:

IP: s=168.71.8.17 (local), d=168.71.5.1 (Serial1), len 100, sending.
IP: s=168.71.8.17 (local), d=168.71.5.1 (Serial1), len 100, sending.
IP: s=168.71.8.17 (local), d=168.71.5.1 (Serial1), len 100, sending.
IP: s=168.71.8.17 (local), d=168.71.5.1 (Serial1), len 100, sending
IP: s=168.71.8.17 (local), d=168.71.5.1 (Serial1), len 100, sending.
```

```
Success rate is 0 percent (0/5)
RouterC#
```

The following output from the *debug ip packet* command on RouterA shows that RouterA receives the pings from RouterC but cannot route the responses. Configuring IP unnumbered incorrectly by applying a different mask on RouterC's Token Ring interface has made connectivity between the two routers impossible.

```
RouterA#debug ip packet
IP: s=168.71.8.17 (Serial1), d=168.71.5.1, len 104, rcvd 4
IP: s=168.71.5.1 (local), d=168.71.8.17, len 104, unroutable
IP: s=168.71.8.17 (Serial1), d=168.71.5.1, len 104, rcvd 4
IP: s=168.71.5.1 (local), d=168.71.8.17, len 104, unroutable
IP: s=168.71.8.17 (Serial1), d=168.71.5.1, len 104, rcvd 4
IP: s=168.71.5.1 (local), d=168.71.8.17, len 104, unroutable
IP: s=168.71.8.17 (Serial1), d=168.71.5.1, len 104, rcvd 4
IP: s=168.71.5.1 (local), d=168.71.8.17, len 104, unroutable
IP: s=168.71.8.17 (Serial1), d=168.71.5.1, len 104, rcvd 4
IP: s=168.71.5.1 (local), d=168.71.8.17, len 104, unroutable
IP: s=168.71.8.17 (Serial1), d=255.255.255.255, len 76, rcvd 2
RouterA#
```

This section has explained why IP unnumbered requires that the same mask be used on all subnets of the same major net. When a different mask is used, routers cannot properly derive the masks for routes they receive. Instead, they resort to installing host routes for these advertisements. As this section has proven, host routes do not allow for full IP connectivity. The next section explains how IP unnumbered works with different major networks.

Using a Different Subnet Mask and a Different Major Net

Using a different major network with no subnet masking on both routers gives similar results to a proper configuration that uses the same major network and the same subnet mask. In the case of different major networks, the routers simply advertise their summarized routes to each other. Each router installs the other's summarized route, and full connectivity is possible.

To avoid repetition, this section begins with a misconfiguration of IP unnumbered. Recall that a misconfiguration of a subnet mask using the same major net on both routers causes connectivity to be broken. In this scenario, connectivity is still possible but the misconfiguration results in some other problems.

A different major network—168.72.0.0—has been configured on RouterC's Token Ring interface; see Figure 4–5. In addition, a subnet mask has been added—255.255.255.0. RouterA still has its original IP unnumbered address of 168.71.5.1 255.255.255.0. Using a subnet mask on both major nets is a violation of the IP unnumbered rule that states as follows: When using different major nets, no subnetting is allowed.

The remainder of this scenario shows how connectivity is still possible even though IP unnumbered has been misconfigured. It also further explains the problems caused by violating the no subnet mask rule.

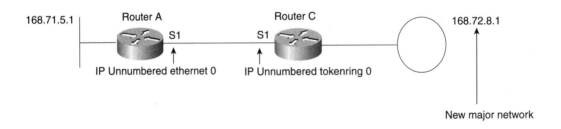

Figure 4–5
RouterC has a new major net on Token Ring 0.

In the following *show interface* command from RouterC, you can see that the new major network has been configured with a subnet mask.

```
RouterC#show interface tokenring 0
TokenRing0 is up, line protocol is up
  Hardware is TMS380, address is 0000.30c8.ab75 (bia 0000.30c8.ab75)
  Internet address is 168.72.8.1 255.255.255.0
  MTU 4464 bytes, BW 16000 Kbit, DLY 630 usec, rely 255/255, load 1/255

RouterC#show interface serial 1
Serial1 is up, line protocol is up
  Hardware is HD64570
  Interface is unnumbered.  Using address of TokenRing0 (168.72.8.1)
```

In the following output of the *show interface* command from
RouterA, you can see that RouterA has the same IP unnumbered configuration as before:

```
RouterA#show interface serial 1
Serial1 is up, line protocol is up
  Hardware is HD64570
  Interface is unnumbered.  Using address of Ethernet0 (168.71.5.1)
  MTU 1500 bytes, BW 128 Kbit, DLY 20000 usec, rely 255/255, load 1/255
```

In the following output of the *debug ip packet* commands from
routers A and C, you can see the two routers sending and
receiving routing updates. Note that a subnet route and a summarized route are sent in both cases.

```
RouterA#debug ip rip
RIP: received update from 168.72.8.1 on Serial1
     168.72.8.0 in 1 hops
     168.72.0.0 in 1 hops
RIP: sending update to 255.255.255.255 via Serial1 (168.71.5.1)
     subnet 168.71.5.0, metric 1
     network 168.71.0.0, metric 1

RouterC#debug ip rip
RIP: received update from 168.71.5.1 on Serial1
     168.71.5.0 in 1 hops
     168.71.0.0 in 1 hops
RIP: sending update to 255.255.255.255 via Serial1 (168.72.8.1)
     subnet 168.72.8.0, metric 1
     network 168.72.0.0, metric 1
```

In the following routing table from RouterA, note the mask on
the subnet route to 168.72.8.0, which is 255.255.255.255.
This is a host route. If RouterA received a packet destined for
168.71.8.2 on its Ethernet interface, the longest match comparison with the route to 168.71.8.0 would fail. This would

occur because the mask associated with the route (255.255.255.255) indicates that in order to match this route, the last octet of the destination IP address should be a 0.

Connectivity is still possible because RouterA has installed a summarized route to 168.72.0.0. RouterA installs this route because it does not have a local connection to 168.72.0.0.

```
RouterA#show ip route
Codes: C - connected, S - static, I - IGRP, R - RIP, M - mobile, B - BGP
       D - EIGRP, EX - EIGRP external, O - OSPF, IA - OSPF inter area
       E1 - OSPF external type 1, E2 - OSPF external type 2, E - EGP
       i - IS-IS, L1 - IS-IS level-1, L2 - IS-IS level-2, * - candidate default

Gateway of last resort is not set

     168.72.0.0 is variably subnetted, 2 subnets, 2 masks
R       168.72.0.0 255.255.0.0 [120/1] via 168.72.8.1, 00:00:20, Serial1
R       168.72.8.0 255.255.255.255 [120/1] via 168.72.8.1, 00:00:21, Serial1
        168.71.0.0 255.255.255.0 is subnetted, 1 subnets
C       168.71.5.0 is directly connected, Ethernet0
RouterA#
```

NOTES

Recall from the section on summarized networks in Chapter 3 that a router should not install a summarized major network route for a major network from which it has a subnet.

In the following *show ip route* command from RouterA, you can see that RouterA will use the summarized major network to route packets destined for 168.72.8.1. RouterA uses this network because the mask on 168.72.8.0 is 255.255.255.255. Even though it looks like a better longest match, it isn't because it has a host mask of 32 bits.

```
RouterA#show ip route 168.72.8.1
Routing entry for 168.72.0.0 255.255.0.0
  Known via "rip", distance 120, metric 1
  Redistributing via rip
  Last update from 168.72.8.1 on Serial1, 00:00:00 ago
  Routing Descriptor Blocks:
  * 168.72.8.1, from 168.72.8.1, 00:00:00 ago, via Serial1
      Route metric is 1, traffic share count is 1

RouterA#
```

The following output from RouterA, which shows it pinging
168.72.8.1, proves that it has connectivity to RouterC because
the pings are successful:

```
RouterA#ping 168.72.8.1
Type escape sequence to abort.
Sending 5, 100-byte ICMP Echos to 168.72.8.1, timeout is 2 seconds:
!!!!!
Success rate is 100 percent (5/5), round-trip min/avg/max = 16/18/20 ms
RouterA#
```

In the following routing table from RouterC, note the mask on
the subnet route to 168.71.5.0. Connectivity is still possible
because RouterC has installed a summarized route to
168.71.0.0. RouterC does so because it does not have a local
connection to 168.71.0.0, as discussed previously.

```
RouterC#show ip route
Codes: C - connected, S - static, I - IGRP, R - RIP, M - mobile, B - BGP
       D - EIGRP, EX - EIGRP external, O - OSPF, IA - OSPF inter area
       E1 - OSPF external type 1, E2 - OSPF external type 2, E - EGP
       i - IS-IS, L1 - IS-IS level-1, L2 - IS-IS level-2, * - candidate default

Gateway of last resort is not set

     168.72.0.0 255.255.255.0 is subnetted, 1 subnets
C       168.72.8.0 is directly connected, TokenRing0
     168.71.0.0 is variably subnetted, 2 subnets, 2 masks
R       168.71.5.0 255.255.255.255 [120/1] via 168.71.5.1, 00:00:02, Serial1
R       168.71.0.0 255.255.0.0 [120/1] via 168.71.5.1, 00:00:02, Serial1
RouterC#
```

In the following *show ip route* command from RouterC, you can
see that RouterC will use the summarized major network to route
packets destined for 168.71.5.1. It will do so because the mask on
168.71.5.0 is 255.255.255.255. Even though it looks like a better
longest match, it isn't because it has a host mask of 32 bits.

```
RouterC#show ip route 168.71.5.1
Routing entry for 168.71.0.0 255.255.0.0
  Known via "rip", distance 120, metric 1
  Redistributing via rip
  Last update from 168.71.5.1 on Serial1, 00:00:16 ago
  Routing Descriptor Blocks:
  * 168.71.5.1, from 168.71.5.1, 00:00:16 ago, via Serial1
      Route metric is 1, traffic share count is 1

RouterC#
```

The following output from RouterC, which shows it pinging 168.71.5.1, proves that it has connectivity to RouterA because the pings are successful.

```
RouterC#ping 168.71.5.1
Type escape sequence to abort.
Sending 5, 100-byte ICMP Echos to 168.71.5.1, timeout is 2 seconds:
!!!!!
Success rate is 100 percent (5/5), round-trip min/avg/max = 16/16/16 ms
RouterC#
```

Note that the previous step of pinging RouterA from RouterC to prove connectivity in this direction was redundant because the pings from RouterA had the source address 168.71.5.1 and the destination address 168.72.8.1. RouterC was able to send ping replies to 168.71.5.1, so there was little doubt that RouterC would be able to originate pings to the same address. However, it never hurts to double-check when you aren't sure.

When to Use RIP or IGRP

When IP unnumbered always works—It will always work with RIP or IGRP when it is properly configured—using the same major networks and the same mask on both ends of the links or two different major networks with no subnet masks at both ends of the links.

When IP unnumbered sometimes works—It will sometimes work with RIP or IGRP when improperly configured in the following way: Different major networks and subnet masks are used at both ends of the links. However, this setup is not recommended.

When IP unnumbered fails—It will always fail with RIP or IGRP when it is improperly configured in the following way: The same major networks and different subnet masks are used on both ends of the links.

When IP unnumbered fails but can be fixed—The most effective way to work around the issues with IP unnumbered is to use static routes. Remember that a static route is one that is manually configured, not dynamically learned.

When IP unnumbered and Frame Relay or ATM are used—IP unnumbered will work on Frame Relay and ATM links for point-to-point subinterfaces. It will not work on multipoint interfaces or multipoint subinterfaces over Frame Relay or ATM.

UNDERSTANDING VLSM

This section provides scenarios on using VLSM and indicates the issues it can cause. Remember that *VLSM* refers to using different masks on the same major net. In Figure 4–6, the major net of 168.71.0.0 has two different masks— 255.255.255.0 and 255.255.255.252.

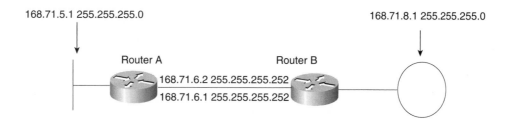

Figure 4–6
168.71.0.0 has two masks.

VLSM Using RIP and IGRP

In general, RIP V1 and IGRP do not support VLSM because they do not include the subnet masks associated with routes in their routing advertisements. This forces routers to derive the correct masks from the interfaces the routes are received over. Using different masks creates the mask ambiguity problem presented in Chapter 3.

NOTES

Recall that *mask ambiguity* is the inability to derive the correct mask for a routing update because it has bits set outside of the range covered by the mask on the interface the route is received over.

It is possible to configure VLSM addresses on routers running RIP or IGRP in some instances. Keep in mind this rule: If the mask for a route in the routing table is different than the mask on the interface the route would be advertised over and they are both part of the same major network, the route will not be advertised. Because of this rule, the routers in this case do not have full IP connectivity.

To make this section more interesting, a configuration that would not normally occur in real life was created. For this configuration, one end of a serial link has a different mask than the other. This allows one router to advertise an unexpected subnet to the other router. This subnet is unexpected because it doesn't match the subnets on the interface the second router is receiving it over (see Figures 4–7 and 4–8).

This section presents two scenarios—one with two routers and another with three routers. Because VLSM behaves in exactly the same manner with RIP and IGRP, only RIP is presented in this section.

VLSM Experiment Using Two Routers

RouterB in Figure 4–7 has been mistakenly configured with the wrong mask on its serial 0 interface in order to clarify the role that the mask on an interface plays when a router is deriving the masks for routing advertisements it receives.

RouterB applies this mask to the routing advertisement for subnet 168.71.5.0 that is received from RouterA. 255.255.255.252 is not an illegal mask for 168.71.5.0. Routing may still work in this situation, and the problem may go unnoticed. However, in a more complicated network, this situation would cause a problem.

The following *show interface* commands from routers A and B show that the mask is not the same on each side of the link. This is not a configuration that would occur normally. However, it is useful for demonstrating how routers derive masks for network addresses and for indicating the problems that can occur when the derived mask is not appropriate. The primary problem in this situation is that incorrect subnet masks are associated with received route advertisements.

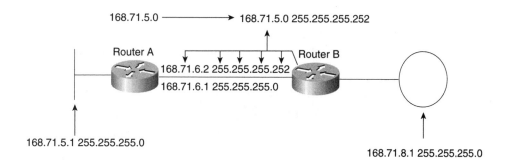

Figure 4–7

RouterB has the wrong mask on serial 0.

```
RouterA#show interface serial 0
Serial0 is up, line protocol is up
  Hardware is HD64570
  Internet address is 168.71.6.1 255.255.255.0

RouterB#show interface serial 0
Serial0 is up, line protocol is up
  Hardware is HD64570
  Internet address is 168.71.6.2 255.255.255.252
```

In the following output of the *show ip route* command from routers A and B, you can see that each router believes 168.71.5.0 has a different mask. In this scenario, the routers' masks will still be inconsistent, but connectivity will still be possible.

```
RouterA#show ip route 168.71.5.0
Routing entry for 168.71.5.0 255.255.255.0
  Known via "connected", distance 0, metric 0 (connected)

RouterB#show ip route 168.71.5.0
Routing entry for 168.71.5.0 255.255.255.252
  Known via "rip", distance 120, metric 1
```

In the following output from RouterB pinging 168.71.5.1 you can see that routing is working for 168.71.5.1:

```
RouterB#ping 168.71.5.1
Type escape sequence to abort.
Sending 5, 100-byte ICMP Echos to 168.71.5.1, timeout is 2 seconds:
!!!!!
Success rate is 100 percent (5/5), round-trip min/avg/max = 4/4/8 ms
RouterB#
```

In this scenario, connectivity was still possible from one router to the other using the assigned IP addresses. However, routing would not work if RouterB received a packet for 168.71.5.10. RouterB could not forward this packet because a longest match lookup for 168.71.5.10 in the routing table would not match against the routing entry for 168.71.5.0 255.255.255.252.

The .10 in the last octet of the IP address 168.71.5.10 has bits set that fall under the range of the mask for the last octet in the routing table entry: .252. This indicates that the host address 168.71.5.10 is not on the subnet covered by 168.71.5.0 255.255.255.252.

See the section in Chapter 8 on determining which subnet a host address falls under if you need more information on this issue.

The following output of the *show ip route 168.71.5.10* command from RouterB shows that RouterB doesn't have a route to 168.71.5.10.

```
RouterB#show ip route 168.71.5.10
% Subnet not in table
RouterB#
```

Note that as far as RouterA is concerned, 168.71.5.1 and 168.71.5.10 are on the same subnet. RouterB, on the other hand, thinks they are on different subnets because of the mask it derived for 168.71.5.0 when it was received from RouterA. The incorrect mask was derived because RouterB has the wrong mask on its serial0 interface—255.255.255.252 instead of 255.255.255.0.

Remember that the correct mask for subnet 168.71.5.0 is 255.255.255.0. RouterB would have been able to match 168.71.5.10 to this route and mask combination. The .10 in the final octet of the IP address (0.0.0.10) falls outside of the range of the bits covered by the subnet mask (255.255.255.0). Therefore, it would have been ignored when RouterB did the longest match lookup.

The next scenario, which uses three routers, shows how an incorrect entry in a routing table can cause the routing table to become corrupted and demonstrates how this can affect network performance.

VLSM Experiment Using Three Routers

This scenario builds on the previous one by bringing RouterC back into the picture. RouterB's serial 0 interface still has the incorrect mask 255.255.255.252, as shown in Figure 4–7. All other masks are 255.255.255.0 (see Figure 4–8).

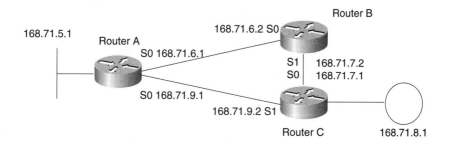

Figure 4–8

Return to the three router topology.

In the following routing table from RouterB, you can see that there are two connected interfaces to major net 168.71.0.0: serial 0 and serial 1. You can also see that every other RIP-derived route now has two entries—one with a mask of 255.255.255.0 and another with a mask of 255.255.255.252:

```
RouterB#show ip route
Codes: C - connected, S - static, I - IGRP, R - RIP, M - mobile, B - BGP
       D - EIGRP, EX - EIGRP external, O - OSPF, IA - OSPF inter area
       E1 - OSPF external type 1, E2 - OSPF external type 2, E - EGP
       i - IS-IS, L1 - IS-IS level-1, L2 - IS-IS level-2, * - candidate default

Gateway of last resort is not set

168.71.0.0 is variably subnetted, 10 subnets, 2 masks
R       168.71.9.0 255.255.255.252 [120/1] via 168.71.6.1, 00:00:00, Serial0
R       168.71.9.0 255.255.255.0 [120/1] via 168.71.7.1, 00:00:26, Serial1
R       168.71.8.0 255.255.255.252 [120/2] via 168.71.6.1, 00:00:00, Serial0
R       168.71.8.0 255.255.255.0 [120/1] via 168.71.7.1, 00:00:26, Serial1
R       168.71.7.0 255.255.255.252 [120/2] via 168.71.6.1, 00:00:00, Serial0
C       168.71.7.0 255.255.255.0 is directly connected, Serial1
R       168.71.6.0 255.255.255.0 [120/2] via 168.71.7.1, 00:00:26, Serial1
C       168.71.6.0 255.255.255.252 is directly connected, Serial0
R       168.71.5.0 255.255.255.0 [120/2] via 168.71.7.1, 00:00:26, Serial1
R       168.71.5.0 255.255.255.252 [120/1] via 168.71.6.1, 00:00:00, Serial0
RouterB#
```

You can see that the entries for the following routing tables from routers A and C are as expected because they both have the correct masks on each interface:

```
RouterA#show ip route
Codes: C - connected, S - static, I - IGRP, R - RIP, M - mobile, B - BGP
       D - EIGRP, EX - EIGRP external, O - OSPF, IA - OSPF inter area
       E1 - OSPF external type 1, E2 - OSPF external type 2, E - EGP
       i - IS-IS, L1 - IS-IS level-1, L2 - IS-IS level-2, * - candidate default

Gateway of last resort is not set

168.71.0.0 255.255.255.0 is subnetted, 5 subnets
C       168.71.9.0 is directly connected, Serial1
R       168.71.8.0 [120/1] via 168.71.9.2, 00:00:03, Serial1
R       168.71.7.0 [120/1] via 168.71.9.2, 00:00:03, Serial1
C       168.71.6.0 is directly connected, Serial0
C       168.71.5.0 is directly connected, Ethernet0
RouterA#
```

```
RouterC#show ip route
Codes: C - connected, S - static, I - IGRP, R - RIP, M - mobile, B - BGP
       D - EIGRP, EX - EIGRP external, O - OSPF, IA - OSPF inter area
       E1 - OSPF external type 1, E2 - OSPF external type 2, E - EGP
       i - IS-IS, L1 - IS-IS level-1, L2 - IS-IS level-2, * - candidate default

Gateway of last resort is not set
168.71.0.0 255.255.255.0 is subnetted, 5 subnets
C        168.71.9.0 is directly connected, Serial1
C        168.71.8.0 is directly connected, TokenRing0
C        168.71.7.0 is directly connected, Serial0
R        168.71.6.0 [120/1] via 168.71.9.1, 00:00:07, Serial1
R        168.71.5.0 [120/1] via 168.71.9.1, 00:00:07, Serial1
RouterC#
```

In this example, if RouterB attempted to ping 168.71.8.1, it would do a longest match lookup and determine that its route to 168.71.8.0 255.255.255.252 via RouterA was the best path to reach this IP address.

The following output of the *show ip route 168.71.8.1* command from RouterB shows that RouterB believes its best route to 168.71.8.0 is via RouterA, not RouterC.

```
RouterB#show ip route 168.71.8.1
Routing entry for 168.71.8.0 255.255.255.252
  Known via "rip", distance 120, metric 2
  Redistributing via rip
  Last update from 168.71.6.1 on Serial0, 00:00:24 ago
  Routing Descriptor Blocks:
  * 168.71.6.1, from 168.71.6.1, 00:00:24 ago, via Serial0
      Route metric is 2, traffic share count is 1

RouterB#
```

RouterB sends the pings to 168.71.8.1 via RouterA. The IP address of the outbound interface is used by default when a router sends a ping, so the IP source addresses in this scenario are all 168.71.6.2, not 168.71.7.2—the IP address on RouterB closest to RouterC. RouterA, which has the correct route and mask for 168.71.8.0, forwards the pings via its serial 1 interface to RouterC. RouterC sends its replies via its serial 0 interface to RouterB, resulting in what is commonly called *asymmetric routing*—two hosts using different paths when sending IP packets to each other.

These last two sections have further explained the function of deriving masks for routes from the interfaces the routes are learned over. They have also shown some interesting situations that can arise when a misconfiguration occurs.

The following section explains what happens when VLSM is properly configured and routing advertisements are blocked entirely.

Correctly Configuring VLSM Blocked Routes

A *blocked route* is a route that is not advertised by a router because it doesn't fit the mask of the outbound interface. In the example in Figure 4–9, the masks and addresses on RouterA's serial 0 have been changed. The new mask is 255.255.255.252. Both routers now have the same mask on this link.

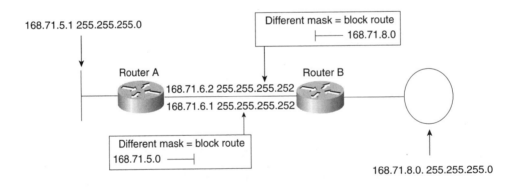

Figure 4–9
VLSM is configured correctly.

In the following output of the *show interface* command from routers A and B, you can see that both ends of the link have the same mask:

```
RouterA#show interface serial 0
Serial0 is up, line protocol is up
  Hardware is HD64570
  Internet address is 168.71.6.1 255.255.255.252
  MTU 1500 bytes, BW 128 Kbit, DLY 20000 usec, rely 255/255, load 1/255

RouterB#show interface serial 0
Serial0 is up, line protocol is up
  Hardware is HD64570
  Internet address is 168.71.6.2 255.255.255.252
  MTU 1500 bytes, BW 128 Kbit, DLY 20000 usec, rely 255/255, load 1/255
```

In the following routing tables from routers A and B, you can see that there are no RIP-derived routes:

```
RouterA#show ip route
Codes: C - connected, S - static, I - IGRP, R - RIP, M - mobile, B - BGP
       D - EIGRP, EX - EIGRP external, O - OSPF, IA - OSPF inter area
       E1 - OSPF external type 1, E2 - OSPF external type 2, E - EGP
       i - IS-IS, L1 - IS-IS level-1, L2 - IS-IS level-2, * - candidate default

Gateway of last resort is not set

     168.71.0.0 is variably subnetted, 2 subnets, 2 masks
C       168.71.6.0 255.255.255.252 is directly connected, Serial0
C       168.71.5.0 255.255.255.0 is directly connected, Ethernet0
RouterA#

RouterB#show ip route
Codes: C - connected, S - static, I - IGRP, R - RIP, M - mobile, B - BGP
       D - EIGRP, EX - EIGRP external, O - OSPF, IA - OSPF inter area
       E1 - OSPF external type 1, E2 - OSPF external type 2, E - EGP
       i - IS-IS, L1 - IS-IS level-1, L2 - IS-IS level-2, * - candidate default

Gateway of last resort is not set

168.71.0.0 is variably subnetted, 2 subnets, 2 masks
C       168.71.8.0 255.255.255.0 is directly connected, TokenRing0
C       168.71.6.0 255.255.255.252 is directly connected, Serial0
RouterB#
```

In this example, 255.255.255.252 and 255.255.255.0 are both legitimate masks for 168.71.5.0, 168.71.8.0, and 168.71.6.0. However, the routers will still not advertise their local LAN interface subnets to each other. It is not sufficient for a mask on an outward bound interface to be legitimate for a particular route. It must be an exact match for the mask the router has stored in its table.

The following output from the *debug ip rip* command on routers A and B shows the RIP process suppressing the updates because they are empty:

```
RouterA#debug ip rip
Oct 30 23:21:46: RIP: sending update to 255.255.255.255 via Serial0 (168.71.6.1)
                                        - suppressing null update

RouterB# debug ip rip
Oct 30 23:21:46: RIP: sending update to 255.255.255.255 via Serial0 (168.71.6.2)
                                        - suppressing null update
```

Proper configuration of VLSM results in routers failing to send any routes in their advertisements, which leads to a total loss of connectivity in many cases.

VLSM Summary

This section has shown the reason RIP and IGRP do not support VLSM (no masks carried in advertisements) and the method used for preventing its use at all (updates over interfaces in the same major net with different masks are suppressed).

SUMMARY

This chapter has covered some of the basics behind using IP unnumbered and VLSM. The use of these functions with routing protocols that don't support them, such as RIP V1 and IGRP, can have varying implications—from using the wrong route to forward packets to total connectivity loss.

The next chapter discusses *default routing* (how hosts and routers route packets off of their local subnet) and some of the complexities surrounding this issue. It provides scenarios based on working and improper configurations.

CHAPTER 5

Default Routing

This chapter discusses end systems' use of a single local gateway or multiple local gateways to reach devices on remote subnets. *Gateways* are routers that forward IP packets from one network or subnetwork to another.

This chapter should not be taken as an exhaustive analysis of all possible ways of solving the problem of reaching devices on remote subnets. An entire book could be written on this issue. I hope this explanation of the fundamental problem and the solutions offered will enable you to apply the solutions where appropriate. When the solutions presented here are not appropriate, the information in this chapter will improve your ability to articulate your particular situation when requesting design assistance.

Before proceeding any further, an initial explanation of some terms is necessary.

INTRODUCTION TO DEFAULT ROUTING

The *gateway of last resort* is the term applied to a routing entry in the Cisco routing table that the router forwards packets to when it lacks a more specific route. The gateway of last resort can be learned from a route provided by another router that is tagged as *candidate default* by the advertising router. The *ip default-network* command is one way to make a router tag a route as a gateway of last resort.

The *ip default-network xxx.xxx.xxx.xxx* command causes a router to treat xxx.xxx.xxx.xxx as a gateway of last resort. A router can have multiple IP default networks entered.

The *ip default-gateway* command is used with routers that have IP routing disabled. It gives them an address to which they can forward packets whose destination IP addresses are not in their address space. 2500s in boot ROM mode are a good example of this situation. The version of Cisco IOS that runs from the 2500 boot ROM doesn't understand the *default-network* command.

HINT

To upgrade a 2500 with a single flash memory partition, you must re-configure the configuration registers so that the router comes up in boot ROM mode the next time it is rebooted.

The *local domain* refers to networks a router has local knowledge (context) of because it has a direct connection to them. Using *secondary addresses* is a way to use the same interface on a router to connect to two or more subnets. A secondary address is sometimes used when all host addresses from one subnet have been assigned and there are still more hosts on the physical network that need an IP address.

If a LAN segment has a subnetted address space of 168.71.2.16 with a mask of 255.255.255.240, only 14 host addresses are available. If more than 14 hosts are attached to the network, another IP address space (subnet) is required. In this situation, hosts in different subnets attached to the same LAN must use the router to forward packets to one another.

GATEWAY OF LAST RESORT

In Figure 5–1, if RouterC did not have an explicit route to subnet 168.72.6.0 or the major network 168.72.0.0, it would need a gateway of last resort to send packets to this subnet.

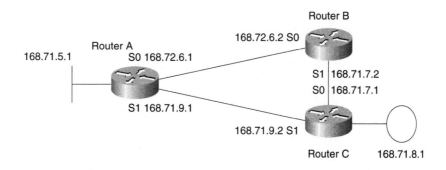

Figure 5–1

The link between RouterA and RouterB has a different major network than all other networks.

In the following routing table from RouterC, you can see that RouterC has installed a gateway of last resort network 10.0.0.0 with a next hop of 168.71.9.1. You can also see that there is no route to 168.72.6.0 or 168.72.0.0.

```
RouterC#show ip route
Codes: C - connected, S - static, I - IGRP, R - RIP, M - mobile, B - BGP
       D - EIGRP, EX - EIGRP external, O - OSPF, IA - OSPF inter area
       E1 - OSPF external type 1, E2 - OSPF external type 2, E - EGP
       i - IS-IS, L1 - IS-IS level-1, L2 - IS-IS level-2, * - candidate default

Gateway of last resort is 168.71.9.1 to network 10.0.0.0

I*   10.0.0.0 [100/82125] via 168.71.9.1, 00:01:06, Serial1
168.71.0.0 255.255.255.0 is subnetted, 5 subnets
C       168.71.9.0 is directly connected, Serial1
C       168.71.8.0 is directly connected, TokenRing0
C       168.71.7.0 is directly connected, Serial0
I       168.71.5.0 [100/10002001] via 168.71.9.1, 00:01:07, Serial1
RouterC#
```

The gateway of last resort is being advertised by RouterA as a candidate default route. It is up to the router receiving a candidate default route to determine whether it should install it as the gateway of last resort. In this scenario, having RouterA advertise 10.0.0.0 as the candidate default route also caused RouterB to send a route to RouterC for 10.0.0.0 that RouterB flagged as a candidate default route.

Figure 5–1 shows that as far as RouterC is concerned, the link between RouterC and RouterA is the best path for reaching 10.0.0.0 because RouterB increases the metric for 10.0.0.0 when advertising it to RouterC. RouterA's metric is smaller than RouterB's. Interestingly enough, as far as reaching 168.71.6.0 is concerned, both of RouterC's physical paths—via RouterA or RouterB—could be of equal cost if all links in the network were the same delay and bandwidth. However, because this scenario relies on using the gateway of last resort to 10.0.0.0 to reach 168.71.6.0, only one path is used even if they are equal cost in theory.

The following configuration from RouterA shows how to enable this function:

```
RouterA
!
interface ethernet0
ip address 168.71.5.1 255.255.255.0
ip address 171.68.207.164 255.255.255.128 secondary
!
interface serial0
ip address 168.72.6.1 255.255.255.0
bandwidth 128
!
interface serial1
ip address 168.71.9.1 255.255.255.0
bandwidth 128
!
router igrp 109
redistribute static
network 168.71.0.0
default-metric 128 2000 255 1 1500
```

```
!
ip default-network 10.0.0.0
ip route 10.0.0.0 255.0.0.0 171.68.207.129
!
```

The following is a step-by-step explanation of enabling a router to advertise a gateway of last resort. The steps do not have to be performed in this exact order, but all steps must be completed.

1. Enter the appropriate *ip default-network* command. In this case, network 10.0.0.0 is used.

   Interestingly, this network does not have to actually exist anywhere in the network. Because IP packets are forwarded on a hop-by-hop basis, it is necessary only to convince a router to send a packet to the next hop to ensure that the packet is making forward progress to its destination. What this command is doing is telling other routers that somewhere there is a router advertising 10.0.0.0 and that the router knows how to reach every other network in the world. Therefore, a packet forwarded in the general direction of this router is on its way to reaching its ultimate destination. This concept was introduced in Chapter 3, "Discontiguous Networks, Summarization, and Subnet 0," in the section on using summarization as a tool.

2. Configure a next hop address to reach the default network. In this case, a host in the secondary address space on Ethernet0 (171.68.207.129) is used. This is a static (manually configured) route.

3. Enable the *redistribute static* command for the routing protocol in use. In this case, IGRP is being used. If you fail to enter this command, the static route is not advertised.

4. Configure a default metric. If you fail to do so, the router uses the unreachable metric (infinity) when advertising this route, which prevents the route from being accepted by other routers.

The *default metric* command takes the following form: bandwidth, delay, reliability, load, and MTU. Review the section on metrics in Chapter 2, "Routing Metrics and Distances," for more information. Remember that by default only bandwidth and delay are used by IGRP. The delay in a route is cumulative, and the minimum bandwidth is used for all links in the path.

Gateway of Last Resort for a Non-Local Domain

The following scenario shows that RouterC uses the gateway of last resort to reach a subnet it has no explicit knowledge of. Remember that a non-local domain is a major network address space that the router has no physical connection to. Refer to Figure 5–1 for the network topology used in this scenario.

In the following output of the *show ip route* command from RouterC, you can see that RouterC does not have a subnet route to 168.72.6.0 or a summarized route to the major net 168.72.0.0:

```
RouterC#show ip route 168.72.6.0
% Network not in table
RouterC#show ip route 168.72.0.0
% Network not in table
RouterC#
```

In the following output from RouterC, you can see that RouterC can ping 168.72.6.1:

```
RouterC#ping 168.72.6.1
Type escape sequence to abort.
Sending 5, 100-byte ICMP Echos to 168.72.6.1, timeout is 2 seconds:
!!!!!
```

```
Success rate is 100 percent (5/5), round-trip min/avg/max = 16/16/16 ms
RouterC#
```

Gateway of Last Resort Fails for a Local Domain

In the scenario shown in Figure 5–2, the link between RouterA and RouterB is now part of the 168.71.0.0 domain that all other networks are using. However, the mask has been changed to 255.255.255.252. This was done to prevent RouterA and RouterB from advertising the 168.71.6.0 subnet. See Chapter 4, "Using IP Unnumbered and VLSM," for more information on VLSM.

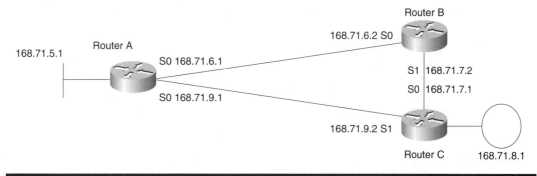

Figure 5–2

The link between RouterA and RouterB has the same major network but a different mask.

In the following routing table from RouterC, you can see that RouterC does not have a route to 168.71.6.0 or a summarized route to 168.71.0.0:

```
RouterC#show ip route 168.71.6.0
% Subnet not in table
RouterC#show ip route 168.71.0.0
Routing entry for 168.71.0.0 255.255.255.0, 4 known subnets
  Attached (3 connections)
  Redistributing via igrp 109

C       168.71.9.0 is directly connected, Serial1
C       168.71.8.0 is directly connected, TokenRing0
C       168.71.7.0 is directly connected, Serial0
I       168.71.5.0 [100/10002001] via 168.71.9.1, 00:00:36, Serial1
```

NOTES

An access list has been applied to the end of this *debug* command, which limits the output of the command to packets that match the access list. Adding the access list affects only the actual debug messages. It is a good idea to add an access list whenever a router with lots of IP traffic is being used to debug a problem related to the forwarding of IP packets. Remember that *debug* commands work only for IP packets that are being process switched. Ping packets generated by a router are always process switched, so adding the access list to the *debug* command will always work in situations similar to this one.

To determine whether access list debugging is available for a certain *debug* command, type a question mark (?) at the end of the command. If access list debugging is available, the prompt indicates that you can enter an access list number.

In the following output of the *debug ip packet* command from RouterC, you can see that RouterC doesn't have a route to use for packets destined to 168.71.6.1:

```
RouterC#debug ip packet 103
IP packet debugging is on for access list 103
RouterC#ping 168.71.6.1
Type escape sequence to abort.
Sending 5, 100-byte ICMP Echos to 168.71.6.1, timeout is 2 seconds:
Oct  8 21:30:32: IP: s=168.71.7.1 (local), d=168.71.6.1, len 100, unroutable.
Oct  8 21:30:34: IP: s=168.71.7.1 (local), d=168.71.6.1, len 100, unroutable.
Oct  8 21:30:36: IP: s=168.71.7.1 (local), d=168.71.6.1, len 100, unroutable.
Oct  8 21:30:38: IP: s=168.71.7.1 (local), d=168.71.6.1, len 100, unroutable.
Oct  8 21:30:40: IP: s=168.71.7.1 (local), d=168.71.6.1, len 100, unroutable.
Success rate is 0 percent (0/5)
RouterC#
```

The following is the content of access list 103:

```
RouterC#show access-lists 103
Extended IP access list 103
    permit ip any 168.71.6.0 0.0.0.255 (5 matches)
RouterC#
```

In the following routing table from RouterC, you can see that RouterC has a gateway of last resort installed. It was ignored because routers do not use a gateway of last resort for

addresses that are part of its local domain—a major network
it has connections to.

```
RouterC#show ip route
Codes: C - connected, S - static, I - IGRP, R - RIP, M - mobile, B - BGP
       D - EIGRP, EX - EIGRP external, O - OSPF, IA - OSPF inter area
       E1 - OSPF external type 1, E2 - OSPF external type 2, E - EGP
       i - IS-IS, L1 - IS-IS level-1, L2 - IS-IS level-2, * - candidate default

Gateway of last resort is 168.71.9.1 to network 10.0.0.0

I*   10.0.0.0 [100/82125] via 168.71.9.1, 00:00:29, Serial1
168.71.0.0 255.255.255.0 is subnetted, 4 subnets
C       168.71.9.0 is directly connected, Serial1
C       168.71.8.0 is directly connected, TokenRing0
C       168.71.7.0 is directly connected, Serial0
I       168.71.5.0 [100/10002001] via 168.71.9.1, 00:00:29, Serial1
RouterC#
```

The solution to this problem is to enter a static route for the
summarized major net that points to the gateway of last resort.
In this case, the fact that 10.0.0.0 is tagged as a gateway of last
resort is not relevant. This scenario would still work if RouterA
advertised 10.0.0.0 without also flagging it as a candidate
default route (capable of being used as a gateway of last resort).
The following configuration from RouterC shows how to add
the static route that will point to the gateway of last resort:

```
RouterC
!
interface tokenring0
ip address 168.71.8.1 255.255.255.0
!
interface serial0
ip address 168.71.7.1 255.255.255.0
bandwidth 64
!
interface serial1
ip address 168.71.9.2 255.255.255.0
bandwidth 128
!
router igrp 109
network 168.71.0.0
!
ip route 168.71.0.0 255.255.0.0 10.0.0.0
!
```

The following routing table from RouterC shows that RouterC has installed the static route for 168.71.0.0 via 10.0.0.0:

```
RouterC#show ip route
Codes: C - connected, S - static, I - IGRP, R - RIP, M - mobile, B - BGP
       D - EIGRP, EX - EIGRP external, O - OSPF, IA - OSPF inter area
       E1 - OSPF external type 1, E2 - OSPF external type 2, E - EGP
       i - IS-IS, L1 - IS-IS level-1, L2 - IS-IS level-2, * - candidate default

Gateway of last resort is 168.71.9.1 to network 10.0.0.0

I*   10.0.0.0 [100/82125] via 168.71.9.1, 00:00:05, Serial1
168.71.0.0 is variably subnetted, 5 subnets, 2 masks
C       168.71.9.0 255.255.255.0 is directly connected, Serial1
C       168.71.8.0 255.255.255.0 is directly connected, TokenRing0
C       168.71.7.0 255.255.255.0 is directly connected, Serial0
I       168.71.5.0 255.255.255.0
           [100/10002001] via 168.71.9.1, 00:00:05, Serial1
S       168.71.0.0 255.255.0.0 [1/0] via 10.0.0.0
RouterC#
```

The following output from the *show ip route* command on RouterC shows that RouterC now has a route it can use to the subnet 168.71.6.0. When queried about its knowledge of a route, it does a longest match lookup in its routing table. In this case, the longest match is to the major net itself.

```
RouterC#show ip route 168.71.6.1
Routing entry for 168.71.0.0 255.255.0.0
  Known via "static", distance 1, metric 0
  Routing Descriptor Blocks:
  * 10.0.0.0
      Route metric is 0, traffic share count is 1
RouterC#
```

NOTES

To ensure that you receive the output for the full destination subnet, use the full IP address of a host on the destination subnet when using the *show ip route* command. You might find that a subnet exists in the routing table that you did not know existed. It is not uncommon to have a routing table with thousands of entries in it. It can be easy to miss a subnet when doing a visual scan. Using the *show ip route xxx.xxx.xxx.xxx* command to scan the table is much easier and less prone to failure.

In the following output from RouterC, you can see that RouterC can now ping 168.71.6.1:

```
RouterC#ping 168.71.6.1
Type escape sequence to abort.
Sending 5, 100-byte ICMP Echos to 168.71.6.1, timeout is 2 seconds:
!!!!!
Success rate is 100 percent (5/5), round-trip min/avg/max = 16/17/20 ms
RouterC#
```

Gateway of Last Resort Still Works When Links Fail

In this scenario (shown in Figure 5–3 and the output that follows), the link between RouterA and RouterC has failed. RouterC has converged on the path via RouterB for its route to the gateway of last resort network (10.0.0.0). 10.0.0.0 is now known via the next hop address of 168.71.7.2 (RouterB's serial 1). Because RouterC's local domain default route (168.71.0.0) is a static route to network 10.0.0.0, it works on the new path for 10.0.0.0 via RouterB as well.

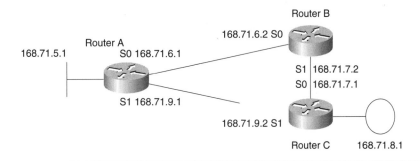

Figure 5–3

The link between RouterA and RouterC has gone down.

```
RouterC#show ip route
Codes: C - connected, S - static, I - IGRP, R - RIP, M - mobile, B - BGP
       D - EIGRP, EX - EIGRP external, O - OSPF, IA - OSPF inter area
       E1 - OSPF external type 1, E2 - OSPF external type 2, E - EGP
       i - IS-IS, L1 - IS-IS level-1, L2 - IS-IS level-2, * - candidate default

Gateway of last resort is 168.71.7.2 to network 10.0.0.0
```

```
I*     10.0.0.0 [100/84125] via 168.71.7.2, 00:01:07, Serial0
I      171.68.0.0 [100/10004001] via 168.71.7.2, 00:01:07, Serial0
       168.71.0.0 is variably subnetted, 3 subnets, 2 masks
C         168.71.8.0 255.255.255.0 is directly connected, TokenRing0
C         168.71.7.0 255.255.255.0 is directly connected, Serial0
S         168.71.0.0 255.255.0.0 [1/0] via 10.0.0.0
RouterC#
```

Using IP Classless

A simpler method for forcing a router to use a gateway of last resort for remote subnets that are part of the local domain is to configure the *ip classless* command. This command causes the router to ignore all aspects of address classes when making routing decisions. The following excerpt from RouterC's configuration shows how *ip classless* has been configured.

```
!
ip classless
!
```

NOTES

ip classless is a global command. It affects all routing protocols in the router. It should be used with caution. A thorough discussion of all of the implications of using this command is beyond the scope of this book. Please refer to your Cisco IOS documentation for more information.

The *ip classless* command will be on by default in Cisco IOS Version 11.3. See bug number CSCdj21662 on CCO (http://www.cisco.com) for more information.

In the following output of the *show ip route* command on RouterC, you can see that, once again, RouterC has no knowledge of how it should route packets for 168.71.6.0:

```
RouterC#show ip route 168.71.6.0
% Subnet not in table
RouterC#
```

In the following output from RouterC pinging 168.71.6.1, you can see that the ping is successful:

```
RouterC#ping 168.71.6.1
Type escape sequence to abort.
Sending 5, 100-byte ICMP Echos to 168.71.6.1, timeout is 2 seconds:
!!!!!
Success rate is 100 percent (5/5), round-trip min/avg/max = 16/17/20 ms
RouterC#
```

As you can see, RouterC can ping a local domain subnet that it has no knowledge of even though the local domain default route pointing to 10.0.0.0 (*ip route 168.71.0.0 255.255.0.0 10.0.0.0*) has not been configured. Remember that this was a required configuration parameter before the *ip classless* command was configured.

In Review

This section provides a quick review of the material just presented. The following section presents a scenario in which an improper use of static routes and gateways of last resort can cause connectivity failures. Figure 5–4 shows the network diagram that will be used for this scenario.

Two types of IP network addresses are under consideration in this section. They are as follows:

- *Non-local domain addresses* (a major network address that the router does not have a physical connection to)—In Figure 5–4, RouterB does not have an explicit route to 168.72.5.0. However, it does have a gateway of last resort of 10.0.0.0. This gateway of last resort is created with a static route to 10.0.0.0 that points at 168.71.6.1 and configures the *ip default-network 10.0.0.0* command. This route is sufficient for RouterB to forward packets to 167.72.5.0 because RouterB has no local context for 168.72.0.0 (it is not a local domain).

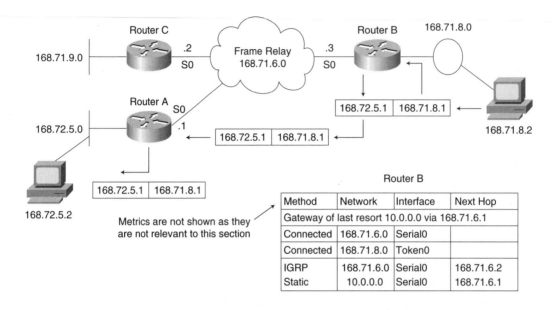

Figure 5–4

A more complicated network configuration is required to make this scenario work properly.

- *Local domain addresses* (a major network address that the router does have a physical connection to)— RouterA must have either an explicit route back to 168.71.8.0 or a static route pointing to 168.71.8.0 with a next hop of 168.71.6.3. A gateway of last resort will not allow RouterA to reach 168.71.8.0 because RouterA is connected to the major net 168.71.0.0. This connection makes 168.71.8.0 part of RouterA's local domain. Routers expect to have explicit routes for all subnets in their local domains. It is possible to get around this by installing a static route to the major network alone. However, this can lead to problems when configured improperly.

USING DEFAULT AND STATIC ROUTES IN COMPLICATED NETWORKS

In this section, several scenarios are presented using static routes and gateways of last resort. These concepts are some of the most difficult for those new to the nuances of IP routing to understand. To truly understand routing, you must have a solid grasp on the fundamentals of local domains versus non-local domains, gateways of last resort, summarized routes, and redistribution of static routes and default metrics.

People who are fully conversant in IP routing can analyze any routing table and determine what will happen when a packet to any possible destination is encountered.

Using Static Routes

In the scenario shown in Figure 5–5, you can see what happens when an improper static route has been entered to fix a routing problem.

In Figure 5–5, RouterA's routing table has been edited to show what happens when an improper static route is added to a router. RouterA has a static route to the major network of 168.71.0.0 via 168.71.6.3. Although this will enable RouterA to forward packets to 168.71.8.0, RouterA cannot reach 168.71.9.0. In fact, if RouterA received a packet for 168.71.9.1 on its Ethernet interface, it would forward it to RouterB. The proper way of doing this is shown in Figure 5–6.

In Figure 5–6, the routing table has been fixed to allow full connectivity to the subnets shown. RouterA now has access to all local subnets of 168.71.0.0. It also has access to a gateway of last resort and a pointer via the summarized route that extends from 168.71.0.0 via 179.12.9.2 to other unknown subnets of 168.71.0.0 that can be found somewhere in the rest of the world.

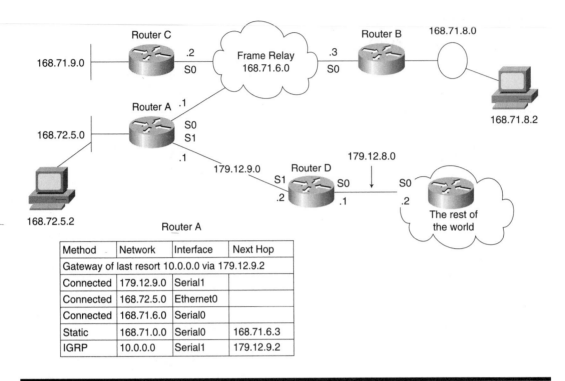

Router A

Method	Network	Interface	Next Hop
Gateway of last resort 10.0.0.0 via 179.12.9.2			
Connected	179.12.9.0	Serial1	
Connected	168.72.5.0	Ethernet0	
Connected	168.71.6.0	Serial0	
Static	168.71.0.0	Serial0	168.71.6.3
IGRP	10.0.0.0	Serial1	179.12.9.2

Figure 5–5

RouterA has an improper static route.

In Figure 5–7, the routing table has been changed to show what would happen if IGRP were used in the local domain to allow full connectivity to the subnets shown and to allow static routes to all other subnets of 168.71.0.0 and other non-local domains. It is easier to use a dynamic protocol than static routes because they are easier to maintain.

RouterA now has access to all local subnets of 168.71.0.0. RouterA also has a gateway of last resort and a pointer via the summarized route that extends from 168.71.0.0 via 179.12.9.2 to other unknown subnets of 168.71.0.0.

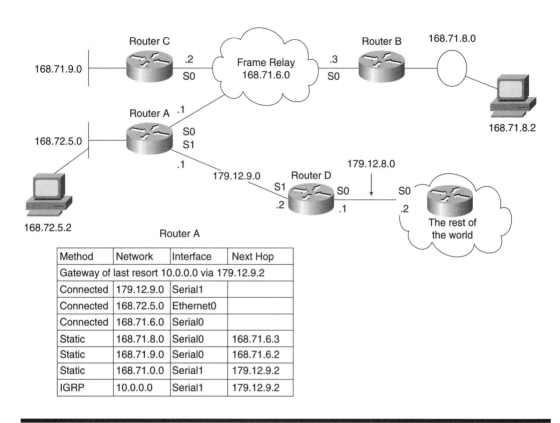

Router A

Method	Network	Interface	Next Hop
Gateway of last resort 10.0.0.0 via 179.12.9.2			
Connected	179.12.9.0	Serial1	
Connected	168.72.5.0	Ethernet0	
Connected	168.71.6.0	Serial0	
Static	168.71.8.0	Serial0	168.71.6.3
Static	168.71.9.0	Serial0	168.71.6.2
Static	168.71.0.0	Serial1	179.12.9.2
IGRP	10.0.0.0	Serial1	179.12.9.2

Figure 5–6
RouterA has working static routes.

Dealing with Too Much Default Routing Information

One of the problems designers of IP networks face is too much default information. By using a route—in this scenario, 10.0.0.0—as both a gateway of last resort for non-local domain routes and a route for unknown subnets of the local domain, packets for networks that do not exist will end up at the router that is advertising this route.

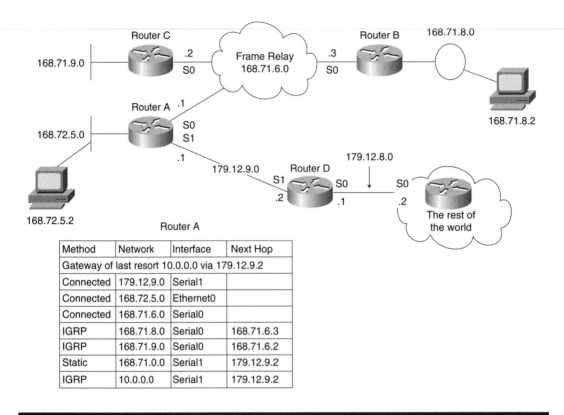

Router A

Method	Network	Interface	Next Hop
Gateway of last resort 10.0.0.0 via 179.12.9.2			
Connected	179.12.9.0	Serial1	
Connected	168.72.5.0	Ethernet0	
Connected	168.71.6.0	Serial0	
IGRP	168.71.8.0	Serial0	168.71.6.3
IGRP	168.71.9.0	Serial0	168.71.6.2
Static	168.71.0.0	Serial1	179.12.9.2
IGRP	10.0.0.0	Serial1	179.12.9.2

Figure 5–7
IGRP has been used for some routes.

This router can forward the packets to its own gateway of last resort—assuming it has one—or drop the packet as unroutable. The problem with dropping the packet is that the router may want to send an ICMP host or network unreachable message for each unroutable packet. This can cause significant overhead if several network users are creating packets for routes that do not exist. That is why Cisco routers send only one ICMP host unreachable message back to the original host for each group of packets that arrive within a short time period.

The following problems can lead to packets arriving for unreachable destinations:

- Incorrectly typed IP addresses in connection attempts for applications, such as Telnet and FTP. Routers forward these via their default routes until their Time to Live (TTL) expires or a router drops them as un-routable.

- Bookmarks in Web browsers for sites that no longer exist.

- Traffic to domain name servers (DNS) that no longer exist. DNS servers are specified by an IP address, not a name. Any change in their IP address can affect the many users who have been using this address to resolve names.

In networks with thousands of users, these kinds of packets happen all of the time. One solution is to configure a route to the null0 interface. This is like /dev/null in UNIX. It is a legitimate interface that accepts the packets and then throws them away. No ICMP host or network unreachable messages are sent for packets forwarded to null0.

In the scenario shown in Figure 5–8, the routing policy for the network containing RouterA, RouterB, RouterC, and RouterD states that no other routers can advertise dynamic routes into this network. This creates a problem because 168.71.29.0 exists outside of this network, even though it is from the local domain address space of this network.

The situation shown in Figure 5–8 can happen when a branch of a company has been moved to another region and has to use a third-party network, such as the Internet, to reach the original corporate site. Ideally, the hosts on this network would have been readdressed, but sometimes connectivity must be provided because there is not enough time to readdress. This situation is resolved by configuring a redistributed static route to 168.71.29.0 in RouterD.

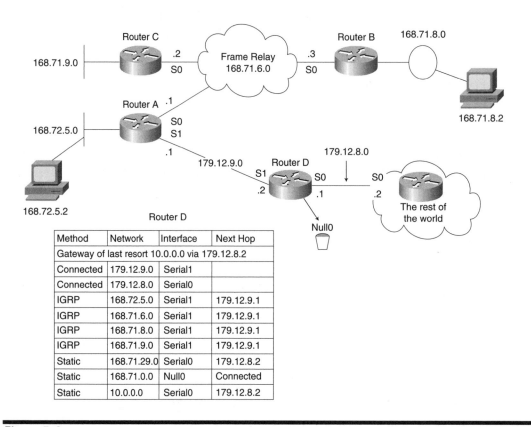

Method	Network	Interface	Next Hop
Gateway of last resort 10.0.0.0 via 179.12.8.2			
Connected	179.12.9.0	Serial1	
Connected	179.12.8.0	Serial0	
IGRP	168.72.5.0	Serial1	179.12.9.1
IGRP	168.71.6.0	Serial1	179.12.9.1
IGRP	168.71.8.0	Serial1	179.12.9.1
IGRP	168.71.9.0	Serial1	179.12.9.1
Static	168.71.29.0	Serial0	179.12.8.2
Static	168.71.0.0	Null0	Connected
Static	10.0.0.0	Serial0	179.12.8.2

Figure 5–8

Using static routes and null0.

In Figure 5–8, RouterD has a redistributed static route to 168.71.29.0 pointing at 179.12.8.2. RouterA, RouterB, and RouterC will use this route, which they learned via IGRP, to forward packets for hosts on 168.71.29.0 in RouterD's direction.

RouterD has a redistributed static route to 10.0.0.0 that points at 179.12.8.2. This route is also tagged as a candidate default. RouterA, RouterB, and RouterC use this route, which they learned via IGRP, to forward packets for hosts on subnets in other major network domains in RouterD's direction. All packets arriving at RouterD for subnets of 168.71.0.0 that RouterD doesn't know about are sent to null0. This is due to the static route of *168.71.0.0 255.255.0.0 null0* that RouterD has configured.

One consequence of using static routes is that routers forward packets toward the next hop router even when the physical network that the static route points to is not operational. In Figure 5–8, RouterD forwards packets for hosts on 168.71.29.0 to the next hop of 179.12.8.2 even if the physical network that 168.71.29.0 is assigned to is down. As long as they have a route, these packets continue to be forwarded from router to router until they reach a router that has learned via a dynamic routing protocol (not a static route) that subnet 168.71.29.0 is no longer reachable.

If all of the WAN links between RouterD and the router with 168.71.29.0 attached to it in Figure 5–8 were high-speed connections, there would be little or no point in attempting to prevent these packets from being forwarded.

On the other hand, if the link between RouterD and the rest of the world were only 56Kbit and usually running at 95–99 percent, it would be useful to prevent these unnecessary packets from flowing across the link. That way, other packets could use the extra bandwidth. However, as previously stated, the policy in this network indicates that no dynamic routes are allowed in from the rest of the world; therefore, nothing can be done. This is a common tradeoff network administrators have to face every day.

This scenario brings up an interesting issue. If a router receives a packet for a subnet it has a connection to and that connection is inactive, the router could forward the packet to a gateway of last resort or a local domain static route. In order for the router to use the gateway of last resort, the subnet on the inactive interface must not be part of the router's local domain. If the subnet in question were part of the local domain, the router would forward the packet only if it had a valid local domain default route configured.

Consider what would happen if the router with the inactive interface had the only connection to the LAN that 168.71.29.0 was assigned to. The packets to hosts on 168.71.29.0 (which the router would be forwarding to its gateway of last resort or local domain default route) would still be forwarded by every other router that they encountered with the same default routes until their TTL values expired.

In other words, packets with no chance of reaching their destinations travel aimlessly around the network until they die. To make matters worse, if the inactive LAN happens to have a lot of popular Web servers or other IP hosts on it, thousands of packets could be roaming around the network wasting bandwidth.

A solution to this issue is to configure a static route to null0 for every subnet a router has an attachment to. This static route must have an administrative distance greater than the distance value associated with any dynamic IP routing protocol that might provide a viable alternative route. In this scenario, the following command would fix the problem: *ip route 168.71.29.0 255.255.255.0 null0 200.*

Fixing a Default Gateway Loop

In the scenario shown in Figure 5–9, a situation has been created in which two routers have installed a gateway of last resort that points to the other router.

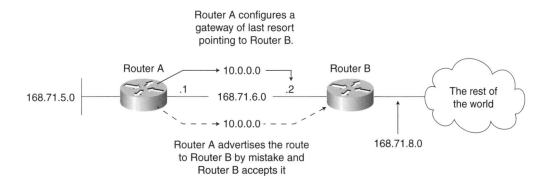

Figure 5–9

Broken gateway of last resort.

The network administrator placed the static route for the gateway of last resort in RouterA instead of RouterB, where it belongs.

RouterA has the *redistribute static* command configured, as well as a default metric. This causes RouterA to advertise the route for 10.0.0.0 to RouterB. This is not a violation of split horizon because RouterA did not actually learn about 10.0.0.0 from RouterB. Having a static route pointing to another router and having a route learned from another router are not the same thing.

In other words, if RouterB had dynamically advertised a route for 10.0.0.0 to RouterA and RouterA had advertised it back to RouterB, that would be a violation of split horizon. In this case, RouterA is telling RouterB about a route that RouterA actually uses RouterB to reach.

Because RouterB doesn't have the static route to 10.0.0.0 statically configured as it should have had, it installs the dynamic route learned from RouterA with the next hop of 168.71.6.1 and tags it as the gateway of last resort.

Packets to unknown destinations that should go to the rest of the world now bounce between the two routers. The following routing table from RouterA shows that its gateway of last resort is pointing to RouterB:

```
RouterA#show ip route
Codes: C - connected, S - static, I - IGRP, R - RIP, M - mobile, B - BGP
       D - EIGRP, EX - EIGRP external, O - OSPF, IA - OSPF inter area
       E1 - OSPF external type 1, E2 - OSPF external type 2, E - EGP
       i - IS-IS, L1 - IS-IS level-1, L2 - IS-IS level-2, * - candidate default

Gateway of last resort is 168.71.6.2 to network 10.0.0.0

S*    10.0.0.0 [1/0] via 168.71.6.2
      168.71.0.0 255.255.255.0 is subnetted, 3 subnets
C        168.71.6.0 is directly connected, Serial0
C        168.71.5.0 is directly connected, Ethernet0
RouterA#
```

The following routing table from RouterB shows that its gateway of last resort is pointing to RouterA:

```
RouterB#show ip route
Codes: C - connected, S - static, I - IGRP, R - RIP, M - mobile, B - BGP
       D - EIGRP, EX - EIGRP external, O - OSPF, IA - OSPF inter area
       E1 - OSPF external type 1, E2 - OSPF external type 2, E - EGP
       i - IS-IS, L1 - IS-IS level-1, L2 - IS-IS level-2, * - candidate default

Gateway of last resort is 168.71.6.1 to network 10.0.0.0

I*    10.0.0.0 [100/82125] via 168.71.6.1, 00:01:21, Serial0
      168.71.0.0 255.255.255.0 is subnetted, 3 subnets
C        168.71.6.0 is directly connected, Serial0
I        168.71.5.0 [100/10002001] via 168.71.6.1, 00:01:09, Serial0
RouterB#
```

In the following output of the *debug ip packet* command from RouterB, you can see the packets entering RouterB on Serial0 and being forwarded back out the same interface. This continues until the TTL expires:

```
RouterB#debug ip packet
IP: s=171.68.207.222 (Serial0), d=168.72.1.1 (Serial0), g=168.71.6.1, len 64, forward
IP: s=171.68.207.222 (Serial0), d=168.72.1.1 (Serial0), g=168.71.6.1, len 64, forward
IP: s=171.68.207.222 (Serial0), d=168.72.1.1 (Serial0), g=168.71.6.1, len 64, forward
IP: s=171.68.207.222 (Serial0), d=168.72.1.1 (Serial0), g=168.71.6.1, len 64, forward
IP: s=171.68.207.222 (Serial0), d=168.72.1.1 (Serial0), g=168.71.6.1, len 64, forward
IP: s=171.68.207.222 (Serial0), d=168.72.1.1 (Serial0), g=168.71.6.1, len 64, forward
IP: s=171.68.207.222 (Serial0), d=168.72.1.1 (Serial0), g=168.71.6.1, len 64, forward
IP: s=171.68.207.222 (Serial0), d=168.72.1.1 (Serial0), g=168.71.6.1, len 64, forward
IP: s=171.68.207.222 (Serial0), d=168.72.1.1 (Serial0), g=168.71.6.1, len 64, forward
IP: s=171.68.207.222 (Serial0), d=168.72.1.1 (Serial0), g=168.71.6.1, len 64, forward
IP: s=171.68.207.222 (Serial0), d=168.72.1.1 (Serial0), g=168.71.6.1, len 64, forward
```

Clearly, the use of gateways of last resort must be carefully planned. Misuse can lead to loss of connectivity and routing loops. If a sufficient number of packets start looping the routers, the links can be overwhelmed and a routing loop storm can be created. A quick fix is a temporary static route pointing to null0 in one of the routers, which vacuums up all of the looping packets. The problem can then be fixed by placing the default routes where they belong.

The 0.0.0.0 Default Route

The 0.0.0.0 default route has special meaning to RIP and IGRP. This section explains what this meaning is and how RIP and IGRP treat it slightly differently.

RIP and 0.0.0.0

For RIP, the 0.0.0.0 route is automatically installed as the local gateway of last resort. No *ip default-network 0.0.0.0* command is required. RIP automatically advertises the route to 0.0.0.0, even when redistribute static and a default metric are not configured (see Figure 5–10).

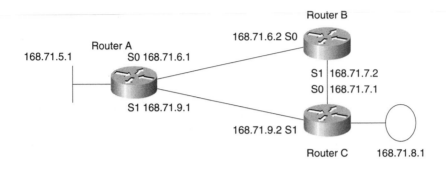

Figure 5–10

Network topology for the RIP and 0.0.0.0 scenario.

The following routing table from RouterC in Figure 5–10 shows that RouterA is advertising a route to 0.0.0.0. It appears that RouterA is the origin of this route, as well as RouterC's next hop, because it has a metric of 1.

```
RouterC#show ip route
Codes: C - connected, S - static, I - IGRP, R - RIP, M - mobile, B - BGP
       D - EIGRP, EX - EIGRP external, O - OSPF, IA - OSPF inter area
       E1 - OSPF external type 1, E2 - OSPF external type 2, E - EGP
       i - IS-IS, L1 - IS-IS level-1, L2 - IS-IS level-2, * - candidate default

Gateway of last resort is 168.71.9.1 to network 0.0.0.0

     168.71.0.0 255.255.255.0 is subnetted, 5 subnets
C       168.71.9.0 is directly connected, Serial1
C       168.71.8.0 is directly connected, TokenRing0
C       168.71.7.0 is directly connected, Serial0
R       168.71.6.0 [120/1] via 168.71.9.1, 00:00:10, Serial1
                   [120/1] via 168.71.7.2, 00:00:04, Serial0
R       168.71.5.0 [120/1] via 168.71.9.1, 00:00:10, Serial1
R*  0.0.0.0 0.0.0.0 [120/1] via 168.71.9.1, 00:00:10, Serial1
RouterC#
```

The following partial configuration from RouterA shows how the route to 0.0.0.0 was created. In this case, null0 was used as the ultimate destination. RouterB and RouterC used 0.0.0.0 as their gateway of last resort and sent all packets for unknown non-local domain networks to RouterA.

Any packets for non-local domain networks arriving at RouterA that RouterA doesn't have a route for are sent to null0:

```
!
hostname RouterA
!
router igrp rip
passive-interface Ethernet0
network 168.71.0.0
!
ip route 0.0.0.0 0.0.0.0 null0
!
```

Notice that it was not necessary to configure redistribute static or a default metric. The metric is assumed to be that of a connected route.

In the following output of the *debug ip rip* command from RouterA, you can see RouterA advertising 0.0.0.0 with a metric of 1:

```
RouterA#debug ip rip
RIP: sending update to 255.255.255.255 via Serial0 (168.71.6.1)
     subnet 168.71.9.0, metric 1
     subnet 168.71.8.0, metric 2
     subnet 168.71.5.0, metric 1
     default 0.0.0.0, metric 1
     RIP: sending update to 255.255.255.255 via Serial1 (168.71.9.1)
     subnet 168.71.6.0, metric 1
     subnet 168.71.5.0, metric 1
     default 0.0.0.0, metric 1
RouterA#
```

In the following scenario, assume that corporate policy dictates that users connected to RouterB have access only to the corporate network. One way to prevent them from accessing the rest of the world is for RouterB to install a gateway of last resort to 0.0.0.0 pointing to null0. Every packet that RouterB receives for networks and subnetworks that it has no explicit knowledge of would be routed to null0.

The following partial configuration from RouterB shows how this is done:

```
hostname RouterB
!
router igrp rip
network 168.71.0.0
!
ip route 0.0.0.0 0.0.0.0 null0
!
```

However, RouterB would advertise that it had a route to the preferred RIP gateway of last resort to RouterA and RouterC (see Figure 5–11).

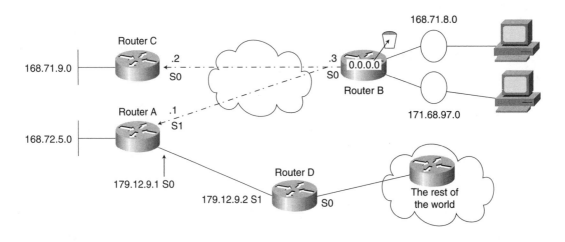

Figure 5–11

RouterB advertises 0.0.0.0 to RouterA and RouterC.

In Figure 5–12, RouterD has the "real" connectivity to the rest of the world and should be the only router advertising the route to 0.0.0.0. However, you now have a problem because both RouterD and RouterB are telling RouterA and RouterC that they have valid routes to all unknown networks.

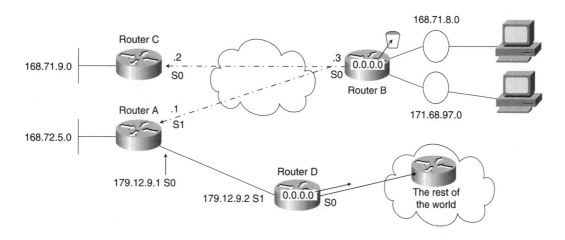

Figure 5–12
RouterD has the real gateway of last resort.

The following partial configuration from RouterD shows its usage of 0.0.0.0:

```
hostname RouterD
!
router igrp rip
network 168.71.0.0
!
ip route 0.0.0.0 0.0.0.0 serial0
!
```

In the following routing table from RouterA, you can see that RouterA has installed two routes to 0.0.0.0:

```
RouterA#show ip route 0.0.0.0
Routing entry for 0.0.0.0 0.0.0.0, supernet
  Known via "rip", distance 120, metric 1, candidate default path
  Redistributing via rip
  Last update from 168.71.6.3 on Serial0, 00:00:01 ago
  Routing Descriptor Blocks:
  * 168.71.6.3, from 168.71.6.3, 00:00:10 ago, via Serial0
     Route metric is 1, traffic share count is 1
    179.12.9.2, from 179.12.9.2 , 00:00:01 ago, via Serial1
     Route metric is 1, traffic share count is 1

RouterA#
```

Figure 5–13 shows how the routes map onto the network topology.

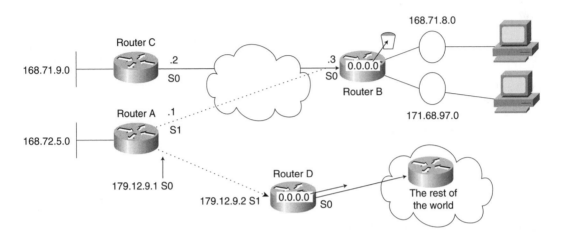

Figure 5–13
RouterA has two routes to 0.0.0.0.

Both routes have the same metric, so they are treated as parallel equal-cost paths. Figure 5–14 shows RouterA load sharing pings over the two links.

In the following output from RouterA pinging 132.10.10.1—an address that lives in the rest of the world—you can see that 40 percent of the pings are lost. These are the ones sent to RouterB:

```
RouterA#ping 132.10.10.1
Type escape sequence to abort.
Sending 5, 100-byte ICMP Echos to 132.10.10.1, timeout is 2 seconds:
!.!.!
Success rate is 60 percent (3/5), round-trip min/avg/max = 16/16/16 ms
RouterA#
```

This is a classic case of a misconfigured default route. You can prove this by configuring a static route in RouterA to 0.0.0.0 via one path and testing it with pings. Then do the same with the other path. The static route overrides the dynamic route to 0.0.0.0. The one that works for 100 percent of the pings is the correct path, and the one that fails completely is the broken path.

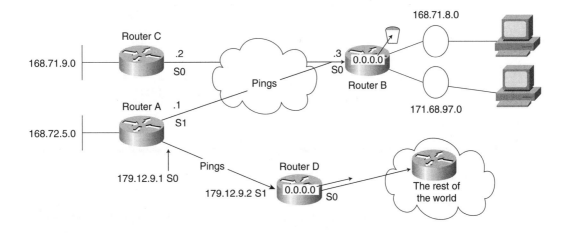

Figure 5–14
RouterA will load share pings over the two routes to 0.0.0.0.

In Figure 5–15, you can see the path that RouterC has installed for 0.0.0.0:

The following routing table from RouterC shows the single route to 0.0.0.0 via RouterB:

```
RouterC#show ip route 0.0.0.0
Routing entry for 0.0.0.0 0.0.0.0, supernet
  Known via "rip", distance 120, metric 1, candidate default path
  Redistributing via rip
  Last update from 168.71.6.3 on Serial0, 00:00:01 ago
  Routing Descriptor Blocks:
  * 168.71.6.3, from 168.71.6.3, 00:00:10 ago, via Serial0
     Route metric is 1, traffic share count is 1
RouterC#
```

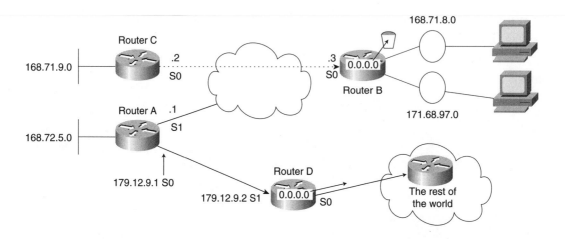

Figure 5–15
RouterC has the wrong path

Note that the metric is 1. The other route via RouterD would
have a metric of 2. In Figure 5–16, you can see the path pings
take for 132.10.10.1 from RouterC.

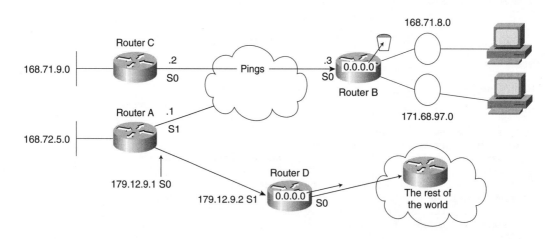

Figure 5–16
RouterC can't ping 132.10.10.1.

In the following output of RouterC pinging 132.10.10.1, you can see that 100 percent of the pings fail:

```
RouterC#ping 132.10.10.1
Type escape sequence to abort.
Sending 5, 100-byte ICMP Echos to 132.10.10.1, timeout is 2 seconds:
...
Success rate is 0 percent (0/5)
RouterC#
```

This proves that RouterC is attempting to use the incorrect route to the gateway of last resort via RouterB because it has a lower metric than the path advertised from RouterD via RouterA.

Having discovered that, in this case, RouterB is causing the problem, your fix is to stop RouterB from advertising the route for 0.0.0.0 to any other routers. Figure 5–17 shows the places the advertisements for 0.0.0.0 need to be blocked.

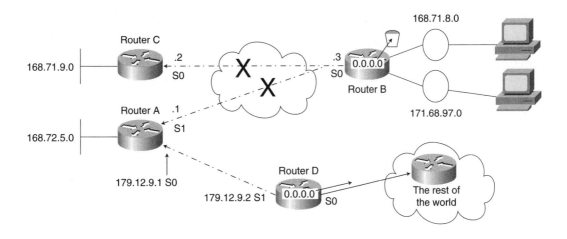

Figure 5–17
RouterB's advertisements for 0.0.0.0 must be blocked.

The following partial configuration from RouterB shows how to do this:

```
!
router rip
network 168.71.0.0
distribute-list 1 out
!
ip route 0.0.0.0 0.0.0.0 null0
!
access-list 1 deny 0.0.0.0 0.0.0.0
access-list 1 permit 0.0.0.0 255.255.255.255
!
```

access-list 1 denies the default route of 0.0.0.0 with the mask of 0.0.0.0, while allowing all other routes with the permit all statement of 0.0.0.0 255.255.255.255.

Remember that all access lists have an implicit deny all at the end. If the goal is to permit some traffic that doesn't meet the test cases earlier in the access list, the final visible line of the access list must permit the traffic to flow. The implicit deny all remains as the last line. Some people add an explicit deny all of 255.255.255.255 0.0.0.0 at the end of access lists to remind themselves of the final deny all issue.

The following output of *debug ip rip* was captured before the configuration to block 0.0.0.0 was added:

```
RouterB#debug ip rip
Oct 15 17:50:39: RIP: sending update to 255.255.255.255 via Serial0 (168.71.6.1)
Oct 15 17:50:39:        subnet 168.71.8.0, metric 1
Oct 15 17:50:39:        subnet 171.68.0.0, metric 1
Oct 15 17:50:39:        default 0.0.0.0, metric 1
Oct 15 17:50:39: RIP: sending update to 255.255.255.255 via Serial0 (168.71.6.2)
Oct 15 17:50:39:        subnet 168.71.8.0, metric 1
Oct 15 17:50:39:        subnet 171.68.0.0, metric 1
Oct 15 17:50:39:        default 0.0.0.0, metric 1
RouterB#
```

The following output of *debug ip rip* was captured after the configuration to block 0.0.0.0 was added:

```
RouterB#debug ip rip
Oct 15 17:51:07: RIP: sending update to 255.255.255.255 via Serial0 (168.71.6.1)
Oct 15 17:50:39:        subnet 168.71.8.0, metric 1
Oct 15 17:50:39:        subnet 171.68.0.0, metric 1
Oct 15 17:51:07: RIP: sending update to 255.255.255.255 via Serial1 (168.71.6.2)
```

```
Oct 15 17:50:39:        subnet 168.71.8.0, metric 1
Oct 15 17:50:39:        subnet 171.68.0.0, metric 1
RouterB
```

As you can see, the access list worked. In the following output
from RouterA pinging 132.10.10.1, you can see that they are
now 100 percent successful:

```
RouterA#ping 132.10.10.1
Type escape sequence to abort.
Sending 5, 100-byte ICMP Echos to 132.10.10.1, timeout is 2 seconds:
!!!!!
Success rate is 100 percent (5/5), round-trip min/avg/max = 16/17/20 ms
RouterA#
```

In the following output from RouterC pinging 132.10.10.1,
you can see that they are now 100 percent successful:

```
RouterC#ping 132.10.10.1
Type escape sequence to abort.
Sending 5, 100-byte ICMP Echos to 132.10.10.1, timeout is 2 seconds:
!!!!!
Success rate is 100 percent (5/5), round-trip min/avg/max = 36/37/40 ms
RouterC#
```

Remember that the goal of this scenario was to create an IP
network routing plan that prevented the hosts on 168.71.8.0
and 168.71.97.0 from reaching any hosts on networks that
RouterB did not have explicit routes for.

The original problem was that RouterB was installing the
dynamic route for 0.0.0.0 from RouterD and then advertising
it to the rest of the network. To fix this problem, a static route
to 0.0.0.0 pointing at null0 was configured in RouterB. This
fixed the original problem but created a new problem.

The new problem was that RouterB started advertising its
static route for 0.0.0.0 to the rest of the network. This caused
some hosts to install this route instead of, or in conjunction
with, their original route to 0.0.0.0, which was being advertised by RouterD. The routers using only RouterB's route to
0.0.0.0, therefore, lost all connectivity to the outside world.

Routers that installed RouterB's route to 0.0.0.0 in conjunction with RouterD's lost 50 percent of their connectivity to the rest of the world.

Using 0.0.0.0 with IGRP

The only difference between the way IGRP uses 0.0.0.0 and the way RIP uses it is that IGRP does not advertise it, even if a *redistribute static* command and a default metric are configured. The solution for creating a local domain default route for IGRP is given in this scenario. The 0.0.0.0 route might be installed as a gateway of last resort by a router running IGRP, even though IGRP—unlike RIP—doesn't treat 0.0.0.0 any differently than any other route. This is because the IP functionality of the Cisco IOS itself installs the route, not IGRP.

A router that has not yet been configured with a dynamic routing protocol still must be able to handle some basic IP functions. In fact, some routers use only static routes and connected routes to maintain the IP connectivity they require. These functions are built into the Cisco IOS to ensure that they are available.

What to Do Instead of Using 0.0.0.0 with IGRP

This section illustrates a previous point about IGRP's behavior when a route to 0.0.0.0 is available. As previously mentioned, the 0.0.0.0 route is automatically installed as the local gateway of last resort for the router by the Cisco IOS. No *ip default-network 0.0.0.0* command is required. Also, as previously mentioned, IGRP does not advertise 0.0.0.0 to other routers, even if *redistribute static* and a default metric are configured. Figure 5–18 shows the network topology used in this scenario.

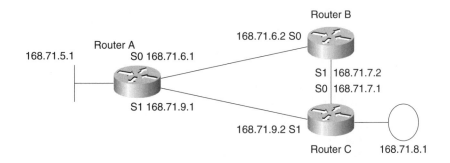

Figure 5–18

The three-router topology.

In the following routing table from RouterA, you can see that the static route to null0 for 0.0.0.0 is entered as the gateway of last resort:

```
RouterA#show ip route
Codes: C - connected, S - static, I - IGRP, R - RIP, M - mobile, B - BGP
       D - EIGRP, EX - EIGRP external, O - OSPF, IA - OSPF inter area
       E1 - OSPF external type 1, E2 - OSPF external type 2, E - EGP
       i - IS-IS, L1 - IS-IS level-1, L2 - IS-IS level-2, * - candidate default

Gateway of last resort is 0.0.0.0 to network 0.0.0.0

     168.71.0.0 255.255.255.0 is subnetted, 5 subnets
C       168.71.9.0 is directly connected, Serial1
I       168.71.8.0 [100/80188] via 168.71.9.2, 00:00:30, Serial1
I       168.71.7.0 [100/82125] via 168.71.9.2, 00:00:31, Serial1
                   [100/82125] via 168.71.6.2, 00:01:23, Serial0
C       168.71.6.0 is directly connected, Serial0
C       168.71.5.0 is directly connected, Ethernet0
S*   0.0.0.0 0.0.0.0 is directly connected, Null0
RouterA#
```

The following partial configuration from RouterA shows how this is done:

```
hostname RouterA
!
router igrp 109
network 168.71.0.0
!
ip route 0.0.0.0 0.0.0.0 null0
!
```

In the following output of the *debug ip igrp transactions* command from RouterA, you can see that RouterA is not advertising 0.0.0.0:

```
RouterA#debug ip igrp transactions
Oct 15 00:42:43: IGRP: sending update to 255.255.255.255 via Serial0 (168.71.6.1)
Oct 15 00:42:43:        subnet 168.71.9.0, metric=80125
Oct 15 00:42:43:        subnet 168.71.8.0, metric=80188
Oct 15 00:42:43:        subnet 168.71.5.0, metric=10000001
Oct 15 00:42:43: IGRP: sending update to 255.255.255.255 via Serial1 (168.71.9.1)
Oct 15 00:42:43:        subnet 168.71.6.0, metric=80125
Oct 15 00:42:43:        subnet 168.71.5.0, metric=10000001
RouterA#
```

Remember that RIP advertised 0.0.0.0 automatically. The following partial configuration from RouterA shows that a default metric has been configured, as well as redistribute static. RouterA still does not advertise 0.0.0.0.

```
hostname RouterA
!
router igrp 109
 redistribute static
 passive-interface Ethernet0
 network 168.71.0.0
 default-metric 128 2000 255 1 1500
!
ip route 0.0.0.0 0.0.0.0 null0
!
```

In the following output of the *debug ip igrp transactions* command from RouterA, you can see that RouterA is still not advertising 0.0.0.0:

```
RouterA#debug ip igrp transactions
Oct 15 00:44:20: IGRP: sending update to 255.255.255.255 via Serial0 (168.71.6.1)
Oct 15 00:44:20:        subnet 168.71.9.0, metric=80125
Oct 15 00:44:20:        subnet 168.71.8.0, metric=80188
Oct 15 00:44:20:        subnet 168.71.5.0, metric=10000001
Oct 15 00:44:20: IGRP: sending update to 255.255.255.255 via Serial1 (168.71.9.1)
Oct 15 00:44:20:        subnet 168.71.6.0, metric=80125
Oct 15 00:44:20:        subnet 168.71.5.0, metric=10000001
RouterA#
```

The following partial configuration from RouterA shows how to get RouterA to use 0.0.0.0 as the local default route. It also

shows how to advertise a different candidate default route—
10.0.0.0—that other routers can consider as a possible gateway of last resort. The *ip default network* command is used to
tag a route as a candidate default:

```
hostname RouterA
!
router igrp 109
 redistribute static
 network 168.71.0.0
 default-metric 128 2000 255 1 1500
!
ip default-network 10.0.0.0
ip route 0.0.0.0 0.0.0.0 null0
ip route 10.0.0.0 255.0.0.0 null0
!
```

A router can have multiple default networks configured; however, 0.0.0.0 is the preferred route when it is in the router's
routing table with an equal or better metric than any other candidate default route. Because both routes in RouterA are static,
they have identical metrics.

The following routing table from RouterA shows both static
routes. Note that the asterisk (*) indicates a candidate default
route.

```
RouterA#show ip route
Codes: C - connected, S - static, I - IGRP, R - RIP, M - mobile, B - BGP
       D - EIGRP, EX - EIGRP external, O - OSPF, IA - OSPF inter area
       E1 - OSPF external type 1, E2 - OSPF external type 2, E - EGP
       i - IS-IS, L1 - IS-IS level-1, L2 - IS-IS level-2, * - candidate default

Gateway of last resort is 0.0.0.0 to network 0.0.0.0

S*    10.0.0.0 is directly connected, Null0
      168.71.0.0 255.255.255.0 is subnetted, 5 subnets
C        168.71.9.0 is directly connected, Serial1
I        168.71.8.0 [100/80188] via 168.71.9.2, 00:00:49, Serial1
I        168.71.7.0 [100/82125] via 168.71.6.2, 00:01:11, Serial0
                    [100/82125] via 168.71.9.2, 00:00:49, Serial1
C        168.71.6.0 is directly connected, Serial0
C        168.71.5.0 is directly connected, Ethernet0
S*    0.0.0.0 0.0.0.0 is directly connected, Null0
RouterA#
```

The following routing table from RouterC shows that RouterC has received RouterA's advertisement for 10.0.0.0 and installed it as a gateway of last resort:

```
RouterC#show ip route
Codes: C - connected, S - static, I - IGRP, R - RIP, M - mobile, B - BGP
       D - EIGRP, EX - EIGRP external, O - OSPF, IA - OSPF inter area
       E1 - OSPF external type 1, E2 - OSPF external type 2, E - EGP
       i - IS-IS, L1 - IS-IS level-1, L2 - IS-IS level-2, * - candidate default

Gateway of last resort is 168.71.9.1 to network 10.0.0.0

I*   10.0.0.0 [100/82125] via 168.71.9.1, 00:00:31, Serial1
168.71.0.0 255.255.255.0 is subnetted, 5 subnets
C       168.71.9.0 is directly connected, Serial1
C       168.71.8.0 is directly connected, TokenRing0
C       168.71.7.0 is directly connected, Serial0
I       168.71.6.0 [100/82125] via 168.71.9.1, 00:00:32, Serial1
                   [100/82125] via 168.71.7.2, 00:00:27, Serial0
I       168.71.5.0 [100/10002001] via 168.71.9.1, 00:00:32, Serial1
RouterC#
```

The 0.0.0.0 route is not as useful for IGRP as it is for RIP. However, it is safer to use with IGRP for the same reasons that it is not as useful.

The simplest way to achieve the same effect for IGRP is to create and redistribute a static route for a fictitious network and flag it as the IP default network. You don't want to use a real network because you may not be able to control where the route for the real network is learned from. It may not always be learned via the path on which you want your traffic to travel.

If you have multiple routers with exit points to other networks that you want to use as redundant links to the outside world, you can configure the same redistributed static route in each of them. If you want one to always be preferred over the others, give it a much better metric. Make certain that, for any router in the network, the metric for the preferred route is better than the metric it receives from another router's candidate default.

USING END SYSTEMS WITH MULTIPLE LOCAL GATEWAYS

Currently, it is not uncommon for an end system to have more than one local gateway. Unfortunately, this is one of the weakest areas of IP routing. It is readily apparent that, when the concept of IP gateways for end systems was being considered by those writing IP protocol stacks, it was not common to have more than one local gateway.

In Figure 5–19, the PC on the Token Ring has two possible gateways to reach 168.71.5.0. Because most PCs running Windows are not usually running a dynamic routing protocol, they are restricted to using a single gateway at a time. In this case, the PC can use either RouterB or RouterC to reach 168.71.5.0—but not both. If RouterA failed while a PC was using it, the PC would have to be reconfigured to use RouterB.

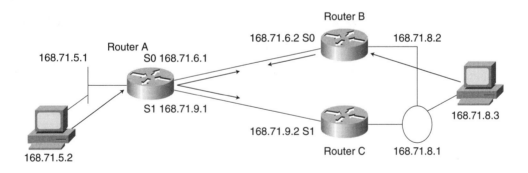

Figure 5–19
A review of the three-router topology.

In addition, the PC cannot load balance traffic between the two routers, even though the links connecting the routers have the same amount of bandwidth (both 56k or T1).

Traffic from the PC on the Ethernet is load balanced because RouterA has two parallel links that are considered to be of equal cost in this example. Note that this PC has only one gateway.

In an ideal world, end systems would be able to dynamically learn how many gateways were available off of their local network, what remote networks each gateway could reach, and the operational status of any gateways.

ICMP Router Discovery Protocol (IRDP) RFC 1256

IRDP RFC 1256 is the ICMP Router Discovery Protocol that runs on routers and end systems so that routers can advertise themselves to end stations and end stations can listen to the advertisements. By listening to these advertisements, end stations can dynamically select a gateway for reaching non-local networks. RFC 1256 allows one router to be preferred over another and provides other options for controlling the behavior of systems running IRDP.

The simplest configuration commands for IRDP in a Cisco router are as follows:

```
!
interface tokenring0
ip address 168.71.8.1 255.255.255.0
ip irdp
!
```

A thorough discussion of RFC 1256 is beyond the scope of this book. See the Cisco IOS documentation for the version of IOS you are using for more information on Cisco's implementation of IRDP.

This RFC is available on any site that makes RFCs available via anonymous FTP. It can be found on Cisco's CCO FTP server as follows: FTP to *cco.cisco.com username=anony-mous, password=your_full_email_address*. The FTP client must run in passive mode. (FTP server assigns the client's FTP port for the session. Go to /pub/rfc/RFC.)

End Systems Using RIP

End systems that can run RIP are somewhat better off. They can listen to routing updates and react to changes in the network accordingly. However, RIP V1 on an end system shares all of the limitations of RIP V1 on a router—no VLSM support, no discontiguous network support, and no capability to understand the actual speed of any network so that two parallel links are always of equal cost even when they are different bandwidths (one 56k and one T1).

In Figure 5–20, the end system on the Token Ring could determine that the path to 168.71.5.0 via RouterB has only one hop, while the path has two. Unfortunately, RIP V1 can't understand that the bandwidth of the one-hop path is much slower, making the two-hop path a better path.

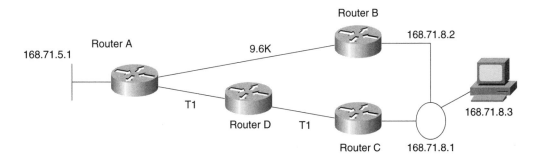

Figure 5–20
The one-hop path is slower than the two-hop path.

In Figure 5–20, RouterA thinks that the one-hop path via RouterB to 168.71.8.0 is faster than the two-hop path via RouterD and RouterC, even though the actual speed of the links between RouterA, RouterD, and RouterC is significantly faster than the link between RouterA and RouterB.

One issue with running RIP, or any dynamic routing protocols on end systems, is that it can result in a lot of routing updates being sent on LANs.

In Figure 5–21, all links are now the same bandwidth. However, the network administrator doesn't want to send all routing information onto the LANs, so the end system cannot figure out for itself that RouterB is the preferred gateway. A candidate default—0.0.0.0—is sent by both routers. The router with the better path—RouterB—has a better default metric configured—in this case, 1 versus 2. It is possible to configure a default metric for use by RIP for the 0.0.0.0 route.

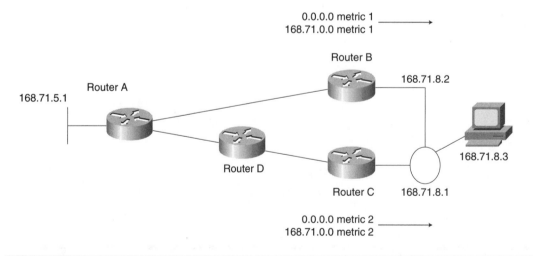

Figure 5–21
Using 0.0.0.0 with different metrics.

The following configurations from RouterB and RouterC show how to make this work:

```
!
hostname RouterB
!
ip subnet-zero
!
interface serial0
ip address 168.71.6.2 255.255.255.0
!
interface serial1
shutdown
!
interface tokenring0
ip address 168.71.8.2 255.255.255.0
!
router rip
network 168.71.0.0
redistribute static
default-metric 1
distribute-list 1 out tokenring0
distribute-list 2 out serial0
!
ip route 168.71.0.0 255.255.255.0 null0
ip route 0.0.0.0 0.0.0.0 null0
!
access-list 1 permit 0.0.0.0 0.0.0.0
access-list 1 permit 168.71.0.0 0.0.0.0
access-list 2 deny 0.0.0.0 0.0.0.0
access-list 2 deny 168.71.0.0 0.0.0.0
access-list 2 permit 0.0.0.0 255.255.255.255
!
```

For RIP V1 and IGRP, the static route to 168.71.0.0 must have the same mask as the Token Ring interface in order for it to be advertised over the Token Ring. (See the VLSM section for more details.) Therefore, the *ip subnet-zero* command must be configured when using RIP V1 and IGRP because the static route 168.71.0.0 255.255.255.0 is pointing at subnet 0 of the 168.71.0.0 major net. This command enables you to use *ip subnet-zero* in a router for static routes or as a subnet on an interface.

The distribute lists ensure that only the 0.0.0.0 and 168.71.0.0 routes are advertised out the Token Ring and that these two routes are not advertised out the serial interfaces.

The access lists are used by the distribute lists. The *default metric* command is used to ensure that the static routes to 0.0.0.0 and 168.71.0.0 advertised by RouterB are preferred over the same routes advertised by RouterC. RouterC uses a default metric of 2.

```
!
hostname RouterC
!
ip subnet-zero
!
interface serial0
shutdown
!
interface serial1
ip address 168.71.9.2 255.255.255.0
!
interface tokenring0
ip address 168.71.8.2 255.255.255.0
!
router rip
network 168.71.0.0
redistribute static
default-metric 2
distribute-list 1 out tokenring0
distribute-list 2 out serial1
!
ip route 168.71.0.0 255.255.255.0 null0
ip route 0.0.0.0 0.0.0.0 null0
!
access-list 1 permit 0.0.0.0 0.0.0.0
access-list 1 permit 168.71.0.0 0.0.0.0
access-list 2 deny 0.0.0.0 0.0.0.0
access-list 2 deny 168.71.0.0 0.0.0.0
access-list 2 permit 0.0.0.0 255.255.255.255
!
```

Cisco's Hot Standby Router Protocol (HSRP)

Hot Standby Router Protocol (HSRP) is a Cisco proprietary protocol for handling multiple gateways on a LAN. It does so by having the gateways share an IP address and a MAC address. One of the gateway's interfaces to the common LAN is in STANDBY mode, while the other's interface is in ACTIVE mode. In the event that the ACTIVE interface or router goes down, the STANDBY interface goes live.

Routers configured for HSRP send information to each other indicating that they will receive even if their interface is in standby mode. This is accomplished by using special functional MAC addresses reserved only for HSRP packets. A router whose interface is in standby mode accepts frames addressed to this MAC address, ignoring all other frames.

HINT

A router configured for HSRP uses its original IP address and MAC address on the interface, as well as the Hot Standby IP address and special MAC address when they are active. Therefore, it is possible to use the original IP addresses for Telnet sessions and SNMP monitoring even when the router is the active HSRP router. In addition, the Hot Standby IP address and the MAC address can be active on only one router at a time.

In Figure 5–22, the end system has two gateways but can use only one at a time. Without HSRP, the end system would have to be reconfigured if the default gateway it was configured for failed. With HSRP, the router with the standby interface learns about the failure of the other gateway because that gateway has ceased sending HSRP packets. This router places its interface into forwarding mode.

Because the HSRP routers are acting as if their interfaces have the same IP address—in this case, 168.71.8.3—and MAC address, the end system keeps using the gateway IP address it was configured with, as well as the MAC address it ARPed for. Remember that the layer two MAC addresses are point to point on the same physical LAN, whereas the layer three IP addresses travel end to end.

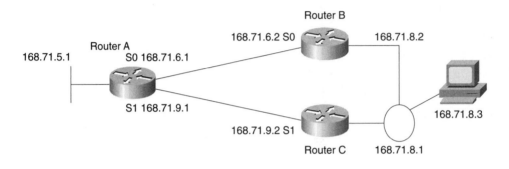

Figure 5–22
Multiple gateways.

The following partial configuration from RouterB shows that RouterB has the highest standby priority and therefore owns the primary HSRP interface in any negotiation between RouterB and RouterC. The standby IP address is 168.71.8.3. This is the address that the end system uses as its default gateway.

```
RouterC#
!
interface tokenring0
 ip address 168.71.8.1 255.255.255.0
 standby preempt
 standby 1 priority 110
 standby 1 preempt
 standby 1 ip 168.71.8.3
!
```

The following output of the *show standby* command from RouterC shows that RouterC is the standby router and that RouterB is the active router:

```
RouterC#sh standby
Tokenring0 - Group 1
  Local state is Standby, priority 110, may preempt
  Hellotime 3 holdtime 10
  Next hello sent in 0:00:00
  Hot standby IP address is 168.71.8.3 configured
  Active router is 168.71.8.2 expires in 0:00:08
  Standby router is local
```

The following partial configuration from RouterB shows RouterB's HSRP configuration commands:

```
RouterB#
!
interface tokenring0
 ip address 168.71.8.2 255.255.255.0
 standby 1 priority 120
 standby 1 preempt
 standby 1 ip 168.71.8.3
!
```

The following output of the *show standby* command from RouterB shows that RouterC is the standby router and that RouterB is the active router:

```
RouterB#sh stand
Ethernet0 - Group 1
  Local state is Active, priority 120, may preempt
  Hellotime 3 holdtime 10
  Next hello sent in 0:00:00
  Hot standby IP address is 168.71.8.3 configured
  Active router is local
  Standby router is 168.71.8.1 expires in 0:00:09
!
```

This was a purposely brief introduction of HSRP. A thorough discussion of HSRP is beyond the scope of this book. See the Cisco IOS documentation for the version of IOS you are using for more information on Cisco's implementation of HSRP.

USING FLOATING STATIC ROUTES

Floating static routes are static routes that are always in the configuration of a router but are only installed in a routing table when a dynamic route to the same network is lost. The dynamic route overrides the static route because the static route is configured with a greater distance. The concept of distance was introduced in the section on metrics and distances in Chapter 2.

This type of static route can be used when the alternative link is a dial-up connection. Dynamic routing information is not usually sent or received over a dial-up link unless the link is intended to be up for a long period of time. Remember that dynamic routing protocols send updates at regular intervals, causing the link to go up and down on a regular basis.

This scenario provides a real-life example of a floating static route being installed in a routing table after the lower-cost (shorter-path or lower-metric) routes are removed.

In Figure 5–23, the link between RouterA and RouterC is now an ISDN connection. This link is used when the primary link between RouterA and RouterB goes down.

The following partial configuration from RouterA shows how to configure a floating static route. The 130 is the distance parameter. It overrides the distance of 120 that RIP uses.

```
RouterA#
!
ip route 10.0.0.0 255.0.0.0 168.71.9.2 130
ip route 0.0.0.0 255.0.0.0 168.71.9.2 130
!
```

In the following routing table from RouterA, you can see that RouterA has installed dynamic RIP routes for networks 10.0.0.0 and 0.0.0.0 via RouterB:

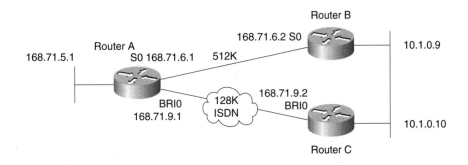

Figure 5–23

RouterA and RouterC have an ISDN connection.

```
RouterA#show ip route
Codes: C - connected, S - static, I - IGRP, R - RIP, M - mobile, B - BGP
       D - EIGRP, EX - EIGRP external, O - OSPF, IA - OSPF inter area
       E1 - OSPF external type 1, E2 - OSPF external type 2, E - EGP
       i - IS-IS, L1 - IS-IS level-1, L2 - IS-IS level-2, * - candidate default

Gateway of last resort is 168.71.6.2 to network 0.0.0.0

R     10.0.0.0 [120/1] via 168.71.6.2, 00:00:00, Serial0
      168.71.0.0 255.255.255.0 is subnetted, 3 subnets
C        168.71.9.0 is directly connected, BRI01
C        168.71.6.0 is directly connected, Serial0
C        168.71.5.0 is directly connected, Ethernet0
R*    0.0.0.0 0.0.0.0 [120/1] via 168.71.6.2, 00:00:01, Serial0
RouterA#
```

In the following routing table from RouterA, you can see that RouterA has not received an update for networks 10.0.0.0 and 0.0.0.0 for almost two minutes. These routes will timeout soon.

```
RouterA#show ip route
Codes: C - connected, S - static, I - IGRP, R - RIP, M - mobile, B - BGP
       D - EIGRP, EX - EIGRP external, O - OSPF, IA - OSPF inter area
       E1 - OSPF external type 1, E2 - OSPF external type 2, E - EGP
       i - IS-IS, L1 - IS-IS level-1, L2 - IS-IS level-2, * - candidate default
Gateway of last resort is 168.71.6.2 to network 0.0.0.0
R     10.0.0.0 [120/1] via 168.71.6.2, 00:01:58, Serial0
      168.71.0.0 255.255.255.0 is subnetted, 3 subnets
C        168.71.9.0 is directly connected, BRI0
C        168.71.6.0 is directly connected, Serial0
```

```
C       168.71.5.0 is directly connected, Ethernet0
R*   0.0.0.0 0.0.0.0 [120/1] via 168.71.6.2, 00:01:59, Serial0
RouterA#
```

In the following output of the *debug ip routing* command from RouterA, you can see the old routes being removed and the new ones being accepted. Note the higher distances (130) in the new routes.

```
RouterA#debug ip routing
*Feb  1 03:53:51: RT: flushed route to 0.0.0.0 via 168.71.6.2 (Serial0)
*Feb  1 03:53:51: RT: no routes to 0.0.0.0, entering holddown
*Feb  1 03:53:51: RT: flushed route to 10.0.0.0 via 168.71.6.2 (Serial0)
*Feb  1 03:53:51: RT: no routes to 10.0.0.0, entering holddown
*Feb  1 03:53:51: RT: flushed route to 168.71.7.0 via 168.71.6.2 (Serial0)
RouterA#
*Feb  1 03:54:45: RT: garbage collecting entry for 0.0.0.0
*Feb  1 03:54:45: RT: garbage collecting entry for 10.0.0.0
*Feb  1 03:55:13: RT: add 0.0.0.0 0.0.0.0 via 168.71.9.2, static metric [130/0]
*Feb  1 03:55:13: RT: add 10.0.0.0 255.0.0.0 via 168.71.9.2, static metric [130/0]
*Feb  1 03:55:13: RT: default path is now 0.0.0.0 via 168.71.9.2
*Feb  1 03:55:13: RT: new default network 0.0.0.0
```

In the following routing table from RouterA, you can see the new routes installed:

```
RouterA#show ip route
Codes: C - connected, S - static, I - IGRP, R - RIP, M - mobile, B - BGP
       D - EIGRP, EX - EIGRP external, O - OSPF, IA - OSPF inter area
       E1 - OSPF external type 1, E2 - OSPF external type 2, E - EGP
       i - IS-IS, L1 - IS-IS level-1, L2 - IS-IS level-2, * - candidate default

Gateway of last resort is 168.71.9.2 to network 0.0.0.0

S    10.0.0.0 [130/0] via 168.71.9.2
     168.71.0.0 255.255.255.0 is subnetted, 3 subnets
C       168.71.9.0 is directly connected, Serial1
C       168.71.6.0 is directly connected, Serial0
C       168.71.5.0 is directly connected, Ethernet0
S*   0.0.0.0 0.0.0.0 [130/0] via 168.71.9.2
RouterA#
```

The dial-on-demand routing (DDR) commands necessary to actually cause RouterA to make an ISDN call to RouterC have not been included. DDR is beyond the scope of this book. The key factor needed for DDR to work is that the router must decide that the dial-up interface is the correct interface to use for forwarding a packet to its next hop.

In this scenario, RouterA has just installed routes that will cause it to forward packets destined to 10.1.0.0 via its ISDN interface. Assuming that the DDR commands are properly configured, the call should be made and a connection should be established.

SUMMARY

This chapter has touched on some fundamental issues regarding IP connectivity to non-local networks. This is probably one of the most complex aspects of IP internetworking. Multiple factors need to be considered when deciding the best way to implement connectivity to non-local subnets.

These factors also come into play when it becomes necessary to troubleshoot an IP connectivity problem. It is not uncommon for a network administrator to discover IP packets wandering aimlessly around the network looking for a home. Sometimes these packets are not worth looking into. Other times, when they are wasting precious bandwidth on low-speed circuits, they need to be tracked down and eliminated. The next chapter discusses the next step—introducing some basic troubleshooting techniques and scenarios.

CHAPTER 6

IP Troubleshooting Scenarios

This chapter covers aspects of troubleshooting IP connectivity problems that have not yet been discussed. It is not intended to be an in-depth analysis of IP network troubleshooting. However, it does cover some of the fundamental skills that anyone supporting an IP network should have.

The troubleshooting methodology presented is very structured. It uses the process of elimination to isolate the failure to the root symptom. Like many network failures, the root cause of the failure in this scenario may never be known.

DEVELOPING A TROUBLESHOOTING ROUTINE

Troubleshooting techniques vary significantly from one network engineer to another. They are part science and part artistry. A good network engineer can simultaneously think in a *linear* fashion (following a logical progression of an event from start to finish) and in a *lateral* fashion (considering events not directly related to the problem at hand but possibly having an effect).

In general, there is no one correct way to determine the root cause of a problem. However, there are a few guidelines you can follow:

- Determine as far as possible exactly what problem you are trying to solve and focus on it. Networks are a lot like cars: You can start out investigating one problem and find 10 other things that may need attention. Make a note of any non-related problems, but focus on investigating the primary problem.

- If several users are reporting problems from different areas of the network at the same time, there is a good chance that they are reporting elements of the same problem. Focus on one area at a time. It can be overwhelming to have 1,000 or more users down at once, but if the same problem is simply reoccurring in multiple parts of the network, you only have to figure it out once.

- Whenever possible, try to duplicate the problem in a lab and troubleshoot it there. Often, the act of troubleshooting a problem has a greater negative impact on the end-user population than the original problem.

- If any test requires reconfiguring a device, ensure that you can roll back the change after the test, or you may find that you have backed yourself into a corner and cannot proceed.

- Use as few tests as possible to isolate and define the problem.

- Ensure that the results of the tests are unambiguous.

- Validate the test results by repeating each one at least twice. Note that running a command to verify a configuration parameter is not considered a test in this sense and therefore doesn't need to be performed twice.

- Document the tests performed and the results in case a bug is found.

- Document any changes made to the network during the troubleshooting procedure so that the network can be properly restored to its original condition.

- Document any workarounds that were left in place so that other support personnel will be able to understand how and why the network changed.

USING A TROUBLESHOOTING SCENARIO

The problem in this fictional scenario is that end systems A and B cannot ping each other. (Assume that the Frame Relay network is fully functional.) End system A is a Sun Classic running Solaris 2.5, and end system B is a PC running Windows 95, as shown in Figure 6–1.

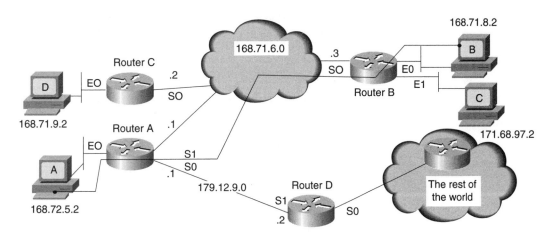

Figure 6–1

A and B cannot ping each other.

Checking the Available Routes

In the following output of the *show ip route* 168.71.8.2 from RouterA, you can see that RouterA has a route to the subnet that PC-B is on:

```
RouterA#show ip route 168.71.8.2
Routing entry for 168.71.8.0 255.255.255.0
  Known via "rip", distance 120, metric 1
  Redistributing via rip
  Last update from 168.71.6.3 on Serial1, 00:00:13 ago
  Routing Descriptor Blocks:
  * 168.71.6.3, from 168.71.6.3, 00:00:13 ago, via Serial1
      Route metric is 1, traffic share count is 1

RouterB#
```

In the following output of the *show ip route* 168.72.5.2 from RouterB, you can see that RouterB has a route to this subnet:

```
RouterB#show ip route 168.72.5.2
Routing entry for 168.71.8.0 255.255.255.0
  Known via "rip", distance 120, metric 1
  Redistributing via rip
  Last update from 168.71.6.1 on Serial0, 00:00:23 ago
  Routing Descriptor Blocks:
  * 168.71.6.1, from 168.71.6.1, 00:00:13 ago, via Serial0
      Route metric is 1, traffic share count is 1

RouterB#
```

The previous test has validated that the two routers have knowledge of the subnets that Sun-A and PC-B are on.

Tracing the Route

Another useful tool is the TraceRoute utility. It is used to trace a route (path) between a device and a host on a remote network or subnetwork address. Most systems with a TCP/IP protocol stack have a version of this utility. In Windows 95, it is called tracert.exe. It is usually found in the Windows directory.

The following output of the *tracert 168.71.8.2* command from SUN-A shows that the trace dies after reaching RouterB. Note

that SUN-A resolved the Domain Name System (DNS) entry
for PC-B before attempting the trace:

```
SUN-A> traceroute 168.71.8.2
traceroute to pc-b.cisco.com (168.71.8.2), 30 hops max, 40 byte packets
 1  routerb (168.71.6.3)  3 ms  3 ms  3 ms
 2  *   *   *
 3  *   *   *
 4  *   *   *
 5  *   *   *
SUN-A>
```

The following output of the *tracert 168.72.5.2* command from
PC-B shows that the trace never really starts. It was necessary
to kill the tracert session by pressing CTRL-C (^C). This typically means that the PC cannot reach its first gateway:

```
c:\windows\ > tracert 168.72.5.2
c:\windows\ >
```

You can test whether the PC is running *tracert* correctly by
tracing the route to itself:

```
c:\windows\ > tracert 168.71.8.2
Tracing route to 168.71.8.2 over a maximum of 30 hops:

 1     2 ms     3 ms     2 ms 168.71.6.3

Trace complete.

c:\windows\ >
```

If, for any reason, the PC fails to run *tracert* correctly, it
appears to freeze after you enter the *tracert* command.

```
c:\windows\ > tracert 168.71.8.2
```

If this happens, you need to terminate the operation by pressing CTRL-C (^C). You can then use the winipcfg.exe utility to
verify that you have an IP address. At a DOS command
prompt, type **winipcfg**, which will bring up the Windows IP
configuration tracking utility. It can tell you everything there is
to know about the IP configuration of the PC (see Figures 6–2
and 6–3).

```
c:\windows\ > winipcfg
```

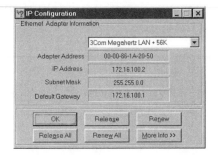

Figure 6–2

The simple view of winipcfg.

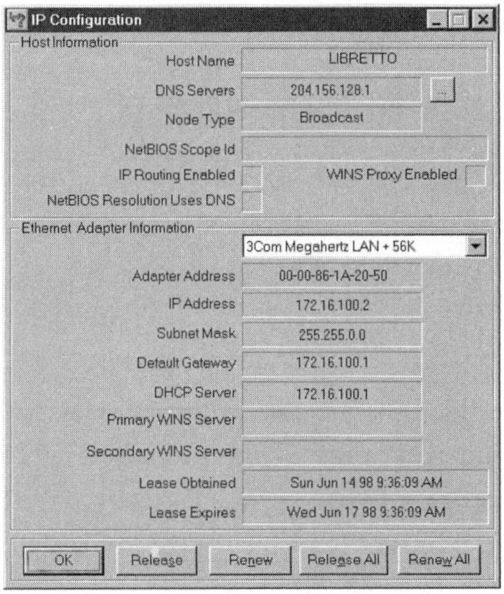

Figure 6–3

The detailed view of winipcfg.

If your IP address appears as 0.0.0.0, your system doesn't have an IP address configured. Contact your system administrator or refer to the Microsoft documentation on configuring the

TCP/IP protocol. If an IP address appears but is not the address you expected, try running *tracert* on this address. It should work.

In this case, PC-B appears to be running tracert.exe correctly. Note that the address was not resolved to a DNS entry, possibly because PC-B could not reach its DNS server.

The problem now appears to be that PC-B cannot reach its local gateway, which prevents PC-B from reaching any hosts on different subnets or networks.

HINT

Cisco routers also have a TraceRoute utility that can be run from a command prompt. The syntax is *traceroute xxx.xxx.xxx.xxx*, where the *x*s represent a host address, a major network, or a subnet. See the Cisco IOS documentation for more information on Cisco's implementation of TraceRoute.

Using Extended Pings to Track Connectivity

Another method for quickly determining whether an end system—such as PC-B—has connectivity to its gateway is to use the extended ping function available on Cisco routers (see Figure 6–4).

Extended ping allows you to select a source address for the pings from any valid IP address in the router. Normally, pings from a router use the address from the interface attached to the subnet that the pings will exit over as the source address. Although a normal ping from a router to an end system proves that IP connectivity exists, it only proves it for the subnet that the end system and the router are connected to.

A more useful test is to determine whether the end system knows how to get packets off of its local network or subnetwork.

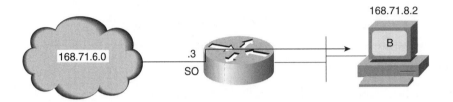

Figure 6–4

Using an extended ping from RouterB.

The following output from RouterB pinging PC-B shows that the pings have failed. Note that the source IP address— 168.71.6.3—is not on the same subnet as PC-B, proving that PC-B is having a problem reaching its gateway.

```
RouterB#ping
Protocol [ip]:
Target IP address: 168.71.8.2
Repeat count [5]:
Datagram size [100]:
Timeout in seconds [2]:
Extended commands [n]: y
Source address: 168.71.6.3
Type of service [0]:
Set DF bit in IP header? [no]:
Validate reply data? [no]:
Data pattern [0xABCD]:
Loose, Strict, Record, Timestamp, Verbose[none]:
Sweep range of sizes [n]:
Type escape sequence to abort.
Sending 5, 100-byte ICMP Echos to 168.71.8.2, timeout is 2 seconds:
...
Success rate is 0 percent (0/5)
RouterB#
```

NOTES

See the Cisco IOS documentation for more information on Cisco's implementation of ping.

Other Possible Problems

It is too early to assume that the problem lies with PC-B's gateway address. Although it might make sense at this point to skip to checking the gateway address of PC-B, doing so would eliminate the opportunity to show some other useful troubleshooting techniques.

An ARP Problem

It is not unheard of to encounter a problem with the ARP process. An ARP entry can be corrupted. Another example is that the gateway interface MAC address changes when someone installs a new interface. The end system's ARP entry for the old IP/MAC address combination might not have timed out yet, which would cause the end system to send packets to the wrong layer two (MAC) address.

Remember that layer two addresses represent point-to-point connectivity on the physical LAN, to which the end system and the gateway are attached. IP addresses, in contrast, represent end-to-end connectivity.

NOTES

Cisco routers do not have the problem of changing the MAC addresses for interfaces when the physical interfaces themselves are changed because Cisco routers download the MAC address for interfaces from a table of addresses held in memory on the system board that holds the CPU. In a 7500-based system, the MAC addresses are held on the RSP.

In the following output from the *show arp* command on RouterB, you can see the IP/MAC addresses in use. On Cisco routers, the *show interface* command shows the MAC addresses assigned to the interfaces. On a Windows 95 system, the winipcfg.exe utility shows the MAC address in use by the PC.

```
RouterB#show arp
Protocol  Address       Age (min)     Hardware Addr   Type   Interface
Internet  168.71.8.1          -        0000.0c0a.50ca  ARPA   Ethernet0
Internet  168.72.8.2          1        0060.9733.e9f5  ARPA   Ethernet0
```

In this scenario, the IP/MAC addresses appear correct. You can compare them to the addresses on PC-B. The *arp -a* command is a fairly universal method for displaying an ARP table on a device running TCP/IP:

```
C:\WINDOWS>arp -a
Interface: 168.71.8.2
  Internet Address   Physical Address      Type
  168.71.8.2     00-60-97-33-e9-f5     dynamic
  168.71.8.1     00-00-0c-0a-50-ca     dynamic
C:\WINDOWS>
```

The following output of *arp -a* from SUN-A is provided for reference only. You already know that SUN-A can reach its local gateway.

```
SUN-A > arp -a
Net to Media Table
Device   IP Address           Mask           Flags      Phys Addr
------  -------------------   ---------------  -----   ---------------
le0    168.72.5.1            255.255.255.255          00:00:0c:32:93:95
le0    168.72.5.2     255.255.255.255     SP    00:80:5f:78:79:71
SUN-A>
```

Because the addresses match, it is probably safe to assume that they are correct. Therefore, the problem lies elsewhere.

Validating End System Routing Tables

The problem now appears to be with PC-B's gateway entry. This section explains how to verify this hypothesis and how to make a temporary change. You previously verified that SUN-A's use of its gateway is correct. The methods for analyzing its routing table are presented in this section for reference purposes only.

Although neither end system is running a dynamic routing protocol, they both still have routing tables. The information in these tables is derived from configuration files when the systems start.

NOTES ———————————————————————

It is possible to manipulate these routing tables temporarily by using the procedures provided in this section. Making the changes permanent requires that the configuration files themselves be modified, which is beyond the scope of this book. Consult the system administrator or the system reference guide for the system in question.

By displaying the routing table on PC-B, you can find the problem. The default route of 0.0.0.0 0.0.0.0 is pointing to the wrong gateway address: 168.71.8.10. The correct gateway is 168.71.8.1:

```
C:\WINDOWS>netstat -rn
Route Table
Active Routes:
   Network Address    Netmask         Gateway Address   Interface    Metric
      0.0.0.0         0.0.0.0         168.71.8.10       168.71.8.2   1
      168.71.8.0      255.255.255.0   168.71.8.1        168.71.8.2   1
      168.71.8.2      255.255.255.255 127.0.0.1         127.0.0.1    1
      168.71.0.0      255.255.0.0     168.71.8.1        168.71.8.2   1
   168.71.255.255     255.255.255.255 168.71.8.2        168.71.8.2   1
      127.0.0.0       255.0.0.0       127.0.0.1         127.0.0.1    1
      224.0.0.0       224.0.0.0       168.71.8.2        168.71.8.2   1
   255.255.255.255    255.255.255.255 168.71.8.2        168.71.8.2   1
Active Connections
   Proto  Local Address       Foreign Address        State
C:\WINDOWS>
```

The following is how you flush existing gateways and add a new gateway dynamically in Windows 95 using a DOS command prompt:

```
C:\WINDOWS>route -f add 0.0.0.0 mask 0.0.0.0 168.71.8.1
```

The following routing table from PC-B shows the correct gateway address in place:

```
C:\WINDOWS>netstat -rn
Route Table
Active Routes:
  Network Address    Netmask           Gateway Address   Interface    Metric
        0.0.0.0      0.0.0.0           168.71.8.1        168.71.8.2   1
      168.71.8.0     255.255.255.0     168.71.8.1        168.71.8.2   1
      168.71.8.2     255.255.255.255   127.0.0.1         127.0.0.1    1
      168.71.0.0     255.255.0.0       168.71.8.1        168.71.8.2   1
  168.71.255.255     255.255.255.255   168.71.8.2        168.71.8.2   1
      127.0.0.0      255.0.0.0         127.0.0.1         127.0.0.1    1
      224.0.0.0      224.0.0.0         168.71.8.2        168.71.8.2   1
  255.255.255.255    255.255.255.255   168.71.8.2        168.71.8.2   1
Active Connections
  Proto  Local Address         Foreign Address         State
C:\WINDOWS>
```

To make the same kind of a change on a Solaris system (and most other UNIX systems), use the following syntax (as ROOT):

```
SUN-A# route add default 168.71.5.1 1
add net default: gateway 168.71.5.1
```

HINT

The second line shown in the previous UNIX output (*add net default: gateway 168.71.5.1*) is SUN-A echoing the command back to the terminal prompt. The word *default* and the address *0.0.0.0* can be used interchangeably.

Again, you use the *netstat -rn* command to display the routing table—the default equals 0.0.0.0:

```
SUN-A# netstat -rn

Routing Table:
  Destination          Gateway               Flags   Ref   Use     Interface
---------------------  --------------------  -----   -----  ------  ---------
127.0.0.1              127.0.0.1             UH      0      80      lo0
224.0.0.0             168.71.5.2            U       3      0       le0
default               168.71.5.1            UG      0      3622
SUN-A>
```

The following output of the *route* command from PC-B shows the various options this command can accept. The syntax on

UNIX systems and NT systems is very similar. You can typically find out the available options by entering the *route* command without any options after it. This is how the information that follows was created.

Remember that these commands are only temporary. Rebooting the PC will restore the defaults.

```
C:\WINDOWS\Desktop>route

Manipulates network routing tables.

ROUTE [-f] [command [destination] [MASK netmask] [gateway]]

    -f          Clears the routing tables of all gateway entries.  If this is
                used in conjunction with one of the commands, the tables are
                cleared prior to running the command.

    command     Specifies one of four commands
                    PRINT     Prints a route
                    ADD       Adds a route
                    DELETE    Deletes a route
                    CHANGE    Modifies an existing route

    destination Specifies the host to send command.
    MASK        If the MASK keyword is present, the next parameter is
                interpreted as the netmask parameter.

    netmask     If provided, specifies a subnet mask value to be associated
                with this route entry.  If not specified, if defaults to
                255.255.255.255.

    gateway     Specifies gateway.

All symbolic names used for destination or gateway are looked up in the
network and host name database files NETWORKS and HOSTS, respectively.  If
the command is print or delete, wildcards may be used for the destination and
gateway, or the gateway argument may be omitted.

C:\WINDOWS\Desktop>
```

Following is an example of adding and then deleting a route on PC-B:

```
C:\WINDOWS>route add 171.68.97.0 mask 255.255.255.0 168.71.8.1

C:\WINDOWS>netstat -rn
Route Table
Active Routes:
  Network Address    Netmask       Gateway Address   Interface    Metric
      0.0.0.0        0.0.0.0         168.71.8.1       168.71.8.2     1
    168.71.8.0     255.255.255.0     168.71.8.1       168.71.8.2     1
```

```
      168.71.8.2   255.255.255.255 127.0.0.1        127.0.0.1   1
      168.71.0.0   255.255.0.0     168.71.8.1       168.71.8.2  1
  168.71.255.255   255.255.255.255 168.71.8.2       168.71.8.2  1
     171.68.97.0   255.255.255.0   168.71.8.1       168.71.8.2  1
       127.0.0.0   255.0.0.0       127.0.0.1        127.0.0.1   1
       224.0.0.0   224.0.0.0       168.71.8.2       168.71.8.2  1
 255.255.255.255   255.255.255.255 168.71.8.2       168.71.8.2  1
Active Connections
  Proto  Local Address          Foreign Address       State
C:\WINDOWS>

C:\WINDOWS>route delete 171.68.97.0 mask 255.255.255.0 168.71.8.1

C:\WINDOWS>netstat -rn
Route Table
Active Routes:
  Network Address  Netmask         Gateway Address  Interface   Metric
         0.0.0.0   0.0.0.0         168.71.8.1       168.71.8.2  1
      168.71.8.0   255.255.255.0   168.71.8.1       168.71.8.2  1
      168.71.8.2   255.255.255.255 127.0.0.1        127.0.0.1   1
      168.71.0.0   255.255.0.0     168.71.8.1       168.71.8.2  1
  168.71.255.255   255.255.255.255 168.71.8.2       168.71.8.2  1
       127.0.0.0   255.0.0.0       127.0.0.1        127.0.0.1   1
       224.0.0.0   224.0.0.0       168.71.8.2       168.71.8.2  1
 255.255.255.255   255.255.255.255 168.71.8.2       168.71.8.2  1
Active Connections
  Proto  Local Address          Foreign Address       State
C:\WINDOWS>
```

It is safe to practice with these commands because they are reset when the PC is rebooted or power cycled.

This section has focused on some basic troubleshooting techniques that are useful when the problem appears to be an end system configuration issue.

SUMMARY

This chapter has introduced some basic troubleshooting techniques and guidelines. The two main ingredients in all network engineers' troubleshooting techniques are as follows:

- Knowledge of the way things are supposed to behave.

- The ability to forget how things are supposed to behave and to have faith that what you are seeing is what is really happening.

The next chapter, which is about bridging IP between different LAN types, seeks to explain a common problem encountered by network engineers attempting to connect different LAN types by bridging. The problem is that in many cases, bridges cannot provide IP connectivity between TCP/IP hosts on different types of LANs. This is because they do not take into account the IP functions occurring at layer three that are needed to establish IP connectivity. Most bridges do not know how to handle these layer three issues because they operate only at layer two (normally the highest layer that bridges are required to understand).

CHAPTER 7

Bridging IP Between Dissimilar Media

This chapter explains why attempting to bridge IP between different media types can fail. In the process of explaining this problem, the concept of mapping layer three (IP) addresses to layer two (MAC) addresses is also presented. For IP, this mapping process is handled by the *Address Resolution Protocol* (ARP), discussed in detail in this chapter.

TRANSLATIONAL BRIDGING

Bridging IP between two different LANs, such as Token Ring and Ethernet, is usually referred to as *translational bridging*. Any layer two frame traveling from Ethernet to Token Ring and vice versa requires translation because Token Ring and Ethernet frames have different formats, as illustrated in Figure 7–1.

Normal bridging forwards layer two frames from one interface to another unchanged. However, the interfaces must be of the same physical type and the layer two encapsulations must be the same. A non-translating bridge cannot change an Ethernet Type II encapsulated frame into an 802.3 encapsulated Ethernet frame. A translating bridge, on the other hand, can. Figure 7–1 shows examples of three common frame types.

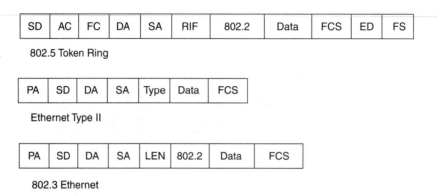

Figure 7–1

Ethernet and Token Ring frames.

MSB Versus LSB

In addition to the difference in the fields the two protocols use, there is a more fundamental issue separating Ethernet (both encapsulations) and Token Ring. Token Ring uses *most significant bit* (MSB) first data transmission and Ethernet uses *least significant bit* (LSB) first data transmission. See Figure 7–2.

Most books on internetworking technology show all IEEE layer two MAC addresses in MSB format. This saves authors from having to add a legend to each written address stating whether it is in MSB or LSB. Essentially, the MSB versus LSB issue means that one physical protocol transmits and receives right to left and the other transmits and receives left to right.

In Figure 7–2, the one representation for Token Ring shows how the addresses are written and transmitted. One of the two representations for Ethernet compares how the addresses are normally written with the way the address bits are actually transmitted. In the other representation for Ethernet, the address is written in the same format in which it is transmitted.

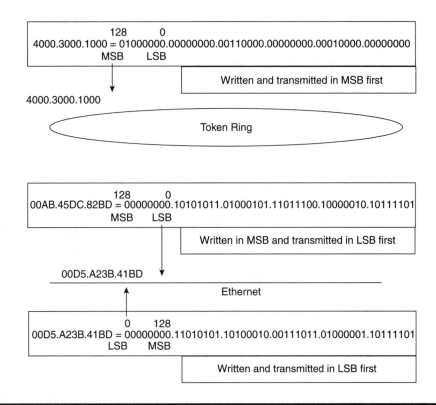

Figure 7–2

MSB versus LSB. By convention, MAC addresses are written in MSB format in most networking books.

Bit Swapping MAC Addresses

When a Token Ring frame is translated into an Ethernet frame (and vice versa), the source and destination MAC addresses are written in the opposite order. An MSB Token Ring MAC address is represented as LSB when it appears on an Ethernet network. This process is known as *bit swapping*.

Bit swapping addresses is not difficult. It is a skill every network administrator or network support analyst should have.

It is not uncommon to encounter layer two frames on a LAN whose MAC addresses do not match any known addresses in the LAN segment on which the problem is occurring. This is often due to the fact that someone has configured translational bridging somewhere in the network, and frames from an LSB type network, such as Ethernet, are showing up on an MSB-type network, such as Token Ring.

HINT ─────────────────────────────────────

When troubleshooting a problem involving unrecognized layer two addresses, it is quite helpful to have the MSB and the LSB formats of the address written down. That way, you can search reports created by a LAN analyzer of traces taken from any network segment for either format of the address.

One problem is that you may not know whether the address you are encountering is LSB or MSB. Fortunately, it doesn't really matter. Because one format is the inverse of the other, there are only two correct answers. Assume that the MAC address is MSB and convert it to LSB. You may have them mixed up as far as what you call them (MSB versus LSB), but you will still have the only two possible combinations.

After you discover which type of media the frame originated from, you will know which is MSB and which is LSB. If you find one version of the address on a Token Ring and the other on an Ethernet, compare the time stamps (assuming you have two analyzers with synchronized time clocks and that you took the traces at exactly the same time). In theory, the one with the earlier time stamp is the one on which the frame originated.

Another way to track this information down is to examine the forwarding tables in the bridges. The MAC addresses should show up as either the MSB or the LSB version in the table. You should never see both versions. This assumes that you have a loop-free bridged network.

Follow these steps:

1. Take the MAC address 4000.3000.1000. Assume it is already in MSB. In order to bit swap it, you have to write it out in binary first. If you are not familiar with binary, refer to Chapter 8, "Hexadecimal and Binary Numbering and IP Addressing." The address becomes 01000000.00000000.00110000.00000000.00010000. 00000000 = 4000.3000.1000.

2. Write the octets in the opposite order you wrote them originally. 01000000 becomes 00000010. The 0s octets do not change. 00110000 becomes 00001100. 00010000 becomes 00001000.

3. Write the octets back together. Remember that the octet order doesn't change, just the bit order within the octets. You now have the binary MAC address 00000010.00000000.00001100.00000000.00001000. 00000000.

4. Express this address back in hexadecimal: 0200. 0C00.0800. For now, you can assume this is the LSB version. Later, you may discover you had it backward.

You now have the only two possible permutations of this MAC address.

ARP EXPLAINED

All layer three network protocols must have a method for mapping layer three addresses to their corresponding layer two addresses (typically a MAC address) for point-to-point data transfer. In this case, point-to-point means that only two hosts are participating in the data transfer. The other options, such as point-to-multipoint (Internet television or radio broadcasting) and multipoint-to-multipoint (TCP/IP-based videoconferencing), are beyond the scope of this book.

Consider an IP host that is trying to initiate a TCP/IP application session, such as FTP with another IP host. The initiating host first checks its *ARP table* (a cache of known IP address/MAC address associations) to see whether it already has the correct MAC address for the destination IP address:

- If it does have the correct address, the IP datagram containing the FTP session initiation request is encapsulated into a layer two frame. The correct MAC address is inserted into the destination MAC address field of the layer two frame, and the frame is forwarded.

- If the host does not have the required MAC address, its TCP/IP protocol stack takes one of two actions, depending on how the vendor that created the stack implemented the ARP function:

  1. Queues the FTP session initiation request while it sends an ARP and resumes sending the request after the required MAC address has been determined.

  2. Drops the FTP session initiation request while it sends an ARP. It assumes that another FTP session initiation request will be sent after the first one times out. After the required MAC address has been determined, the next FTP session initiation request is forwarded.

A thorough discussion of ARP and the issues surrounding it is beyond the scope of this book. IP addresses must be mapped to layer two addresses for every type of network capable of carrying IP datagrams: Token Ring, FDDI, Ethernet, ISDN, ATM, and PPP, for example. Some use similar mapping methods, whereas others have their own unique methods.

I hope that by presenting a general introduction to ARP, as well as supplying a common problem ARP has when faced with different LAN media, you will understand that ARP is a crucial function. Its behavior must be understood for all media types before IP can be implemented successfully. The common problem ARP has is presented in the next section.

Translating Bridges and ARP Frames

A translational bridge converts the frame fields from Token Ring to Ethernet II or 802.3. It also handles the bit ordering (MSB versus LSB) problem. However, unless the bridge has special functionality built into it, IP hosts on the bridge's Token Ring still cannot communicate with IP hosts on the bridge's Ethernet interface. This is because the Address Resolution Protocol (ARP) (RFC 826) that IP uses to map layer two addresses to layer three addresses transmits MAC address information in fields higher than layer two. These fields do not normally get bit swapped when a layer two frame is translated between different media by a translating bridge. See Figure 7–3 for an example of an ARP frame.

NOTES

Cisco routers do not transitionally bridge IP between media that use different bit ordering and frame formats. Cisco switches such as the catalyst 5xxx series can do this.

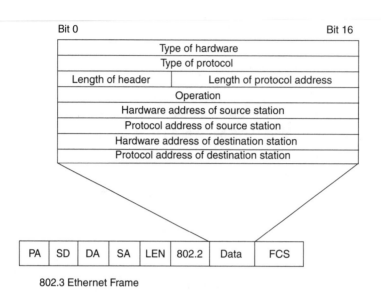

Figure 7–3

An ARP frame.

ARP in Action

When a host running IP needs to determine the layer two address (MAC) for a layer three (IP) address, it sends out an ARP request. In Figure 7–3, the Operation field would be set to the hex number indicating an ARP request. If the target host responded with an ARP reply, the target's layer two (MAC) address would appear in two places in the reply: in the layer two frame's Source Address (SA) field and in the ARP reply's *Hardware Address of Source Station field*.

The host that sent the request and receives the reply determines the target host's layer two (MAC) address from the ARP reply's *Source Hardware Address field*, not the layer two frame's Source Address (SA) field. As long as the two addresses are the same, this doesn't cause a problem. See Figure 7–4.

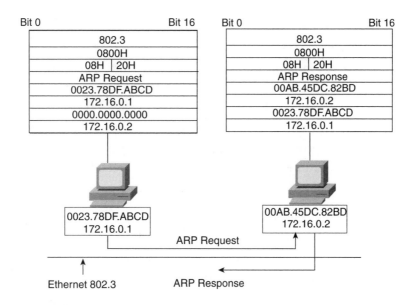

Figure 7–4

An ARP request.

NOTES

It is important to note that ARP packets are not IP packets. They have an Ethertype (protocol identification code) of their own: 0806h. ARP packets do not cross routers. They will, however, cross a bridge.

Look at the ARP structure in Figure 7–4. Notice that it has the hardware address (MAC address) and protocol address (IP) of the sending station. It has fields for the same information for the destination station.

When an IP host sends an ARP request to another IP host in order to determine its MAC address, the source information is that of the sending station. The field for the hardware address of the destination station is typically set to all 0s. The field for the protocol (IP) address of the destination station is set to the

IP address of the host whose layer two (MAC) address is being sought.

Another important point is that the layer two destination (MAC) address in the frame itself is set to the broadcast address FFFF.FFFF.FFFF.FFFF (all 1s). This causes every station on the network to receive the ARP and check whether the protocol (IP) address of the destination station matches its own address. If it does match, the receiving host responds. If it doesn't match, it ignores the ARP.

If a host decides to respond to an ARP, it uses the MAC address received in the hardware address of the ARP's source station field as the layer two destination MAC address for the ARP response. The host then inserts its hardware (MAC) address and its protocol (IP) address as the source information in the ARP response. The host inserts its MAC address in the layer two frame's source address MAC field. Finally, it sends the layer two frame to the station that sent the ARP request. See Figure 7–5.

The station sending the ARP reply derives the destination address for that reply using the hardware address of the source station from the ARP request's data portion. This means that the address used in the destination layer two MAC address is in MSB format on the Ethernet side of the bridge. The bridge bit swaps this address to the LSB format as it translates the frame to Token Ring.

Figure 7–5 shows that the destination MAC address on the Token Ring is incorrect. The IP hosts will not receive this frame. No IP connectivity will be possible.

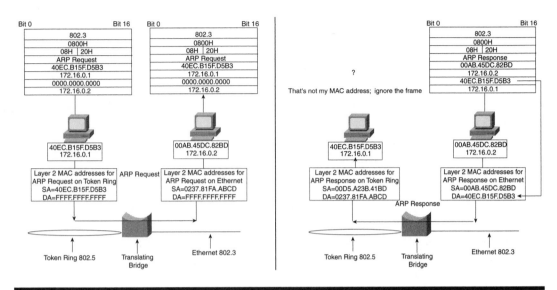

Figure 7–5

The destination MAC address for the ARP Response on the Token Ring is incorrect.

Vendor-Specific Solutions to ARP

Some vendors offer the capability to translate the information in the hardware address fields in ARP requests and ARP replies. This solution allows systems to communicate on media that use different bit transmission orders. See Figure 7–6.

In Figure 7–6, the bridge has pre-swapped the hardware addresses. The hosts think they are using the correct MAC addresses when they transmit their IP packets, but they are using the opposite versions. However, the bridge bit swaps the MAC addresses to the correct versions and thus makes connectivity possible.

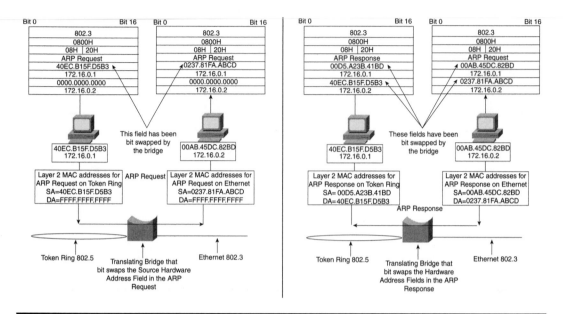

Figure 7–6

Bridge pre-swapping bits.

In Figure 7–7, you can see an FTP session initiate a request that is received by the host on the Ethernet.

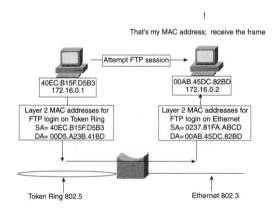

Figure 7–7

IP connectivity works bits.

Static ARPs

Another solution when the bridges do not support IP ARP bit swapping is to implement static ARPs on the IP hosts. However, this can be a tremendous administrative burden in a large network.

The remainder of this section shows how to configure and delete a static ARP in Windows 95.

Displaying the Parameters of the ARP.EXE Command

To display the parameters of the ARP.EXE command, enter **arp** at the DOS command prompt:

```
C:\>arp
Displays and modifies the IP-to-Physical address translation tables used by
address resolution protocol (ARP).
ARP -s inet_addr eth_addr [if_addr]
ARP -d inet_addr [if_addr]
ARP -a [inet_addr] [-N if_addr]
  -a            Displays current ARP entries by interrogating the current
                protocol data.  If inet_addr is specified, the IP and Physical
                addresses for only the specified computer are displayed.  If
                more than one network interface uses ARP, entries for each ARP
                table are displayed.
  -g            Same as -a.
  inet_addr     Specifies an internet address.
  -N if_addr    Displays the ARP entries for the network interface specified
                by if_addr.
  -d            Deletes the host specified by inet_addr.
  -s            Adds the host and associates the Internet address inet_addr
                with the Physical address eth_addr.  The Physical address is
                given as 6 hexadecimal bytes separated by hyphens. The entry
                is permanent.
  eth_addr      Specifies a physical address.
  if_addr       If present, this specifies the Internet address of the
                interface whose address translation table should be modified.
                If not present, the first applicable interface will be used.
C:\>
```

Displaying the Current ARP Entries

To display the current ARP entries, enter **arp –a** at the DOS
command prompt:

```
C:\>arp -a
Interface: 171.68.16.69
  Internet Address       Physical Address        Type
  171.68.16.65           00-00-0c-32-93-95       dynamic
C:\>
```

How to Create a Static ARP Entry and Display It

To create a static ARP entry and display it, enter the following
command at a DOS prompt:

```
C:\>arp -s 171.68.16.67  02-00-0c-00-08-00 171.68.16.69
C:\>arp -a
Interface: 171.68.16.69
  Internet Address       Physical Address        Type
  171.68.16.65           00-00-0c-32-93-95       dynamic
  171.68.16.67           02-00-0c-00-08-00       static
```

Deleting Static ARP Entries

The following output shows how to delete a static ARP entry
and how to show that it has been deleted:

```
C:\>arp -d 171.68.16.67
C:\>arp -a
Interface: 171.68.16.69
  Internet Address       Physical Address        Type
  171.68.16.65           00-00-0c-32-93-95       dynamic
C:\>
```

If the static ARPs you create do not reappear after the PC is
restarted, you need to create a batch file or script containing
the required commands and run it every time the system starts.
Consult your Windows 95 documentation for instructions on
this procedure.

SUMMARY

This chapter has provided a brief introduction on layer three to layer two address mapping. The TCP/IP Address Resolution Protocol (ARP) was presented in more detail in order to explain the problem of bridging IP between networks that use different bit ordering. The concept of bit swapping layer two addresses was presented as well. If you are involved in supporting a TCP/IP-based network, you should have a thorough understanding of the material in this chapter.

More information on ARP can be found in the related RFC (RFC 826). See Appendix A, "RFCs," for more information on RFCs and how to obtain them.

Chapter 8, "Hexadecimal and Binary Numbering and IP Addressing," introduces the concepts of binary numbering and hexadecimal numbering. It also provides more information on subnetting IP addresses and other IP address issues.

Hexadecimal and Binary Numbering and IP Addressing

This chapter helps you understand the structure of IP addresses and how to use subnetting and supernetting, a newer concept, to more effectively control major network address space. The chapter is broken into the following sections:

- Binary numbering versus decimal numbering

- Hexadecimal numbering versus decimal numbering

- Introduction to the 32-bit IP address

- Understanding subnet masks, subnetting, and supernetting

BINARY NUMBERING VERSUS DECIMAL NUMBERING

Binary numbering uses only 0s and 1s. It is a base-2 numbering system in which one is the largest digit that can be used in any position. This is the same as having nine be the largest number that can be used in any position in a decimal number.

Each digit in a binary number is multiplied by 2 to the power of the digit's position in the binary number, with the first position being the power of (0). Any number to the power of 0 is 1. Therefore, $(1*(10^0))=1=(1*(2^0))$.

Consider the binary number 1010. It can written in the more explicit form of $1*(2^3) + 0*(2^2) + 1*(2^1) + 0*(2^0)$. This is one way to convert a binary number to a decimal number. In this case, $1*(2^3)$ equals decimal 8, $0*(2^2)$ equals decimal 0, $1*(2^1)$ equals decimal 2, and $0*(2^0)$ equals decimal 0, resulting in the following formula: 8+0+2+0=10. Therefore, 1010 in binary is 10 in decimal format.

Compare the binary (base-2) number 1010 with the decimal (base-10) number 1010. You write out the base-10 number using the same system as the base-2 number, resulting in $1*(10^3) + 0*(10^2) + 1*(10^1) + 0*(10^0)$, which gives you the formula $(1*1000) + (0*100) + (1*10) + (0*1)=1010$. This is also written as 1010.

You now need to consider eight-digit numbers (bytes or octets) because this is the unit most commonly used by computer addressing schemes. Extend the concept of powers and position discussed previously to add four more digits.

First, consider the binary number 10101010. You can write it out using the same system as before: $1*(2^7) + 0*(2^6) + 1*(2^5) + 0*(2^4) + 1*(2^3) + 0*(2^2) + 1*(2^1) + 0*(2^0)=170$ in decimal format. How do you arrive at this answer? Look at the following method for writing out the same number:

$$1*(2^7) \quad = \quad 128$$

$$+ 0*(2^6) \quad = \quad 0$$

$$+ 1*(2^5) \quad = \quad 32$$

$$+ 0*(2^4) \quad = \quad 0$$

$$+ 1*(2^3) \quad = \quad 8$$

$$+ 0*(2^2) \quad = \quad 0$$

$$+ 1*(2^1) = 2$$

$$+ 0*(2^0) = 0$$

$$= 170$$

Some people prefer to think about octets in terms of the values represented by each position. The positions are 7, 6, 5, 4, 3, 2, 1, and 0. These are the powers that the base is raised to for each position. For binary, the resulting values in decimal format are 128, 64, 32, 16, 8, 4, 2, and 1. Once again, $2^7=128$, $2^6=64$, $2^5=32$, $2^4=16$, $2^3=8$, $2^2=4$, $2^1=2$, and $2^0=1$.

Compare this to the decimal values for the same eight positions using base 10: 10,000,000; 1,000,000; 100,000; 10,000; 1,000; 100; 10; 1. Once again, $10^7=10,000,000$; $10^6=1,000,000$; $10^5=100,000$; $10^4=10,000$; $10^3=1,000$; $10^2=100$; $10^1=10$; and $10^0=1$.

Just as the decimal numbering system has a ten thousands place, a one thousands place, and a thousands place, the binary numbering system has a 128 place, a 64 place, a 32 place, and so on.

NOTES

One final note on binary octets: If every digit in an octet is set to 1, the resulting number in decimal format is 255. 128+64+32+16+8+4+2+1=255. This is a key point to understand because it plays a significant part in IP addressing.

An easy system for changing decimal numbers into binary numbers uses iterative division, dividing by 2 until a remainder of 1 is achieved. You can convert 170 in decimal form to its binary equivalent. You start by dividing the number to be converted (170) by 2. The result is divided by 2 again, while the remainder is written off to the side. Remainders are written from right to left.

170/2 = 85 R 0. Binary result so far 0.

85/2 = 42 R 1. Binary result so far 10.

42/2 = 21 R 0. Binary result so far 010.

21/2 = 10 R 1. Binary result so far 1010.

10/2 = 5 R 0. Binary result so far 01010.

5/2 = 2 R 1. Binary result so far 101010.

2/2 = 1 R 0. Binary result so far 0101010.

1/2 = 0 R 1. Binary result so far 10101010.

HEXADECIMAL NUMBERING VERSUS DECIMAL NUMBERING

Hexadecimal (Hex) numbering uses 0–F (A=10, B=11, C=12, D=13, E=14, and F=15). It is a base-16 numbering system. F is the largest digit that can be used in any position. This is the same as having 9 be the largest number that can be used in any position in a decimal number.

Each digit in a hex number is multiplied by 16 to the power of the digit's position in the hex number, with the first position being the power of (0). Any number to the power of 0 is 1. Therefore, $(1*(10^0))=1=(1*(16^0))$.

Consider the hex number AA. It can be written in the more explicit form of $A*(16^1) + A*(16^0)$, which is one way to convert a hex number into a decimal number. In this case, $A*(16^1)$ equals decimal 160, and $A*(16^0)$ equals decimal 10, resulting in the formula 160+10=170. AA in hex equals 170 in decimal.

Notice that it takes eight binary digits—10101010—to write the binary equivalent of 170 (decimal), but it takes only two hex numbers. This is one reason why hex is such a popular numbering system.

The primary use of hex numbering in addressing schemes is to provide a shorthand method of writing binary octets. You seldom have to deal with hex numbers greater than two digits. Layer two Media Access Control (MAC) addresses are typically written in hex. For Ethernet and Token Ring, these addresses are 48 bits, or six octets. Because these addresses consist of six distinct octets, they can be expressed as six hex numbers instead.

Instead of writing 10101010.11110000.11000001.11100010.01110111.01010001, you can write the much shorter hex equivalent: AA.F0.C1.E2.77.51. To make handling hex versions of MAC addresses even easier, the dots are placed only after each four digits, as in AAF0.C1E2.7751.

Here is an easy way to manipulate hex numbers that can help when you need to convert hex to binary in a hurry and don't have a calculator handy. Break the two-digit hex number into two distinct sections: AA becomes A.A. Write the binary equivalent of each number: 1010.1010 (1010=10=A). Then put them back together again: 10101010=AA. Try another one: FA=F.A=1111 to 1010=11111010.

Although it is unusual to work with hex numbers larger than two digits, the concept of manipulating a four-digit hex number is presented here in order to provide an advanced discussion on hex numbering.

Consider the hex number FADE. You can write it using the same system as before: $F*(16^3) + A*(16^2) + D*(16^1) + E*(16^0) = 64222$

in decimal. How do you arrive at this answer? Look at the following method for writing out the same number:

$$F*(16^3) = 61440$$

$$+ A*(16^2) = 2560$$

$$+ D*(16^1) = 208$$

$$+ E*(16^0) = 14$$

$$= 64222$$

Some people prefer to think about hex numbers in terms of the values represented by each position. The positions in this example are 3 2 1 0. These are the powers the base is raised to for each position. For hex, the resulting values in decimal are as follows: 4096 256 16 1. Once again, 16^3=4096, 16^2=256, 16^1=16, and 16^0=1.

Compare this to the decimal values for the same four positions by using base-10: 1,000 100 10 1. Once again, 10^3=1,000; 10^2=100; 10^1=10; and 10^0=1. Just as the decimal numbering system has a ten thousands place, a one thousands place, and a thousands place, the hex numbering system has a 4096 place, a 256 place, a 16 place, and so on.

The system for changing hex numbers into binary numbers is the same as changing decimal numbers into binary numbers. It uses iterative division by 2 until a remainder of 1 is achieved. Let's convert AA in hex to its binary equivalent. You start by dividing the number to be converted (AA) by two. The result is divided by two again, and the remainder is written off to the side. Remainders are written from right to left.

AA/2 = 55 R 0 Binary result so far 0.

55/2 = 2A R 1 Binary result so far 10.

2A/2 = 15 R 0 Binary result so far 010.

15/2 = A R 1 Binary result so far 1010.

A/2   = 5 R 0 Binary result so far 01010.

5/2   = 2 R 1 Binary result so far 101010.

2/2   = 1 R 0 Binary result so far 0101010.

1/2   = 0 R 1 Binary result so far 10101010.

You can do this again using the decimal equivalents of the hex numbers to make it easier to see what is going on:

170/2 = 85 R 0 Binary result so far 0.

85/2 = 42 R 1 Binary result so far 10.

42/2 = 21 R 0 Binary result so far 010.

21/2 = 10 R 1 Binary result so far 1010.

10/2 = 5 R 0 Binary result so far 01010.

5/2   = 2 R 1 Binary result so far 101010.

2/2   = 1 R 0 Binary result so far 0101010.

1/2   = 0 R 1 Binary result so far 10101010.

INTRODUCTION TO THE 32-BIT IP ADDRESS

An IP address consists of four sets of octets (eight bits per octet), or 32 bits. IP addresses are typically written in a format referred to as *dotted decimal format*. In other words, the number base is decimal and the sections are denoted by dots (.). A Class B address representation is as follows: 10.1.23.19.

```
    10.      1.      23.     19 (decimal)
00001010.00000001.00010111.00010011 (binary)
```

10.1.23.19 is much easier to work with than its binary equivalent, 00001010.00000001.00010111.00010011. It is important to note that they both have the exact same meaning.

Classes of Addresses

These four octets are broken down to provide an addressing scheme that can provide for large and small networks. Although there are five different classes of networks (A to E), you will only be considering classes A to C. To differentiate between different classes of addresses, look at the first octet of the dotted-decimal address:

```
*  Class A:  1 - 127 (e.g. 10.1.23.19) (0.0.0.0 and 127.0.0.0 are reserved)
*  Class B:  128-191 (e.g. 172.16.19.48) (128.0.0.0 and 191.255.0.0 are reserved)
*  Class C:  192-223 (e.g. 193.18.9.10) (192.0.0.0 and 223.255.255.0 are reserved)
```

NOTES

The reserved addresses used in the section on IP address classes are commonly referred to as *martian networks*. Routing protocols such as RIP and IGRP running on IP connectivity devices, such as routers, should ignore routing advertisements for martian networks. The reserved addresses given represent the minimum set of martian networks that should be recognized. It is possible to add additional martian networks as requirements dictate. If you are interested in learning more about martian networks, try using your favorite Web search engine. Search on martian networks or *GATED (Gateway Routing Daemon)*. GATED is the application used on UNIX systems and some routers to manage dynamic routing information. A *DAEMON* is a background process that monitors incoming IP packets for system requests it should service. Just as GATED handles dynamic routing information, *NAMED* handles Domain Name Service (DNS) requests.

Note that classes D and E exist but are reserved. Class A addresses have the first octet dedicated as "network" or Internet portion, with octets 2, 3, and 4 available for local subnets and hosts. The concept of subnetting is explained later in this chapter. Allocation of Class A addresses is severely restricted due to the limited number available.

Class B addresses have the first two octets dedicated as the Internet portion, with octets 3 and 4 available for local subnets and hosts. These Class B addresses are typically used for intermediate-sized networks that have between 256 and 65,536 hosts. Obtaining a Class B address is becoming very difficult because there are so few left.

Class C has the first three octets dedicated as the Internet portion, with octet 4 available for local subnets and hosts. Class C addresses are perfect for those networks with fewer than 254 hosts. Class C addresses remain fairly easy to acquire. Companies that have more than 254 hosts need to request multiple Class C addresses. Example network numbers are illustrated as follows:

```
*   Class A: assigned network 10.0.0.0
*   Class B: assigned network 172.16.0.0
*   Class C: assigned network 192.151.10.0
```

See RFC 1918, "Address Allocation for Private Internets," for more information on available IP addresses and strategies for implementing IP addressing in your network. Appendix A, "RFCs," has information on where to obtain this and other RFCs.

Default Subnet Masks for Class A, B, C, and D Addresses

All classes of IP addresses have a default mask, often referred to as the netmask. The default netmasks are as follows:

```
* Class A: Network mask 255.0.0.0
* Class A: 0.255.255.255 Host bits
* Class B: Network mask 255.255.0.0
* Class B: 0.0.255.255 Host bits
* Class C: Network mask 255.255.255.0
* Class C: 0.0.0.255 host bits.
```

These masks are sometimes referred to as *subnet masks*, although technically this is not accurate. They are really *network masks*. These masks only cover the range of bits reserved by default for the class of address in question. The concept of a subnet mask is "to further subdivide a (major) network into smaller (sub) networks." Hence the terms subnetwork and subnetwork mask, which are usually shortened to subnet and subnet mask, respectively. Thankfully, most people use the term subnet mask to refer to either a network mask or a subnet mask. The next section explains what subnet masks are and how they are used.

UNDERSTANDING SUBNET MASKS, SUBNETTING, AND SUPERNETTING

The network addresses previously discussed represent only one physical network. If you have all of your hosts connected to the same piece of physical network equipment, such as an Ethernet 10BaseT hub, you only need one network address. In this case, you could decide to use 125.0.0.0 as your network address and assign host addresses from 125.0.0.1 to 125.255.255.254.

You can't use 125.255.255.255 because this is the all hosts address. Any packets with this destination address will be received by every host in the 125.0.0.0 network. This is otherwise known as the broadcast address for network 125.0.0.0. It requires that all digits in the second, third, and fourth octets be set to 1. The broadcast address for a Class B address, such as 171.54.0.0, would be 171.54.255.255. The broadcast address for a Class C network, such as 220.34.145.0, would be 220.34.145.255.

If you have hosts in two or more locations, and the locations are connected by a router, you cannot use the 125.0.0.0

address in more than one location. This is because systems running IP consider the portion of the address covered by the netmask to be the "network" address and consider the remainder of the address to be the "host" portion. Each network must be unique because that is how systems such as routers—which connect physical networks together and provide layer three connectivity—determine where the IP networks are located.

Consider a router with two Ethernet ports, 0 and 1. If the IP address on port 0 were 125.0.0.1 and the IP address on 1 were 125.0.0.2, the router would not be able to determine which interface a host with the IP address of 125.0.0.3 was reachable over using only layer three information. This is because the router only stores the network portion of the address in its routing table—in this case, 125.0.0.0.

The routing table is the database the router uses to keep track of all available networks. Looking at a packet destined for 125.0.0.3, the router would discover that it is a host system on the 125.0.0.0 network. The router would then query its routing table to determine which interface it knows about network 125.0.0.0 over. In this example, it would discover that both Ethernet 0 and Ethernet 1 have connections to 125.0.0.0. The only logical conclusion the router could reach is that both interfaces are actually connected to the same physical network. In this case, the router should be able to pick either interface to forward the packet over.

The other choice is to send two copies of the packet—one over each interface. Sending duplicate packets is usually not a good idea. They waste processing power on the system receiving them, so the router is likely to randomly select one of the interfaces. If 125.0.0.3 is connected to the physical network the router selects, the packet is received. If it is not, the packet is not received.

With the exception of parallel WAN links using HDLC encapsulation, Cisco routers do not allow the same network address to be applied to more than one interface. This applies to subnets as well.

Think about telephone area codes in the U.S. phone system. Each area code must be unique. Otherwise, the phone system would not be able to deliver the calls successfully.

However, the host portions of an address can be the same on different networks. Just as the phone system allows for numbers such as 408 555 1212 and 650 555 1212, IP networks allow for addresses such as 10.1.2.3 255.0.0.0 and 11.1.2.3 255.0.0.0. The phone system routes the call based on the area code and lets the local office keep track of its available numbers (telephones). The routers in an IP network route IP packets based on their network addresses and let the final router in the path deliver the packet to its final destination (IP end system).

The two solutions to this problem are as follows:

- Select a different network address for each location. Use the default network mask for each address. In this case, you could use 126.0.0.0 and 130.0.0 for the next two locations. Remember that 127.0.0.0 and 128.0.0.0 are reserved.

- Use subnetting. In this case, you need to come up with what is known as a subnet mask. What you are basically doing is creating subnetworks from a major network.

NOTES

The term *major network* or *major net* is simply a reference to the default network portion of an IP address based on its class. The major net of the Class A host address 125.0.0.1 is 125.0.0.0. (Class A networks reserve only the first octet.) The major net of the Class B host address 168.92.0.1 is 168.92.0.0. (Class B networks reserve the first and second octets.)

Because a Class A address uses the first octet as the network portion and the final three octets as host bits, the only way to create additional networks from the original network address is to somehow steal some of the hosts bits. Keep in mind that in the previous example, the "125" portion of address 125.0.0.1 was fixed. If you were to change it to, say, 126.0.0.1, you would use a completely different Class A address, which is not your goal. Your goal is to create more networks from the original 125.0.0.0 network.

If you understand that the default mask of 255.0.0.0 for a Class A indicates that the first octet is fixed and that the remaining bits can be set to any value except 255.255.255, you are well on your way to understanding the solution to subnetting. Consider the following:

```
255.0.0.0
125.0.0.0
```

The 255 overlays the first octet. What would happen if you extended the default mask by another octet?

```
255.255.0.0
125.0.0.0
```

You would be indicating that both the first and the second octet are now fixed—the first one because of the default mask for a Class A address, and the second one because you added a subnet mask. In this case, the default mask is 255.0.0.0 and the subnet mask is 0.255.0.0. The combination of the two creates a mask of 255.255.0.0. Now, a change in the second octet creates a new subnet.

125.1.0.0 with a mask of 255.255.0.0 and 125.2.0.0 with a mask of 255.255.0.0 are different subnets. Consider the following:

```
255.255.0.0
125.1.0.0
255.255.0.0
125.2.0.0
```

Both addresses are now using the first two octets as a combined network portion of the address (network and subnetwork). Both addresses still have the last two octets available as host addresses.

You can now create 253 different subnetworks of the major net 125.0.0.0. They range from 125.1.0.0 255.255.0.0 (subnet 1) to 125.254.0.0 255.255.0.0 (subnet 254). Using subnet 125.0.0.0 255.255.0.0 (subnet 0) is discouraged. It is easily confused with the major network 125.0.0.0 255.0.0.0 by routers running routing protocols such as RIP or IGRP, which do not store the subnet masks associated with networks they know about. See the section on subnet 0 in Chapter 3, "Discontiguous Networks, Summarization, and Subnet 0."

Following is an example of subnetting a Class B address to illustrate how subnetting works.

Assume that you were assigned the Class B address 172.16 from the Network Information Center (NIC). The first things you would need to determine would be how many subnets you needed and how many nodes per subnet you needed to define. A typical (and the easiest to use) Class B subnet mask would be 8 bits. Because the third octet is the first "free" octet for Class B, you can start there.

An 8-bit subnet mask would be 255.255.255.0. This would mean that you would have 254 subnets available and 254 addresses for nodes per subnet. In other words, your subnets would range from 172.16.1.0 to 172.16.254.0. Your host addresses on each subnet would range from 172.16.X.1 to 172.16.X.254, where X is the subnet applied. For subnet 1 (172.16.1.0), the host addresses would range from 172.16.1.1 to 172.16.1.254.

There is a mathematical formula for determining the number of subnets and hosts a subnet mask will allow for. In the previous example of 172.16.0.0 255.255.255.0, eight bits in the third octet are available for creating subnets, so $2^8 = 256$. You have to subtract 1 for subnet 0 (172.16.0.0 255.255.255.0) and another for the broadcast address (172.16.255.0—the all 1s subnet). Remember that the all 1s address is always a broadcast address, regardless of whether it is a subnet of all 1s, a host address of all 1s, or both. Therefore, the formula becomes $(2^8) - 2 = 254$.

The exact same formula is used for determining the quantity of host addresses available. In this example, you again have one octet—the forth octet—available for host addresses. Therefore, $(2^8) - 2 = 254$ host addresses are available on each subnet of 172.16.0.0.

Determining What Subnet Is Being Used

Sometimes it is not as easy as the previous example may have led you to believe to determine which subnet a host address is part of. Subnets do not have to be created on octet boundaries. Consider the following perfectly valid host address:

```
172.16.32.1 255.255.240.0
```

This is not a host on the 32nd subnet of major net 172.16.0.0. As you will discover in a moment, it is the third subnet of 172.16.0.0 when using a mask of 255.255.240.0. However, it is still fairly easy to determine that a host address such as 172.16.32.1 is part of subnet 172.16.32.0. Consider the following host address:

```
172.16.44.1 255.255.240.0
```

What subnet is it part of? Unlike the previous example, in which any bit changed in the third octet represented a new subnet, this example has only reserved the first four bits of the third octet. This allows for $(2^4) - 2 = 14$ subnets and $(2^{12}) - 2 = 4094$ hosts.

Look at the address and mask in binary:

```
11111111.11111111.11110000.00000000 (mask)
10101100.00010000.00101100.00000001 (host address)
```

Notice that in the third octet of the host address, only one bit is set to one in the bits covered by the subnet mask. Remember that the subnet mask reserves bits for creating unique subnets. Because the remaining three bits that are set to 1 in the third octet of the host address are outside of the reserved bits, they must be host bits. Therefore, host address 172.16.44.1 is also in subnet 0.0.32.0 of the major net 172.16.0.0.

A certain logical (Boolean) formula can be used to determine what subnet a host address is part of. It requires a logical AND operation. Performing an AND operation means that any time you AND a 0 value to another 0 or a 1 value, the result is 0. Only a 1 ANDed with another 1 value will result in a 1 value. This is illustrated as follows:

```
0    0    1
0    1    1
-    -    -
0    0    1
```

Start by representing the bits in binary. You can drop the 1 in the last octet of the host address because the mask stops half-way through the third octet. Therefore, any bits set in the fourth octet must be host bits, not subnet bits.

```
172.16.44.0    = 10101100.00010000.00101100.00000000
255.255.240.0  = 11111111.11111111.11110000.00000000
Results of AND = 10101100.00010000.00100000.00000000
```

The resulting value is 172.16.32.0. Therefore, this is subnet 0.0.32.0 of the major net address 172.16.0.0.

The Shorthand Subnet Mask Indicator

Many TCP/IP devices have adopted a shorthand method for indicating the subnet mask associated with a network address. The format is 171.68.0.0/16. This is the shorthand version of 171.68.0.0 255.255.0.0. The /16 indicates that 16 bits are reserved for the subnet mask. 171.68.0.0/24 is shorthand for 171.68.0.0 255.255.255.0. As a final example, consider the Class C address 193.65.200.0/30, which is shorthand for 193.65.200.0 255.255.255.252. As you can see, this is a much easier method for representing IP network addresses and their associated masks.

NOTES

The /16 is also used with the term *prefix*, as in "the address 171.68.0.0/16 has a 16-bit prefix." Prefix is a shorthand way of referring to the number of bits in the address that are covered by the associated subnet mask. A non-subnetted Class C address has a 24-bit prefix by default. A subnetted Class C address with a mask of 255.255.255.240 has a /28 bit subnet mask and a 28-bit prefix.

Introduction to Supernetting

Supernetting is another term that anyone supporting an IP network should be familiar with. It is almost the opposite of subnetting. Subnetting refers to making additional smaller (sub) networks out of a major network. Supernetting, on the other hand, refers to making one large (super) network out of two or more smaller networks. The smaller networks can be major nets, such as 220.100.100.0/24, or subnets, such as 220.67.87.0/32.

Consider a company (Catco, Inc.) that has been granted the following registered Class C addresses: 220.220.1.0 through 220.220.255.0. Assume that Catco has assigned (used) 220.220.1.0 through 220.220.100.0. Catco does not need to advertise the entire list of 100 individual Class C addresses to the Internet. Instead, Catco can supernet the addresses to a shorter prefix: 220.220.0.0/16. This results in a 99 percent reduction in the number of routes that need to be advertised to the Internet. Full connectivity from the Internet to the 100 assigned Class C addresses is still possible because Catco has control of every possible network with the 16-bit supernet prefix of 220.220.0.0 (220.220.1.0, 220.220.2.0, . . . , 220.220.254.0 and 220.220.255.0).

HINT

You must configure the global command *ip classless* on a Cisco router in order to implement supernetting.

Supernetting is part of the broader concept of *classless interdomain routing* (CIDR). See Appendix A for a list of RFCs that provide more information on CIDR and supernetting.

This has been an intentionally brief introduction to the concept of supernetting. If you want to implement supernetting, you should consult the relevant RFCs. The book *Internet Routing Architectures* by Bassam Halabi, published by Cisco Press (ISBN 1-56205-652-2), is another excellent source of information on this subject.

Calculating Subnet and Host Combinations

Cisco Systems has a tool on CCO that makes subnetting much easier. Log on to CCO with your username and password and then access the following URL: `http://www.cisco.com/techtools/ip_addr.html`.

The Net3 Group has a Windows tool that can help you perform subnet and hosts calculations. See the URL `http://www.net3group.com/ipcalc.html-ssi` or search Net3's main home page at `http://www.net3group.com`.

SUMMARY

This chapter has provided a brief introduction on binary and hexadecimal numbers. IP address concepts and issues were presented as well. If you are involved in supporting an IP-based network, you should have a thorough understanding of this material.

Appendix A contains a list of RFCs that provide additional information on the concepts presented in this book.

RFCs

This appendix contains titles and brief introductions for the RFCs referenced in this book. It also contains some RFCs that are useful for people just getting started in TCP/IP-based internetworking and the Internet. Some of these RFCs explain the standards bodies and their policies. Others explain fundamental concepts that are useful to understand. A couple—such as RFC 1149—show the humorous side of the RFC world.

A full index of RFCs can be found at the following URL: `http://www.cis.ohio-state.edu/htbin/rfc/rfc-index.html`. If this URL is unavailable for any reason, search with the keyword **RFC** in your favorite Web search engine.

How RFCs Work

RFCs are numbered based on when they were written, not by title or content. Occasionally, a group of related RFCs are all updated and posted at the same time. In this case, they are numbered sequentially. The simplest way to find an RFC on a particular subject is to open the RFC index in a word processor or a Web browser and search for a keyword.

For example, to find all RFCs related to RIP, search with the keyword **RIP**. Be sure to make your search case sensitive. Otherwise, you will get hits on words such as "postscript."

Because the RFCs are indexed in the order in which they are written, you can search from the top of the index to find the latest versions first.

Whenever you are reading an RFC, look for a statement that says *(Obsoleted by RFCxxx)*. If you see this statement, you are reading an outdated copy. When in doubt, always refer to a recent copy of the RFC index. It always indicates whether a newer revision of an RFC is available.

RFCs RECOMMENDED FOR FURTHER STUDY

The RFCs selected for this list were chosen in a highly subjective and arbitrary fashion. Note, for example, that entire topics—such as the Simple Network Management Protocol (SNMP) and the Post Office Protocol (POP3)—have been omitted. Clearly, some topics had to be left out. Otherwise, this appendix would have been a rewrite of the index itself. RFCs that would help you build a solid technical foundation, as well as the RFCs that explained the inner workings of the Internet standards bodies, are included.

NOTES

Consult the RFC index for the latest versions of these RFCs before you start studying those listed here. These numbers become outdated very quickly.

RFC 2235: Hobbes' Internet Timeline

This RFC provides a history of the major events that shaped the Internet into what it is today.

RFC 2200: Internet Official Protocol Standards

This RFC covers some of the processes involved in creating RFCs. It also explains some of the terms found in RFCs and their usage. This is a "must read" for anyone involved in supporting IP networks.

RFC 2151: A Primer on Internet and TCP/IP Tools and Utilities

This name is pretty self-explanatory. RFC 2151 is an introduction to some of the fundamental tools and utilities available. Traceroute, PING, Finger, and others are covered. This is another "must read."

RFC 2101: IPv4 Address Behavior Today

This RFC clarifies the current interpretation of the IP V4 32-bit IP address space. It also provides some background on IP V6.

RFC 2031: IETF-ISOC Relationship

This RFC explains the relationship between the IETF and the Internet Society.

RFC 2028: The Organizations Involved in the IETF Standards Process

This is pretty much what it says it is—an explanation of the organizations involved in the IETF standards process.

RFC 2027: IAB and IESG Selection, Confirmation, and Recall Process: Operation of the Nominating and Recall Committees

Again, this is pretty self-explanatory; it's an introduction to the process of selecting members for, and managing the membership of, the IAB and IESG.

RFC 2026: The Internet Standards Process: Revision 3

This is another RFC that explains RFC processes and other background information.

RFC 2008: Implications of Various Address Allocation Policies for Internet Routing

This RFC discusses some of the older policies for allocating IP address space. It suggests ways they can be changed to reflect the Internet changes that have occurred since they were originally drafted.

RFC 1935: What Is the Internet, Anyway?

An informational RFC discussing the Internet and what it means to different people and organizations.

RFC 1925: The Twelve Networking Truths

This is a humorous RFC about life and networking.

RFC 1923: RIPv1 Applicability Statement for Historic Status

This RFC discusses the current status of RIP V1 (RFC 1058) and some of its limitations. Anyone running a network with RIP V1 should read this.

RFC 1918: Address Allocation for Private Internets

This RFC provides background on the allocation of IP addresses for private Internets. It also provides implementation guidelines for companies that want to implement IP but do not want full connectivity to the Internet. This is a "must read" for anyone involved in supporting an IP network.

RFC 1917: An Appeal to the Internet Community to Return Unused IP Networks (Prefixes) to the IANA

This RFC discusses the limited amount of IP addresses available for allocation. It also explains how companies that have addresses they no longer require can return them.

RFC 1878: Variable Length Subnet Table for IPv4

This is a useful table of the various subnets that can be derived from the 32-bit IP address space.

RFC 1812: Requirements for IP Version 4 Routers

This RFC explains some of the functions that routers must perform when routing IP V4. This is a "must read" for anyone involved in supporting an IP network that uses routers.

RFC 1631: The IP Network Address Translator (NAT)

This RFC explains the function of IP address translation and some of the requirements that must be met by a device implementing NAT. This is a "must read" for anyone involved in supporting an IP network that uses NAT when accessing the Internet.

RFC 1601: Charter of the Internet Architecture Board (IAB)

This is pretty self-explanatory; it is the charter of the IAB. Useful reading for anyone interested in the function of the IAB.

RFC 1580: Guide to Network Resource Tools

Similar to RFC 2151 in intent but not in content. This is more focused on information-finding tools, such as Gopher, WAIS, and USENET. This is a "must read" for anyone using the Internet to find or disseminate information.

RFC 1393: Traceroute Using an IP Option

This RFC provides background on the Traceroute utility. It also suggests some enhancements. This is useful reading for those responsible for troubleshooting IP network problems.

RFC 1256: ICMP Router Discovery Messages

This RFC explains IRDP and discusses how IP systems can use it to find and use IP gateways (routers) off of their local network. Some third-party TCP/IP stacks for Windows 95 and Windows NT support IRDP. SUN Solaris 2.5 does as well. Those exploring how to enable hosts to use multiple local gateways should read this.

RFC 1180: A TCP/IP Tutorial

This RFC is a solid introduction to the TCP/IP protocol suite. It discusses the multiplexing of various applications over TCP and UDP. It also explains some related applications, such as Telnet and FTP. This is a "must read" for anybody just getting started in implementing an IP-based network. Experienced IP support engineers may find some new information as well.

RFC 1178: Choosing a Name for Your Computer

This RFC covers some of the pitfalls of using inappropriate computer names and suggests some naming strategies.

RFC 1149: A Standard for the Transmission of IP Datagrams on Avian Carriers

This is another humorous RFC.

RFC 1058: Routing Information Protocol

This is "the" RFC for RIP V1. It is a "must read" for supporters of IP networks with routers because this is where it all started.

RFC 826: An Ethernet Address Resolution Protocol

This is the RFC on ARP. This is a "must read" for those involved in supporting IP networks.

RFC 1700: Assigned Numbers

This RFC contains references to the registered numbers that are assigned for various functions—such as TCP Port numbers for applications such as Telnet (23). Those involved in internet-working to any degree should be familiar with the material contained in this RFC.

RFC 1534: BOOTP

This RFC explains how certain TCP/IP configuration parameters, such as IP addresses, default gateways, and DNS servers, are passed from servers to workstations while the workstations are booting up. This allows network administrators to centralize the administration of this information. BOOTP has been superseded by the Dynamic Host Configuration Protocol (DHCP), which is referenced later in this appendix.

RFC 2283, RFC 1966, RFC 1965, RFC 1774, RFC 1773, RFC 1772, RFC 1771, RFC 1745: Border Gateway Protocol V4 (BGP4)

BGP4 is the latest version of this protocol. It specifies how routing information is passed between *autonomous systems*. Autonomous systems are groups of networks (which are typically very large) under the control of a single organization or a group of cooperating organizations. Internet Service Providers (ISPs) that control the backbone of the Internet typically have their own autonomous systems. ISPs use BGP to link these autonomous systems to other ISPs' autonomous systems.

For more information on this subject, see *Internet Routing Architectures* by Bassam Halabi, published by Cisco Press (ISBN 1-56205-652-2).

RFC 1817, RFC 1520, RFC 1519, RFC 1518, RFC 1517: Classless Interdomain Routing (CIDR)

CIDR replaces the standard network masks applied to classes of IP addresses. For example, instead of using a mask such as 255.255.0.0 for network 171.68.0.0, a mask of 255.0.0.0 could be applied. This would shorten the prefix of 171.68.0.0 to 171.0.0.0. If all of the networks that have 171 as their first octet were under the control of a single autonomous system, the autonomous system managers could limit their advertisements to other autonomous systems to an 8-bit prefix.

Instead of sending 16-bit prefixes, such as 171.1.0.0, 171.2.0.0, 171.2.0.0, and 171.253.0.0, to an adjacent autonomous system, the manager can just send 171.0.0.0. Because there are 254 possible 16-bit prefixes starting with 171.0.0.0, advertising can be saved on up to 253 networks (you still have to advertise 171.0.0.0), depending on how many of the available 171.0.0.0 networks are actually assigned.

The application of CIDR in the Internet has greatly reduced the numbers or routes (networks) that need to be advertised between and within autonomous systems.

RFC 2132, RFC 2131, RFC 1534: Dynamic Host Configuration Protocol (DHCP)

This RFC explains how certain TCP/IP configuration parameters, such as IP addresses, default gateways, and DNS servers, are passed from servers to workstations while the workstations are booting up. This allows network administrators to centralize the administration of this information. DHCP supersedes BOOTP, which was referenced previously.

RFC 2308, RFC 2230, RFC 2219, RFC 2182, RFC 2181, RFC 2136, RFC 2052, RFC 1996, RFC 1995, RFC 1912, RFC 1794, RFC 1713: Domain Name System (DNS)

This is the application that allows IP hosts to be referenced by names instead of explicit IP addresses. For instance, instead of entering `c:\ftp 192.31.7.130` to start a Windows FTP session to Cisco's FTP site, you can enter `c:\ftp ftp.cisco.com`.

If your PC's DNS server(s) is configured properly, your PC sends a DNS query to its DNS server(s) (it can have more than one in case one fails) requesting the IP address associated with the system name ftp.cisco.com. After the reply is received, the FTP application uses the IP address it contains (192.31.7.130) to establish an FTP session.

RFC 2178, RFC 1745, RFC 1587, RFC 1586, RFC 1585, RFC 1584: Open Shortest Path First (OSPF)

These are the latest RFCs containing information on OSPF. OSPF is an open (not proprietary) standard. It is what is commonly known as an Interior Gateway Protocol (IGP). IGPs are typically used within autonomous systems. IGP was created to overcome some of the significant limitations of the Routing Information Protocol V1 (RIP), such as lack of VLSM support and lack of discontiguous network support.

RFC 1931, RFC 1293: Reverse Address Resolution Protocol (RARP) Inverse RARP

These protocols perform the opposite function of the Address Resolution Protocol (ARP). ARP maps layer three IP addresses to layer two MAC addresses. RARP, on the other hand, maps layer two MAC addresses to layer three IP addresses.

RFC 2092, RFC 2091, RFC 1723, RFC 1722, RFC 1721, RFC 1582, RFC 1581: RIP

RIP V1 was one of the original IP routing protocols. RIP V2, which is now available on many TCP/IP systems, overcomes some of the significant limitations of RIPV1, such as lack of VLSM support and lack of discontiguous network support.

The RIP V1 protocol specification (RFC 1058) is provided in the previous section. The other RFCs refer to RIP V2 and other RIP enhancements.

RFC 2072, RFC 2071: Router Renumbering

These informational RFCs explain the concept of renumbering IP networks and indicate when this may be necessary.

RFC 2001: TCP/iP (TCP) Slow Start

TCP is the connection-oriented transport layer protocol in the TCP/IP protocol suite. It has flow control and error correction built in. It is used by TCP/IP applications, such as Telnet and FTP.

The TCP Slow Start algorithm forces a new TCP session to assume there is congestion on the network. This results in using a smaller packet size, a smaller *window size* (number of outstanding, unacknowledged packets), and a longer *timeout* (how long TCP will wait for acknowledgments before assuming a packet has been lost).

After the session is established, TCP starts increasing the packet size and the window size, while decreasing the timeout period. When TCP determines that the maximum values have been reached (the timeout period starts to expire for some packets), it reduces the packet sizes and the window, while increasing the timeout period. However, these numbers are not immediately dropped to their original Slow Start values.

RFC 1470: TCP/IP Debugging Tools

This RFC has valuable information on many tools and techniques for troubleshooting TCP/IP networking problems.

SUMMARY

This appendix has provided information on obtaining and using RFCs. RFCs are the lifeblood of the Internet. Nothing happens without them. They represent the conception of new ideas (proposals). They track the ideas through their gestation period (the ratification process) and finally document their birth (as an Internet standard).

After a standard has been established, RFCs track their evolution as well. Anybody supporting an IP network should check out the RFC index at least twice a year to look for emerging standards, as well as newer versions of RFCs for applicable technologies.

Index